From Holy Laughter to Holy Fire

America on the Edge of Revival

Michael L. Brown

Destiny Image® Publishers, Inc.
P.O. Box 310
Shippensburg, PA 17257-0310

"Speaking to the Purposes of God for This Generation
and for the Generations to Come"

ISBN 1-56043-181-4

For Worldwide Distribution
Printed in the U.S.A.

First Printing: 1996   Second Printing: 1996

From Holy Laughter to Holy Fire

America on the Edge of Revival

Other Books by Michael L. Brown

Israel's Divine Healer
(Studies in Old Testament Biblical Theology)

It's Time to Rock the Boat:
A Call to God's People to Rise Up and
Preach a Confrontational Gospel

Our Hands Are Stained With Blood:
The Tragic Story of the "Church" and the Jewish People

Whatever Happened to the Power of God:
Is the Charismatic Church Slain in the Spirit
or Down for the Count?

How Saved Are We?

The End of the American Gospel Enterprise

Compassionate Father or Consuming Fire?
Who Is the God of the Old Testament?

For information on ICN Ministries, or for a listing of other books and tapes by Michael L. Brown, write to:

ICN Ministries
P.O. Box 7355
Gaithersburg, MD 20898-7355
Phone: 301-990-4303
FAX: 301-990-4306

Dedication

Dedicated to the memory of Leonard Ravenhill, a dear friend and father in the faith. Surely we who live in this day will reap the rewards of the tears he shed for revival for more than 60 years.

Destiny Image books are available through these fine distributors outside the United States:

Christian Growth, Inc.
Jalan Kilang-Timor, Singapore 0315

Vine Christian Centre
Mid Glamorgan, Wales, United Kingdom

Omega Distributors
Ponsonby, Auckland, New Zealand

WA Buchanan Company
Geebung, Queensland, Australia

Rhema Ministries Trading
Randburg, Rep. of South Africa

Word Alive
Niverville, Manitoba, Canada

Salvation Book Centre
Petaling, Jaya, Malaysia

This book and all other Destiny Image
and Treasure House books
are available at Christian bookstores everywhere.

Call for a bookstore nearest you.
1-800-722-6774
Or reach us on the Internet: **http://www.reapernet.com**

Contents

Foreword

Is God visiting His people again?

At the edge of the twentieth century and the dawn of the next millennium, the subject of revival is once again engaging the hearts and minds of the people of God. Strange things are happening again in our churches.

Michael Brown (the author of this study and many others) is an anomaly. He knows what it is like to survive in the streets from where he came and to stir a sleeping church to which he is surely sent. *"He that is forgiven much loves much."* He is generally a gentleman (except when it comes to dealing with religious sin), and he is certainly a scholar (he writes simply). He seeks to be one of those few who soak their ministries in much prayer, Scripture, and Christian history. He is also both properly Hebrew and prophet-hearted and thus doubly dangerous. He passes A.W. Tozer's test of the prophet's heart with flying colors: *"Does he make me feel uncomfortable?"*

This work is a snapshot of the blessings and dangers of such a visitation. Michael Brown believes that revival is more than a series of meetings which begins Monday and finishes Sunday. You will find much in this book that commends it to serious students of the Holy Spirit's work in history, but you find something else here too: the dealings of God with our culture in our time. Something is going on again in the churches of our Western world.

Jesus is passing by.

Jesus is visiting His people again. Like the man born blind (who met with a miracle before he ever saw the face of the Messiah), another generation of harvest is coming to the Lord of light. The man born blind had no religious past and no theological explanation for what happened. He was disbelieved and questioned by his former friends and neighbors, left to fend for himself by his parents, and finally quite soundly rejected by the current religious leaders of his time. They "cast him out." *But he got new eyes from the hand of Him who first made man from clay and with them he saw the Lord.*

What Jesus did then, He is doing again in our time. Michael's timely book is a scroll from one of the new breed of the once-blind that have been touched by the Hand of the Master and "cannot but tell" what has happened to them.

Winkie Pratney

Preface

This book is an expanded edition of *High-Voltage Christianity*, published in 1995 by Huntington House. When the first edition of the book was released, the subject of revival was becoming red hot. Now, it is white hot. This is the day we have longed for! Revival is knocking at the door. How will we respond?

There is an excitement in much of the Church of America today, a rising faith, a new expectancy, a fresh desire to see radical spiritual change, an awareness of the importance of divine visitation. Pastors seem more and more willing to "throw out the clock," to hold protracted renewal meetings, and to call their congregations to prayer and fasting for a real outpouring. And many are being touched and blessed. Could this be the beginning of a truly *national* awakening?

It seems that God has sovereignly brought the subject of revival to the attention of His people, with leaders of all persuasions cracking open books about past visitations in America, and with writer after writer (including this present writer!) quoting the views of Jonathan Edwards on revival. Obscure examples that I both read and wrote about some years ago are now popping up everywhere, even on the Internet. Yes, revival is a hot topic of the hour.

But divine visitation will not come automatically, and there is no guarantee that we will go from "refreshing" to revival. We must remove the roadblocks! There is quite a mixed bag out there today going under the name of "revival"—from the silly to the sacred, from the hollow to the holy—and the responses have been just as varied.

Three of the most common responses to the current "renewal" movements in North America can be classified as cavalier, cautious, and critical. The *cavalier* response buys into everything, hardly exercising any discernment. It asks, "How can you argue with the blessing?", diving into the streams without even looking, often cheapening that which ought to be consecrated and precious. The *cautious* response wants to believe that God is at work and recognizes the danger of an arrogant, judgmental attitude. Still, it is troubled by many of the manifestations and much of the message. It stands on the shorelines, occasionally wading into the waters, not quite sure whether to take the plunge or to take off. The *critical* response dismisses the whole thing as either demonic, fleshly, or both. "This is *not* from above," it categorically declares. It denies that God is in the waters at all, often without getting anywhere near the river. It has no need to investigate the facts; it is right. Often acting as a "ministry," it is adept at critiquing whatever new thing God *is* doing, specializing in throwing the baby out with the bathwater.

This book is meant to challenge the cavalier and the critical, while at the same time encouraging the cautious. There is *much* to be concerned about in *some* of the current moves, but there is *much* to rejoice about also. These are days of mighty outpouring! America could be on the verge of the greatest revival our nation has ever seen. But it will require us to deepen our commitment, purify our message, press in to God like never before, lay down our lives for the gospel, and pray and obey as if there were no tomorrow. Either the glory comes down or the nation folds up. It's simple. A hyped-up placebo will not take the place of the holy Presence.

America is rotten to the core, the Church has not risen to the occasion, and this generation is in the balance. There is no political solution for the problems of the hour, nor can any man-made "Christian" antidote provide the cure. Revival is our only hope—yet there is hope for revival! Now is the time to believe.

But do we know what visitation really means? Are we looking for the Lord to simply add greater blessing to our plans and programs? Do we think of revival merely as the means through which our churches will grow and our ministries will prosper? Do we realize that revival means upheaval? Do we understand that visitation comes with radical consequences? Do we fathom just how deeply the Spirit moves in times of national awakening? Are we ready?

Since 1982 (and in some ways, although without much understanding, since my first days in the Lord in the early 1970's), the whole thrust of my life has been the message of repentance and the promise of revival. Nothing consumes me more than a desire to see the Lord exalted in power in the midst of a holy people. How I long to see the *real thing* in our day—not some high-tech, slickly-marketed, superficial version, but a heaven-sent tidal wave. May it sweep across our land! May it help us to reap an awesome harvest. May it prepare us for hard times to come.

It is with the goal of helping us see revival in our day that this book has been written, often under an intense burden of the Spirit. My heart has been ablaze, and much prayer has gone up to the throne of God, asking the Lord to use this message to ignite revival fires in many lives. May He stir *you* as you read!

This new, expanded edition contains three additional chapters: "The Prophets of the Thirteenth Year" (written in May and June of 1996 in Cheltenham, England and Pensacola, Florida); "God Wants All of Me" (also written in June, 1996); "To Judge or Not to Judge?" (written in the Fall of 1994); and a lengthy poem, "The Rhyme of the Modern Parishioner" (begun in the Fall of 1994). A few additional quotes and paragraphs have also been added in the text of the other chapters; otherwise the text is the same, aside from minor, editorial changes.

The dedication of this book to Leonard Ravenhill reflects my conviction that any true spiritual awakening in our day will be due in part to his tears and broken heart. His writings deeply impacted me in 1982-83, and it was my wonderful privilege to have been adopted by him as a spiritual son in 1989, becoming the recipient of his prayers and his influence until he went to be with the Lord late in 1994. May his dear wife Martha be encouraged that their travail has not been in vain.

My precious wife Nancy has also longed for true revival for many years. With all my heart, I believe that the glorious visitation for which she has so often wept is at the door. May our generation live to see the glory of God sweep our land. May our children be caught up in the divine tidal wave. Come Lord! It's time.

Michael L. Brown
August 1996

The Rhyme
of the Modern Parishioner

It happened in the vestibule
At ten one Sunday morn;
A haggard-looking church-goer
Sat plaintive and forlorn.

Then suddenly he rose and found
A hungry-looking Christian;
He took his hand, took him aside,
And asked him a straight question:

"You've read the Word; you know the Book;
The promises are clear.
But have you seen the living God?
Have you found Him here?

Have you experienced holy fire
The Spirit in His power,
A mighty wave, a rushing wind,
A flame that does devour?

Is there something more you're seeking,
So high, so wide, so deep?
Do you find yourself frustrated?
Is church putting you to sleep?

Then listen well, your heart is ripe;
My tale I will tell.
This story is your story too,
And it's your tale as well.

For thirty years I've been in church,
It seemed like a good show.
But now I've got to meet with God—
Do *you* know where to go?

I'm trapped in mundane worship times,
The praises have grown cold;
The preaching's dry and dusty,
The teaching stale like mold!

Each service feels like a rerun,
The songs all sound the same;
The prophecies are so hollow—
Not worthy of the name!

Words, more words—they're everywhere,
But oh there is a stink!
Words, more words—they're everywhere,
But none to make us think!

We lack the heavenly Presence,
It's clear we're in a rut;
I'm desperate for revival—
It burns within my gut!

I'm love-sick for my Jesus,
So hungry for my Lord;
Just longing for my Savior;
God knows that I'm so bored!

Is there someone who can help me,
Who's touched the real thing?
A man who's heard from heaven—
With a word from God to bring?

Are there prophets burning with fire,
Servants who are ablaze?
Anointed and overflowing,
Appointed for these days?

Do they carry the Spirit's burden,
And breathe the Lord God's breath?
Are they set apart and holy,
Obedient to death?

I hear the words of the Master,
'Come follow Me,' He said.
If some Christians go their own way;
I'll go with Him instead!

Oh please, don't do as I have done,
And waste so many years.
Don't wait and wait for endless months;
Move on! Outgrow your fears!

Forget the twelve step programs;
A seminar won't do.
You need a touch from heaven,
To fill you through and through.

There must be change in *your* life—
A work of God that's real.
Don't fool yourself with worn clichés—
Don't let the devil steal!

Don't miss out on God's Presence
Or let these hours pass;
Don't stop your soul from hungering;
Get out of the morass!

Dear friend, you are not crazy;
Dear saint, you are not mad;
There really is a problem,
It's true, you have been had!

There's more! There's more! Believe it!
There is *that place* in God.
There are holy visitations,
New paths that must be trod.

Will you get up like old Pilgrim,
And seek that better way?
Will you go forth on that journey
No matter what men say?

Will you go out now and meet Him,
And leave the crowd behind,
Forsaking dead traditions,
If Jesus you will find?

It's not in another meeting,
A nicely packaged hour;
Another harmless service,
Devoid of heaven's power.

It's not in another teaching,
Three points to fill your head.
The Word is always vibrant;
But this stuff is so dead!

We need God to send His Spirit,
To fully take control,
To transform every member,
To come and make them whole!

Enough with man's religion;
Enough with earthly plans;
Enough with our new programs;
Produced by fleshly hands."

Just then in strode the pastor
His calling to fulfill;
Just doing his weekly duty—
Then he became frozen still.

For astir was that parishioner
He grasped the preacher's clothes,
And grasped the preacher's soul as well—
And in that grasp he froze.

"Oh pastor, enter the prayer room
And shut yourself inside.
Be emptied of competition,
And crucify your pride!

Pray for holy visitations,
Caught up alone with Him,
Consumed with heavenly vision—
That's where you must begin!

You won't find Him in a textbook,
Buried on page twenty-two.
He is the living God who acts—
He wants to move in you!

It's not only the 'apostles'
He'll bless and send and use;
He will saturate your own soul,
If you will not refuse.

So arise, get up, pursue Him,
Jesus your true best Friend!
He is worthy of devotion;
He's faithful to the end!

Why should you starve on crusty bread,
And crawl along the ground?
Your Savior is your source of life,
Seek *Him*, let joy abound!

Renew your life, refresh your heart,
Press in, take hold, pray through.
Put first things first, make God your goal;
What else have you to do?

Your Bible schooling stole your zeal,
Church life has drained you dry;
You used to have such childlike faith,
Now budgets have your eye!

You used to be so passionate,
So innocent and free
Now you've become professional;
You'll preach for a good fee!

Oh, set your sights on higher goals
And not on dollar bills.
Live in the light of Judgment Day;
Ambition always kills!

Let Jesus be your daily Guide,
Put Him where He belongs;
And soon His presence will arrive;
His praise will fill your songs!

Simplicity will be your style,
Devotion your new goal;
Communion will become your aim,
God's life will flood your soul!

Oh, take your eyes off numbers,
Church growth can be a trap!
Go out and make disciples.
Go out and bridge the gap!

Pour your life out for broken lives—
Let God *your* heart break too.
Take up the cross, deny yourself;
Just live His will to do!

Wake up, be brave, be honest;
Today—oh hear His voice!
Be ruthless with your schedule;
Seek GOD. Make that your choice.

You won't find Him in your planner,
No committee has the key.
You'll find Him when your soul cries out,
'There must be more for me!'

'There must be more than building funds,
And sessions past midnight,
And endless talks with leadership,
Disputing who is right.

Somehow I know I've been misled;
The model doesn't work.
I'm not called as an executive,
Nor should I be a clerk.

I'm called to be a man of God,
A man who's Spirit-led,
A healer of the sick and lame
Someday to raise the dead!'

And with that cry new life will rise,
Your heart will be revived;
Heaven's light will flood your soul—
You will not be denied!"

The parishioner then turned his gaze
Away from flesh and blood:
He looked to Him who sends the showers,
To Him who sends the flood.

"Today, O Lord, do hear our voice,
And pour Your Spirit out.
Saturate the thirsty ground.
End this spiritual drought!

Revive us with Your Presence,
Renew us from above;
Touch the flock called by Your name;
Come fill us with Your love!

Do greater works in our day,
Than that which You have done.
Bring the fullness of Your rains,
And glorify Your Son!"

That old church-goer spoke no more.
Another voice was heard.
Yet not the voice of flesh and blood:
It was our Father's word.

And if you listen closely,
Beyond this little rhyme,
You'll hear Him speaking clearly:
"My children, it is time."

And it will be said: "Build up, build up, prepare the road! Remove the obstacles out of the way of My people." For this is what the high and lofty One says—He who lives forever, whose name is holy: "I live in a high and holy place, but also with him who is contrite and lowly in spirit, to revive the spirit of the lowly and to revive the heart of the contrite."

Is. 57:14-15

A voice of one calling: "In the desert prepare the way for the LORD; make straight in the wilderness a highway for our God. Every valley shall be raised up, every mountain and hill made low; the rough ground shall become level, the rugged places a plain. And the glory of the LORD will be revealed, and all mankind together will see it. For the mouth of the LORD has spoken."

Is. 40:3-5

You promised us a baptism of fire.
But here we are bogged down in slothful mire,
Thy people fat, content, increased in goods,
Resentful if we prod them from their moods.
Forgive them, Father, oh, forgive!
Shake them awake! And let them live
Upon the plane of Pentecostal power—
Less enduement cannot meet this hour.
Before You come to take Your spotless Bride,
We trust You for a world revival tide!

Leonard Ravenhill, *Revival God's Way*

I hail in the twentieth century, the blessing of our age restored—a Church holy in life, triumphant in faith, self-sacrificing in service with one aim, to preach Christ crucified "unto the uttermost part of the earth."

John Hyde, written in 1901

Chapter One

Remove the Stumbling Blocks!

God is on the move! His Spirit is being poured out around the earth, and multitudes are being ushered into the Kingdom. A vast harvest is being reaped and the Bride is making herself ready. Even in America, in the midst of divine judgments, shakings, and purgings, there are signs of revival at hand.

Now is the time to awake! Now is the time to dive in! Now is the time to remove every hindrance, every roadblock, every barrier that stands in the way of the pure and holy moving of God. Do we really have any choice? Without sweeping revival in our generation there is little or no hope for America.

How tragic it would be if the Lord visited Russia, China, Sudan, Argentina, India, and other nations around the globe yet bypassed the United States of America. How tragic it would be if America—the country that has sent out and financed more missionaries than any other country in history— would be left out. How tragic it would be if the fruit of our terrible, corporate disobedience outweighed and overshadowed the fruit of our corporate faith. But it doesn't have to be that way! This could be the generation that experiences the glory of God. This could be the season of refreshing.

Of course, we must not fool ourselves. America is in desperate trouble, and if God did not judge us with severity for more than 30 million abortions, for 20,000 homicides a year, for every kind of sexual perversion, for the idols of materialism and greed, for birthing an endless stream of false religions and cults, then He would not be God. He would be no better than the corrupt judges who rule in many of our courts today.

Perish the thought! God *will* pour out His wrath on our country and we *will* be shaken to the core. Don't let any so-called prophet tell you that America will be spared from experiencing a strong measure of the Lord's justice and holy anger. But in answer to the prayers of countless thousands of saints who have faithfully cried out for days and weeks and years, and in keeping with His love and compassion, in wrath the Lord will remember mercy (Hab. 3:2). Times of outpouring will come! Torrents of revival will fall!

Even now, the first drops are trickling down, and churches are being renewed. Even now, many believers are experiencing personal revival, and their lives are being supernaturally changed. But already in some circles there is a mixture: There is something of heaven and something of Hollywood. Often the beautiful Presence of God must compete with the big personalities of the great. Instead of the human vessels being effaced, they are being exalted.

It is sad but true: Some of this "Holy Ghost outpouring" is coming to the rich and famous—the superstar ministers, the megachurch kingdoms, the carnal-prosperity preachers—without producing radical, lasting change. The emphasis is still on success instead of sacrifice and on exciting signs instead of enduring surrender. There are manifestations and there is merchandising. The old wineskins (or, in some cases, pseudo-wineskins) remain the same. *That is not revival!*

Almighty God wants to send a flood. The Lord of heaven and earth wants to bring a visitation. He wants to display His glory. He wants to magnify His Son! He wants to get for Himself a humble, holy, radical, revived, overcoming, obedient people. We've hardly seen anything yet, and yet we have no guarantee we'll see anything more—unless we remove the stumbling blocks and clear the paths. The carnal show must stop. We need a pure move from heaven.

But this sword cuts both ways. Carnality is not the only problem. Religiosity is just as bad—if not worse. In fact, "religious spirits" have stopped and sidetracked more revivals than have carnal spirits. No sooner does the Lord begin to move in power than some of His "leaders" begin to put on the brakes. The revival is not sophisticated enough for them; it's not to their theological liking; it doesn't fit into their denominational straightjackets; it's not coming where they expected it to come, or when they expected it to come, or how they expected it to come, or through whom they expected it to come; therefore it can't be God.

They are unable to see what the Lord is doing because their perspective is so limited, and they instantly write off the whole thing with a know-it-all judgmental spirit. They throw out the baby—and sometimes it is just a tiny baby—with the bathwater. Yet their churches languish while those whom they criticize are being blessed. How dangerous it is to be spiritually stiff! Revival would almost mean resurrection for some of these petrified preachers.

As for the sincere, Spirit-filled leaders who react to the early excesses and extremes, God looks at their hearts. And if they are pure in His sight, they will not be left out. They may be offended by the pollution in the first flowing streams, but they will dive in when the holy waves come. (Some holy waves are already here!)

And then will there be perfect unity and balance? Not yet! Even at flood tide, there will be all too many carnal believers who just want to party and more than enough critical believers who can only seem to pout. It's so easy to go to extremes!

How do we avoid spiritual foolishness and fleshly spirituality without becoming religiously rigid and suffocatingly sanctified? How can we see everything the Lord wants to do in our day without being fascinated with false fire or despising the true fire? The answers, as always, are simple—and costly. But if we press in to God with submissive, hungry, teachable hearts, we *will* hear His voice.

And when He speaks to you, put your defenses down. Don't resist God! Do what He says. Then you will be blessed. Nothing will stop revival from coming to you. So let's remove the stumbling blocks!

This is what our age needs, not an easy-moving message, the sort of thing that makes the hearer feel all nice inside, but a message profoundly disturbing. We have been far too afraid of disturbing people, but the Holy Spirit will have nothing to do with a message or with a minister who is afraid of disturbing. You might as well expect a surgeon to give place to a quack who claims to be able to do the job with some sweet tasting drug, as expect the Holy Spirit to agree that the tragic plight of human souls today can be met by soft and easy words. Calvary was anything but nice to look at, blood-soaked beams of wood, a bruised and bleeding body, not nice to look upon. But then Jesus was not dealing with a nice thing; He was dealing with the sin of the world, and that is what we are called upon to deal with today. Soft and easy words, soft-pedalling will never meet the need.

Rev. Robert Barr, in Duncan Campbell's
The Price and Power of Revival

I fear the Preachers have been more studious to please than to awaken, or there would have been a deeper work.

John Wesley, Journal, Oct. 12, 1774,
reflecting on his ministry near Swanage, England

"Turn us again, O God": it is not so much said, "turn our captivity," but "turn *us*." All will come right if we are right. When the Lord turns his people he will soon turn their condition.

Charles Spurgeon, commenting on Ps. 80:3

Chapter Two

The Prophets
of the Thirteenth Year

Josiah was eight years old when he became king, and he reigned in Jerusalem thirty-one years. He did what was right in the eyes of the LORD and walked in the ways of his father David, not turning aside to the right or to the left. In the eighth year of his reign, while he was still young, he began to seek the God of his father David. In his twelfth year he began to purge Judah and Jerusalem of high places, Asherah poles, carved idols and cast images. (2 Chron. 34:1-3)

Notice the chronology carefully. Josiah began to reign at the age of eight. Eight years into his reign, at the age of sixteen, he began in earnest to seek the Lord. Then, four years later, at the age of twenty and in the twelfth year of his reign, he began to act, bringing a mighty reformation to Judah and Jerusalem. And so it was that one of the greatest revivals in Old Testament history was birthed—in the twelfth year of Josiah's reign.

But something even more significant began in the thirteenth year of his reign:

The words of Jeremiah son of Hilkiah, one of the priests at Anathoth in the territory of Benjamin. The word of the LORD

came to him in the thirteenth year of the reign of Josiah....
(Jer. 1:1-2)

Jeremiah's prophetic ministry began in the first year of Josiah's reformation! What an incredible fact. In the very infancy of national revival, at the birth of a sweeping renewal movement, Jeremiah, the preacher of repentance, the weeping prophet of judgment and restoration, the ambassador of the New Covenant, received his call. This is of critical importance for the Church today. Where are the prophets who begin to speak in the thirteenth year of Josiah? Where are the repentance preachers in these infancy years of renewal and revival?

There is no question but that we are at the beginning of an international awakening of huge proportions. The prayer movements of the 1980's and early 1990's have given way to the outpourings and stirrings of the mid-1990's. Revival is at hand! Visitation is at the door! But where are the Jeremiahs? Where are those who will summon us to go deeper, challenging our comfortable commitment, confronting us with the whole counsel of God, and calling us to holy service by life or by death? Where are the unsettling voices?

It really is a shame that we are so polarized. Those who see the superficial side of things and who cry out for something more often reject *everything* the Spirit is doing because it is so mixed with flesh and frivolity. On the other hand, those whom God *is* using in renewal often reject every form of constructive criticism because of all the extraordinary fruit they have seen. We need both! We need those who are grieved and those who are aggressive, those who watch and weep along with those who dive in and delight. We need refreshing *and* repentance, charisma *and* correction, empowering *and* purifying, blessing *and* burden, anointing *and* agonizing. Otherwise—and mark this carefully—we will end up choosing between "correct" religion that is more dead than alive and fading "renewal" that sputters, stagnates, and eventually stinks.

Josiah and Jeremiah were both called by the Lord. In fact, *both* Josiah's movement and Jeremiah's message were founded on repentance. But the prophet called the people deeper. Josiah helped to delay the coming judgment; Jeremiah prepared them for the judgment that had to come. We need to learn the lessons from the past! We need the prophets of the thirteenth year. In the midst of reformation and renewal the Lord said through Jeremiah that, "Judah did not return to Me with all her heart, but only in pretense" (Jer. 3:10). Are *we* returning to Him with all our hearts today, or are we getting caught up in the excitement of the latest, greatest Holy Ghost happening?

The Jesus People movement was an international work of God, but its lasting fruit was greatly diminished because of the massive lacks in the Church of the early 1970's. The Charismatic Renewal was another genuine move of the Spirit, but for many, gifts more than God formed the center of their experience. Therefore what could have been was not to be. Beyond these moves of the Spirit, there were genuine revivals in the past that had a real impact, but then the fire faded, the new wine waned, and only a few went on in power while the rest lived on a memory. May it not happen to us! This is the hour we have longed for. This *is* the day. I am desperately jealous for "the real thing."

In spite of what many are saying today, "this" is not yet "that." We have not yet seen 3,000 *converted* and *added to the Body* through a single message (Acts 2). We have not yet seen public miracles that cause citywide shaking (Acts 3). We have not yet seen the real persecution begin (Acts 4), or couples like Ananias and Sapphira dropping dead in our services because of their deception (Acts 5), or men like Stephen stoned because of their witness (Acts 6–7). But we're getting there! I genuinely believe that in some churches in America, we are now seeing the "it" (as in, "This is it!") that could turn into "that" (as in, "This is that!"). Those who feel God has called them to "correct" the current renewal would do well to first search their own hearts.

1. It would be a real error to reject the current work of the Spirit, even in its initial stages. In the well-known words of the prophet Zechariah, "Who despises the day of small things?" (Zech. 4:10a) If we despise the small, we may never see the grand. Let us nurture rather than negate.

2. It is dangerous to exaggerate the past. (Read Ecclesiastes 7:10!) This is almost as bad as excusing the present. It's time for realism—past, present, and future. God has moved, God is moving, and God will continue to move. Just how wide-ranging and deep that move will be depends on our humble, prayerful, wholehearted response.

3. We must guard against a cynical, never-satisfied attitude. When the trickle comes, this attitude says, "This is hardly a river," and when the river comes it says, "This is hardly a flood," and when the flood comes it says, "Floods are dangerous!"

4. "Orthodox" critics should put up or shut up. Abstract, theological "truth" that tears down without building up is of no use at all. To quote James 2:18b, "Show me your faith without deeds, and I will show you my faith by what I do." Or, in the words of Ecclesiastes, "even a live dog is better off than a dead lion!" (Ecc. 9:4b) Let's see the fruit of your "orthodox" faith—in

your ministry, in your church, and around the world. The gospel gives life.

Still, there are some deep concerns in this "thirteenth year of Josiah." Search this out, and see if the Lord has something to say to you. There are problems that *must* be addressed.

1. How much stress is placed on the issue of personal sin in the life of the believer? As Andrew Murray wrote, "The need of revival always points to previous decline, and decline was always caused by sin. Humiliation and contrition have [therefore] ever been the conditions of revival."[1] We preach repentance because we need revival. We need revival because we are backslidden. We are backslidden because we have sinned. What are the sins that caused so many American believers to become compromised or carnal or selfish or sluggish or religious or rigid? Those are the sins that must be addressed, and that is where repentance must begin for each of us individually. Then revival—not just refreshing or renewal—will come. Targeted preaching will hit the mark.

2. Many have had an experience instead of an encounter. What starts well ("I was so blessed last night. I've grown so much more in love with Jesus!") quickly gets off track ("I need to get blessed again! I need another touch.") Nothing less than hunger *for God* will bring lasting fullness.

3. The peripheral in past revivals has frequently become the central here. Manifestations in past revivals were the *result* of the preaching, while many of today's manifestations are the *object* of the meeting, becoming the *focus* of the teaching, the *proof* of the praying, and the *showcase* of the service. There is a

difference between falling under conviction and falling under the power, between being delivered and being zapped. We need to be careful in our comparisons!

4. John Wesley said that "they that bring most holiness to heaven will find most happiness there...." In the current renewal, many have become happy in the Lord, leading to holy living. But what happens when the happiness halts? What happens when the euphoria ends? A more biblical emphasis would be on holiness leading to happiness (in other words, repentance leading to refreshing). Then both will last. Of course, the key to repentance is often a fresh, renewing touch from heaven, but we have almost completely forgotten that a piercing word from heaven is also part of the package!

5. Pastors from around the nation are getting excited about revival. They've had it with church activity and business, and they're desperate for divine visitation. But are they desperate for the divine Visitor? He is still a consuming Flame. He is still a refiner's Fire. Do you want *Him*?

6. Where is the holy, "take off your shoes" Presence of God? Why so much frivolity if the majestic God is so near?

7. So many say, "More blessing, Lord," but do not pray, "A deeper burden, Lord." The extent of their vision seems to be spiritual fun and games. Or, to express this to the tune of "Ring Around the Rosy," many think that revival is merely a matter of:

> Line up at the altar.
> Time to laugh and falter.

"Ushers! Ushers!"
We all fall down!

But far from our church altar
Nations quake and falter
And starving boys lay dying
And homeless girls lay crying
With missionaries groaning
And saints in prison moaning
And terrorists still toiling
While the Middle East is boiling
And America collapses
As morality relapses
And fetal brains are sucked out
Tiny organs neatly plucked out
While gays prance down our streets
And we hold Christian retreats....
Yes, the world is going mad,
But not us. Oh no, we're glad.

For now it's party time:
Believers get in line!
"Ushers! Ushers!"
We all fall down!

I absolutely, emphatically, and without reserve believe in people falling under the Spirit's power and being supernaturally touched. I have experienced it personally and it has happened to thousands we have prayed for. We have seen them stagger, collapse, shake, weep, and laugh. That is not the problem. But something is often missing in our motivation and our method. We need to grow up!

8. With so much stress placed on outward, physical manifestations, it's only fair to ask what will happen when they stop. Who will seek God while in the valley and fast for dying souls while in the desert? How

deep are we? Manifestations are often glorious, but maturity is the goal.

9. Much teaching in the current renewal caters to our easy-believe, "what's in it for me?" mentality. We want empowering to get instead of empowering to give. The great missionary Jonathan Goforth asked if Jesus would have continued to multiply the fishes and loaves for the 5,000 hungry people if His disciples kept feeding and refeeding those seated in the first few rows. And will God continue to pour His blessing into us if we don't pour it out on others?

10. Is the *emphasis* on "getting drunk" on God's new wine reflective of the heart and soul of New Testament Christianity? The question is not whether God sometimes overwhelms His people with an outpouring of the Spirit to the point that we are accused of drunkenness. Let the inundation come, and let the critics howl! The question is whether we should build our theology on the words of the mockers who say, "These men are drunk," instead of saying with Peter, "These men are *not* drunk"—and then, like Peter, bringing a withering word to both the critical and the convicted. Doesn't the New Testament urge us to be alert, sober, and watchful? Of course, we can never get enough of the joy of the Lord (at least, I can't!) and we can never have too much of the Spirit. But we *can* major on the outward instead of the inward; we can miss the heart of the Word.

Why not emphasize fullness instead of drunkenness? The difficulty is not so much with the nature of the manifestations. The difficulty is with our emphasis.

We spotlight the sensational and underscore the unusual, and then we wonder why people aren't focusing on Jesus. The bottom line is that the Church in this hour doesn't need more folly. Filling, yes; folly, no. Rejoicing, yes; revelry, no. We are called to go into all the world and make disciples, not drunkards.

11. The Church still has little or no prophetic voice to the nation. The outpouring of the Spirit has certainly drawn the attention of the media, and to some extent, the world *has* been touched. Backsliders have returned to the Lord and sinners have been saved. But the Church hardly has a *voice*. Someone must sound the trumpet! Those who have been awakened must in turn become awakeners. Who will call our nation to account?

12. For some, the "blessing" could become a curse. (There are churches that have completely bought into "the renewal" that are already in serious decline. Danger!) God forbid that we make the Spirit into a spectacle and turn holy excitement into Hollywood entertainment. If you concentrate on the laughter more than the Lord and on the shaking more than the Savior, take heed. You may get what you want. Instead of soaring with the Spirit you may end up slobbering in the Spirit. Instead of "soaking" you may find yourself sinking. Watch out!

The fact is that even now, there are leaders around the world saying, "Where do we go from here?" There are Christians asking, "Is this it?" I believe that the Spirit is saying, "Dig deeper! Believe for more! This is only the beginning. It's time for a brand new day."

I for one don't want to miss out. How about you?

The contemporaries of [George] Fox and [William] Penn regarded their way of life with extreme repulsion; their response to it was terrible hatred, and years of bloody persecution.... It is wild and unbridled enthusiasm [i.e., fanaticism], said the people of that time, who found it so disquieting; but nowadays we regard it as a mighty movement of the Spirit, albeit mixed up with many strange features.

W. Nitsch, in W.J. Hollenweger's *The Pentecostals*

Can you find in your hearts to be like [those] Jews, who prayed and longed for the coming of the Messias, and when He came, rejected and crucified Him, because He came not in the way their prejudices led them to look for Him?

James Robe, in Arthur Wallis'
In the Day of Thy Power

There is a general tendency to err on the side of prejudice, suspicion and unbelief; and this attitude is nowhere countenanced in the New Testament. Where there is doubt, let there be a patient waiting upon God until the true character of the work is manifest, for the tree will be known by its fruit. Let all take heed. If we indulge in hasty criticism we may be speaking against the Holy Spirit; if we oppose we may "be found even to be fighting against God."

Arthur Wallis, *In the Day of Thy Power*

"Not from Above but from Below"

From the Berlin Declaration of 1907,
in which the leaders of the German
Evangelical Church rejected the
modern Pentecostal movement
as inspired by the devil

"A sham...a mockery, a blasphemous travesty of the real thing."

Peter Price, a leading Welsh pastor,
reacting to the 1904 Revival

Chapter Three

Are You "Religious"?

Religion can be a good word or a bad word. James in the New Testament used it in the sense of true godly living (see James 1:26-27). That kind of religion is good. But for the most part, "religious" people give God a hard time. Just ask Jesus! It was the religious leaders who rejected Him, opposed Him, misunderstood Him, and handed Him over to be killed. Sinners heard His teaching and were elated; the religious heard Him and were enraged. The people wanted to crown Him; the religious leaders wanted to crucify Him.

It is no different in our day and age. "Religious" people don't like the One whom Jesus sent—the Holy Spirit! They have the outward form yet resist the inward fire. They are externally pious yet internally pompous. "Religious" people are hypocrites. Are you "religious"?

Notice these amazing passages from Matthew's Gospel. First, Matthew 14:34–15:2:

> When they had crossed over, they landed at Gennesaret. And when the men of that place recognized Jesus, they sent word to all the surrounding country. People brought all their sick to Him and begged Him to let the sick just touch the edge of His cloak, and all who touched Him were healed. Then some Pharisees and teachers of the law came to Jesus from

Jerusalem and asked, "Why do your disciples break the tradition of the elders? They don't wash their hands before they eat!"

Do you see it? Jesus, the Son of God, heals the sick. The long-awaited Messiah brings deliverance to the captives and release to the oppressed. Glory and honor to God! The time of fulfillment is at hand. Israel's prayers are finally being answered. The long night of her suffering is coming to an end. Jesus the Savior is here! The Lord is visiting His people.

The scene is almost indescribable. A man who was lame leaps for joy, dancing and skipping and laughing. A father holds his children in his arms and sobs uncontrollably: His blind eyes have been opened! For the first time in years, he can see the faces of his precious little ones. Another man shouts, "I'm clean! I'm clean!" His leprosy has vanished in an instant. A young mother falls to her knees in worship. Her dying daughter is whole! The promised Deliverer has come.

But that's not what these Pharisees saw. Jesus was breaking their religious traditions! "Your disciples don't wash their hands before they eat!" Who cares about the miracles? Who cares about the mighty moving of the Spirit? Who cares about the tangible demonstration of the power of God? Who cares about all these desperate people being touched? He's violating our customs; He can't be from God. Our traditions go back for generations. Who does He think He is? That, my friend, is a hypocritical, religious spirit.

Now look at Matthew 19:2-3:

> Large crowds followed Him, and He healed them there. Some Pharisees came to Him to test Him. They asked, "Is it lawful for a man to divorce his wife for any and every reason?"

That is the religious mentality: "Forget about the fact that none of us have ever seen such a display of mercy and compassion in our lives. Forget about the crowds being healed. Instead, focus in on one thing only: What is Jesus' doctrinal position on a controversial side issue? That's what we care about!"

Does it sound extreme? It is, but it is extremely common! The Spirit falls dramatically on an entire congregation, hundreds are touched and transformed, and religious believers get offended. Why? Because their sacred traditions were violated. The preacher didn't use the King James Bible (or, in some circles, his sin was that he *did* use the King James). People jumped, or fell, or laughed, or cried; they were too loud, or they were too quiet. The service lasted for five hours, or the sermon lasted for five minutes. The sick were prayed for before the message (or, maybe there wasn't even a message). "That's not how we do it in our church!"

You would think we would have more sense. In one group, men and women are judged for wearing suits and dresses to the meeting. In another group, they're judged for coming in jeans and sneakers. And if the Spirit happens to move in one of these groups that doesn't adhere to our dress code…"It can't be God," we say. "The pastor wasn't wearing a tie." Or, "The pastor *was* wearing a tie." And we can make all these foolish judgments subconsciously, not realizing for a moment that is why we reject their ministries. May the Lord help us to grow!

Do you think I'm exaggerating? Hardly! One movement I know rejected the ministry of a visiting pastor, in spite of hundreds of hungry souls that flocked to the altar to be saved. What was the problem? The pastor was dressed up (they were casual); he liked to sing the old, classic hymns (they preferred modern choruses); he shouted and got emotional as he preached (their leaders *taught* instead of preached, and they were *laid back* in their delivery); he spoke against sin clearly (they thought this was condemning). And so his ministry to them was cut short, but it was God who sent him and anointed him to minister to them! (And, yes, I've seen almost the exact flip side of this religious bigotry also. I'm sure I've been guilty of it too!)

Jesus is being wonderfully exalted in one church group, and we reject it as being emotionalism or even demonic without so much as asking God for His side of the story, and for the most part, basing our positions on hearsay—on secondhand stories and unconfirmed reports. Why are we so sure? Because that group doesn't agree with our end-time scheme! They say that Jesus is returning before the tribulation (or, after the tribulation; or, there will not be a specific seven-year tribulation), or, they don't share our view on divine healing, therefore they can't be receiving an outpouring of the Spirit. And has it ever occurred to us that, based on *their* doctrine, *we* can't receive an outpouring either? Oh that God would deliver us from our religious narrowness!

Finney said it clearly:

Now it is remarkable that so far as my knowledge extends, all the seasons of great revivals with which the church has been blessed from the very first, have been broken up and the revival influence set aside by an ecclesiastical and sectarian jangling, to preserve what they call the purity of the church and the faith once delivered to the saints. I believe it to be a truth, that ministers as a class, have always been responsible for the decline of revivals; that their own sectarianism, ambition and prejudice have led them to preach and contend, to run to synods, councils, and other ecclesiastical meetings, until the churches, at first pained and even shocked with this tendency of things, have come to adopt their views, imbibe their spirit, and get entirely away from God.[1]

As one man of God once said, speaking of an area that missed out on revival, "I verily believe revival would have come to _____ at that time if prayerful sympathy, instead of carnal criticism, had been shown."[2]

And when an awakening came to Lewis Island in 1949, Duncan Campbell said that the exact same thing took place; critics quickly believed rumors claiming that the revival was giving birth to doctrinal error: "As in [the previous] case, so also in Lewis, criticism was based on hearsay—never a wise procedure. If only those who opposed had gone to hear for themselves, how different the story might have been today!"[3]

Remember this well: Jonathan Edwards was a staunch Calvinist and Charles Finney was a committed Arminian, yet God mightily used them both in revival in our land—although that hasn't stopped some Calvinists from belittling Finney and some Arminians from disparaging Edwards. And have you ever stopped to wonder what would have happened if the Arminians (or, the Calvinists) sat on God's throne and controlled revivals? One of these men of God (or maybe even both of them) would not have been used: "Sorry! We won't bless you. Your doctrine doesn't agree with ours." (Of course, *our* doctrine is faultless and complete. We've got it all!)

The two prominent figures in the great eighteenth century revivals in England were John Wesley and George Whitefield. At one point in their lives, these close friends completely split up because of their Arminian-Calvinist doctrinal differences. But who can think of two more effective vessels of revival in the history of the Church? How glorious it would be if the Lord gave us a thousand Wesleys and

Whitefields, Edwards and Finneys in our day. Could we receive from them all? (Maybe God sends us so many different messengers because He knows we'll only receive from one or the other!)

Pentecostals and Charismatics need to remember that the revivals in Wales in 1904 to 1905 and in the Hebrides in 1949 to 1950 had great, deep movements of the Spirit, with virtually no emphasis on speaking in tongues. But non-Pentecostals and non-Charismatics need to acknowledge that the awesome, unprecedented outpourings of the Spirit that have taken place around the world in recent years (e.g., in South America and China) have almost always been marked with tongues, signs, wonders and miracles.[4]

Let's not be so quick to judge a moving of God based on the doctrine of those involved. The Spirit is sweeping millions into the Kingdom, and some of the Lord's self-appointed "truth sentries" glibly sit by and say, "This is not from God. It's too fast, too big, too much." God looks at *them* and says, "It's too bad you don't know how to be blessed!" The windows of heaven are open wide, but the hearts of heaven's future inhabitants are too often fastened shut.

Of course, doctrine is *critically* important, especially for the long-term health of the Body. Faulty foundations make for unstable structures. But we must never miss out on true revival because of doctrinal differences. Does God love that believer with whom we disagree enough to answer their prayers? Does He care enough for them to shower them with His grace? Then why can't He bring revival to them—or through them?

After years in revival ministry, Finney had this to say:

Another thing that is working an immense evil in the present day is the growing sectarianism of the church. It seems to me that the leading denominations that have heretofore been most zealous and successful in promoting revivals of religion, are within the last ten years, becoming highly sectarian in their spirit and measures....

Now this is certainly a great evil; and unless a counteracting influence can be brought to bear on the churches; unless ministers cease from this sectarian spirit—cease from these janglings and strife of words—cease from creating prejudices—cease from heresy-hunting, and all the management of ecclesiastical ambition, and give themselves up directly to promoting brotherly love, harmony in the church, the conversion of sinners and the sanctification of the saints, it is certain that revivals of religion cannot exist and go forward in purity and power.[5]

What are *we* promoting in our day? What will *our* ministry patterns lead to? Some of us have become so sound that we are now soundly asleep!

Obviously, we can't ignore major doctrinal error. We need to stand for the truth without compromise and expose that which denies the faith. We must confront heresy and never back down. There are absolute essentials—dealing with the inspiration of Scripture, the nature of God, the person of Jesus, His virgin birth, His atoning death, His resurrection, salvation only through Him, the resurrection of the saved and the lost, to name just a few—that are non-negotiable. God won't use a rank heretic to refresh His Church.

As for the genuine believers He *does* use, they're not perfect yet! Even "mighty men of God" have blind spots, and outpourings do not guarantee accuracy. There's nothing that says we can't disagree with parts of the message or differ with the minister's manners and methods, but we must be very careful not to throw out the baby with the bathwater. If

God sent it, it's good—even if it needs to be cleaned up, dusted off, and fine-tuned a little.

The vessel being used may be a little immature. He may have a lot more spiritual "schooling" ahead and need further training in the Word. Still, he can be mightily used in revival. He may be strong in faith, strong in zeal, and powerfully anointed, yet lacking in experience. But let's not write off and reject a servant of the Lord—clearly bearing much fruit and radically affecting lives—because he hasn't "arrived" yet. Let's receive what the Spirit is doing through him while helping him to grow and mature. Do you think Evan Roberts at 26 years old made any mistakes in his ministry? Yet he was the central figure, the divine detonator, so to speak, handpicked by God, without a doubt, behind the awesome spiritual explosion in Wales in 1904. And as for the rest of us in ministry, are we without fault? How perfect is our delivery and style? Do we always do things *exactly* the way Jesus would have us do them?

Of course, we must *never* tolerate the presence of moral transgression among God's people, regardless of whether these "sinning saints" claim to be "eternally secure"—and no matter how much they seem to be "anointed." One mark of true revival is that it will wash away habitual sin in its wake. In fact, if it *doesn't* lead to holiness, it wasn't sent from heaven. Make no mistake! Deep revival goes hand in hand with dramatic reformation.

But let's beware of a judgmental, dogmatic spirit on the nonessentials—on the things that will not keep us out of heaven or greatly affect our daily walk here. It's one thing to preach and teach what we believe with all our hearts, giving careful attention to all the major truths of the Scripture. Systematic and in-depth teaching of biblical doctrine is fundamental. (Of course, everybody thinks their doctrine is biblical. What teacher says, "Don't listen to me. I'm preaching error. I'm making the whole thing up!") But we must never lose sight of the fact that if someone is saved, they are a part of God's family, bound for heaven, and destined for glory—in spite of their doctrinal imperfections.

Should it surprise us that our Father would want to bless them in this world, before they get to heaven? Would it offend us if the Lord bypassed us in our doctrinal stiffness and dead orthodoxy and stood by those whose hearts were wholly His (see 2 Chron. 16:9)—even if they didn't know any Hebrew or Greek?

How tragic that we despise the gift because we don't like the packaging. What a shame that we miss the Spirit because we don't like the style. What a pity that we fashion ourselves to be so deep when, in point of fact, we're often so dull. We call it discernment; God calls it judgment, and judgment steals the blessing every time!

Can we be honest with ourselves? What makes us think we would have followed John the Baptist? How many of us would have felt more at home with the Pharisees and teachers of the Law, the seasoned religious leaders, the men in the know, those with a sacred tradition of truth? Why trade in such a good thing for a fanatical, offensive, brash, revival preacher in the wilderness? Plus, siding with the religious crowd was acceptable; joining with John might cause us to wind up in prison. "Religion" is so much more comfortable than revival!

How can we be so sure that we would have laid our lives down to become disciples of Jesus? After all, the Sadducees were the keepers of the Temple and preservers of the Torah. The Pharisees were deeply observant men, pious even in the smallest details of eating and drinking, rigidly faithful in prayer and giving. Jesus was a radical! His teaching was controversial, His methods sometimes shocking, His lifestyle unnervingly nonconformist. The religious leaders must have had good reasons for rejecting Him. Why should I venture out into the deep? It's nice and safe snuggled here on the shore!

What about you? Are you hungry for revival, or are you happy with religion? Do you want the fire, or are you satisfied with a form? Do you desire a tidy little service, or are you desperate for torrents of the life-giving Spirit?

On the day of Pentecost, would you have been among those God-fearing Jews who had ears to hear what the Spirit was saying ("we hear them declaring the wonders of God in our own tongues!" [Acts 2:11b]), or would you have been among those God-fearing Jews who mocked, saying, "They have had too much wine" (Acts 2:13b)? After all, what was the historic precedent for the events that unfolded that glorious day? Where was the clear scriptural justification? Where were supernatural tongues ever mentioned in the Hebrew Scriptures? Prophecy, yes; tongues, no. As for people speaking in foreign languages in Israel, that was a sign of judgment in the Old Testament! And just who were these wild-eyed fishermen and tax collectors anyway? Who ordained them?

The religious stood back and got sanctimonious; the humble pressed in and got saved. How easy it is to be so right that we end up right outside the blessing of God!

We quote John the Baptist and Jesus, yet we follow in the footsteps of the hypocrites who opposed them. We pray for the Spirit's rain and thunder but get uncomfortable at the first sign of clouds. May God loosen us up and deliver us from our spiritual stiffness. It's hard to move freely in such starchy shirts!

Consider the example of Smith Wigglesworth. Raised in an impoverished family, he was working twelve-hour days by the age of six. His wife taught him to read the Bible when he was in his twenties, and for the rest of his life (he died in 1947 at the age of 87), God's Word was the only book he read. He was radical in his methods, blunt in his manners, and awesomely effective in his ministry: winning the lost, delivering the demonized, healing the sick, and even raising the dead.

Yet most evangelical preachers today who claim to revere Peter and John—"unschooled, ordinary men" according to Acts 4:13—reject or ignore Wigglesworth because he was an unschooled, ordinary man. He didn't have the proper theological training; he wasn't a polished speaker; he was too Pentecostal. And yet the same things that made Peter and John different (they had walked closely with Jesus and were anointed with His power) are the very things that caused Wigglesworth to stand out in his generation.

What makes these modern preachers so sure they would have liked the apostles? Maybe Peter wouldn't have passed their doctrinal test. Maybe John would have been too simple. And as for Matthew, wasn't he really a layman? (Of course, the shoe can be on the other foot too: Some of our Pentecostal and Charismatic friends would have had a hard time with Paul. He was too intellectual and had *too much* theological training. A man like that couldn't possibly flow in the Spirit. Oh, how narrow we are!)

The only way we can prove our openness to the Holy Spirit is by welcoming Him afresh when He comes—however, whenever, and through whomever that may be. Listen to this story that Wigglesworth tells about a young man who received the baptism of the Spirit—with speaking in tongues—at a Pentecostal meeting. His own group wasn't too happy!

> The brethren were very upset about this and came to the [young man's] father and said to him, "You must take your son aside and tell him to cease." They did not want any disturbance. The father told the son and said, "My boy, I have been attending this church for twenty years and have never seen anything of this kind. We are established in the truth and do not want anything new. We won't have it." The son replied, "If that is God's plan I will obey, but somehow or other I don't think it is." As they were going home the horse stood still; the wheels were in deep ruts. The father pulled at the reins but the horse did not move. He asked, "What do you think is up?" The son answered, "It has got established." God save us from becoming stationary.[6]

And God save us from getting stuck in the ruts. It is possible to get too established!

None of us has seen it all; none of us knows it all; and none of us has it all. We are small, individual parts of a great big Body. None of us are "it." (There's only one "big shot" here—and He doesn't have to take out two-page ads in *Charisma* or *Christianity Today* to get His point across.) All of us need to learn more, receive more, and grow more. All of us need some things added to us, other things taken away from us, and still other things corrected within us. We all need to be revived sometime, somewhere, somehow. And we need one another!

Then why are we so stubborn? Why are we so resistant to the fresh wind of the Spirit? It is true that some believers simply can't sort out the good from the bad. They quickly get confused and become unsure. Others have been disappointed so many times before that they're afraid to get their hopes up again. But for many of us, it's that stifling, proud, religious mentality that gets in the way. It killed the prophets, and it can kill us too. So I ask you again (as I ask myself for the hundredth time): Are you "religious"?

The God of the Bible—and the God of revival—is a God of life. May we live and thrive in Him! This is no time for dead religion.

As for new religions, beyond the numbering of a busy man, they come and go—especially in Los Angeles. They come with the blare of trumpets out of tune and harmony, but lustily blown with all the power of human or inhuman lungs; they shine with phosphorescent gleam, strangely, like that of brimstone, and with color more or less tainted; they distract the affrighted atmosphere with a bewildering jargon of babbling tongues of all grades—dried, boiled and soaked; they rant and jump and dance and roll in a disgusting amalgamation of African voodoo superstition and Caucasian insanity, and will pass away like the nightmares of hysteria that they are.

Rev. R.J. Burdette, denouncing the Azusa Street revival

When God moved among a group of Christians in Madras in 1940 the churches at first were supportive until they realized that the man God was using was Bahkt Singh. Suddenly the ministers' conference came to a decision: "We in the Indian Ministers' Conference have met and passed a resolution never again to make any place available to this Punjabi preacher. Our objection is that he is not an ordained minister, and therefore had no right to baptize anyone."

Brian Edwards, *Revival: A People Saturated With God*

Five churches have already been denied me, and some clergy, if possible, would oblige me to depart out of these coasts.

George Whitefield, after preaching in America
on the reality of the new birth

Woe to you, teachers of the law and Pharisees, you hypocrites! You shut the kingdom of heaven in men's faces. You yourselves do not enter, nor will you let those enter who are trying to.

The Lord Jesus, Matt. 23:13

Chapter Four

The Hypocrite's Checklist (I)

In Matthew 23, Jesus pronounced seven woes on the Pharisees and scribes. His words were scathing, His denunciations severe, His accusations scalding. It is a shattering chapter to read. Unfortunately, we've gotten used to Matthew 23. After all, these were the Pharisees! They were just a bunch of hypocrites, right?

Well, we have to admit from the Gospels that there were some good Pharisees who stood with Jesus and supported Him, but weren't the rest of them just bold-faced liars? Weren't they deceivers? Wasn't it obvious to everyone that these religious leaders were empty inside? Not necessarily. They were highly respected by many of the people. They weren't like the pastor who runs off with his secretary or the TV preacher who makes fraudulent miracle claims. They were super-committed, super-devoted, and super-serious about God's law.

But for many of them, pride entered their lives. Their religion became a performance, their piety a show. Outwardly they were spotless; inwardly they were stained. They did not practice what they preached, and when Jesus came, He saw through their souls. He read their hearts like open mail, and He infuriated them with His ways and words. In fact, very early in His ministry, some of these leaders began to plot how they could *kill* the Son of God (see Mark 3:6). He exposed their hypocritical religion, and there is nothing that will oppose revival like hypocritical religion.

Now consider this carefully: *The same roadblocks that stand in the way of revival often bar the way to heaven.* That which robs you of the blessing of God in this world can steal eternal life from you in the world to come. Religious hypocrisy is dangerous! Religious hypocrisy destroys.

Some of us seem to think that it is only particular religious groups and denominations that have a monopoly on religious hypocrisy. The fact is, we've got some skilled, seasoned, full-time hypocrites in our own midst, along with plenty of part-time hypocrites, whatever our religious or denominational persuasion may be. Where there is religion, there will be hypocrisy.

Here's a checklist for self-examination. If you fail completely, you probably need to get saved! Otherwise, rejoice where you pass the test and repent and ask for grace to change where you fail. (By the way, if you find yourself getting angry or defensive as you read, maybe God is trying to speak to you. I've already been through the coals in my own life in the process of writing this!)

1) A religious hypocrite claims to have an exclusive corner on the truth, even among God's people. A vicar in the Church of England once said to Leonard Ravenhill, "We don't recognize your ordination." Ravenhill answered, "The Church of Rome doesn't recognize yours." "But we have the apostolic succession!" came the strong reply. "The only proof of apostolic succession," said the clear-headed Ravenhill, "is apostolic success." That's where the rubber meets the road!

So many groups (and individuals) think that they and they alone have it all. "We have the true interpretation. We have the unbroken chain of revelation. We have the orthodox doctrine." How familiar this sounds!

> Then they hurled insults at him [i.e., the blind man Jesus healed] and said, "You are this fellow's disciple! We are disciples of Moses! We know that God spoke to Moses, but as for this fellow, we don't even know where He comes from." (John 9:28-29)

The latest wave of doctrinal arrogance in America today is coming from the predestination camp: "The problems in the church can be traced back to the fact that we have departed from Calvinism! That alone is God-centered truth. That alone is pure Bible."

No, "Reformed" doctrine doesn't have all the answers either, even though some modern Calvinistic teachers on the radio and in print will tell you they've got the key. And some of them, like the religious leaders of old, are not afraid to hurl insults around at their non-Reformed brethren, damning to hell those believers who dare disagree with them. Careful! Those who claimed to be Moses' disciples 2,000 years ago had a hard time following Jesus, the Prophet who was like Moses, when He came.

Proverbs 3:7-8 is the antidote for elitism:

> Do not be wise in your own eyes; fear the LORD and shun evil. This will bring health to your body and nourishment to your bones.

Pride kills.

2) A religious hypocrite is self-righteous. Remember, the fundamental attitude of religious hypocrisy is that it wants to be something in the sight of man.

> ...You are the ones who justify yourselves in the eyes of men, but God knows your hearts. What is highly valued among men is detestable in God's sight. (Luke 16:15)

Religious hypocrisy measures itself by human standards:

> To some who were confident of their own righteousness and looked down on everybody else, Jesus told this parable. (Luke 18:9)

Religious hypocrisy is self-deceived and fails to see the depth of its poverty. Therefore, it cannot be healed. It says, "I'm not sick!" Because it trusts in its own righteousness, it cannot receive the righteousness that comes from God alone.

> Some Pharisees who were with Him heard Him say this and asked, "What? Are we blind too?" Jesus said, "If you were blind, you would not be guilty of sin; but now that you claim you can see, your guilt remains." (John 9:40-41)

> It is not the healthy who need a doctor, but the sick. But go and learn what this means: "I desire mercy, not sacrifice." For I have not come to call the righteous, but sinners. (Matt. 9:12b-13)

How did the Pharisee pray in Luke 18:11? "God, I thank you that I am not like other men...." I'm religious! I'm better!

> But the tax collector stood at a distance. He would not even look up to heaven, but beat his breast and said, "God, have mercy on me, a sinner." I tell you that this man [said Jesus], rather than the other, went home justified before God. (Luke 18:13-14a)

In whose eyes do *you* want to be justified?

3) A religious hypocrite is a slave to human praise and criticism. He is not free to please God, since the fear of man binds him up and the praise of man builds him up. This kind of attitude makes faith and bold public confession virtually impossible:

> How can you believe if you accept praise from one another, yet make no effort to obtain the praise that comes from the only God? (John 5:44)

> Even after Jesus had done all these miraculous signs in their presence, they still would not believe in Him. ... Yet at the same time many even among the leaders believed in Him. But because of the Pharisees they would not confess their faith for fear they would be put out of the synagogue; for they loved praise from men more than praise from God. (John 12:37,42-43)

Contrast this with the attitude of Paul:

> Am I now trying to win the approval of men, or of God? Or am I trying to please men? If I were still trying to please men, I would not be a servant of Christ. (Gal. 1:10)

The fear of man is a snare! For true believers in the glorious Lord Jesus, it is insanity.

> The Jew[ish leaders] still did not believe that he had been blind and had received his sight until they sent for the man's parents. "Is this your son?" they asked. "Is this the one you say was born blind? How is it that now he can see?" "We know he is our son," the parents answered, "and we know he was born blind. But how he can see now, or who opened his eyes, we don't know. Ask him. He is of age; he will speak for himself." His parents said this because they were afraid of the Jew[ish leadership], for already the Jew[ish leaders] had decided that anyone who acknowledged that Jesus was the Christ would be put out of the synagogue. That was why his parents said, "He is of age; ask him." (John 9:18-23)

I wonder how those parents are feeling today.

4) A religious hypocrite is jealous, envious, and competitive. Instead of rejoicing that the Kingdom is being advanced through others, that the name of Jesus is being exalted, that people are being blessed, religious hypocrites get angry and judgmental because the ministry isn't coming through them. Soon enough, they oppose it. People of God, beware: This kind of attitude can be disastrous; it caused the religious leaders to reject Jesus and the apostles. Be on your guard! "For he [Pilate] knew it was out of *envy* that they had handed Jesus over to him" (Matt. 27:18).

> The apostles performed many miraculous signs and wonders among the people. And all the believers used to meet together in Solomon's Colonnade. No one else dared join them, even though they were highly regarded by the people. Nevertheless, more and more men and women believed in the Lord and were added to their number. As a result, people brought the sick into the streets and laid them on beds and mats so that at least Peter's shadow might fall on some of them as he passed by. Crowds gathered also from the towns around Jerusalem, bringing their sick and those tormented by evil spirits, and all of them were healed. Then the high priest and all his associates, who were members of the party of the Sadducees, were *filled with jealousy*. They arrested the apostles and put them in the public jail. (Acts 5:12-18)

> On the next Sabbath almost the whole city gathered to hear the word of the Lord. When the Jews saw the crowds, they were *filled with jealousy* and talked abusively against what Paul was saying. (Acts 13:44-45)

Where does the spirit of envy and competition come from?

> ...if you harbor bitter envy and selfish ambition in your hearts, do not boast about it or deny the truth. Such "wisdom" does not come down from heaven but is earthly, unspiritual, of

the devil. For where you have envy and selfish ambition, there you find disorder and every evil practice. (James 3:14-16)

One night, during the Welsh Revival,

Evan Roberts was preaching with great difficulty. His sensitive spirit could detect the difference between the enmity of a sinful heart and opposition from a decided will. Recognizing the opposition in this case to be caused by the latter, he stopped preaching and said, "There is willful opposition here to the Word of God and to the Spirit of God. It hinders His manifestation in our midst. Let us all go to prayer and ask that those who oppose the Holy Spirit will either repent or leave the service."

During the prayer four men got up and left. Mr. Roberts felt the change in atmosphere and continued to preach. *All four of the men who left were ministers.* Perhaps they had allowed jealousy from the abyss to take hold of their hearts. Maybe they were saying, "Why can such a simple miner do these things which are our right?"[1]

How dare this young, inexperienced man draw such crowds! How dare he be so blessed!

Look closely at John 11:

Then the chief priests and the Pharisees called a meeting of the Sanhedrin. "What are we accomplishing?" they asked. "Here is this man performing many miraculous signs. If we let Him go on like this, everyone will believe in Him, and then the Romans will come and take away both our place and our nation." (John 11:47-48)

The modern version of this is, "We've got to do something quickly about this new ministry in town! People are getting saved, delivered, and healed there. If we don't discredit it and work against it, soon we'll lose all our people—and all their money too." (There is, of course, another common alternative. We'll copy what the new ministry is doing. We'll put on the same show. We'll emphasize the same things. So what if God hasn't called us or anointed us to minister like they do. At least they won't get our people.)

How carnal we can become! The Lord of the harvest thrusts forth laborers into His harvest field, and rather than rejoicing, we attack. Whose side are we on anyway?

Why not adopt the attitude of Paul? Imprisoned in Phillipi, knowing that people were preaching Jesus with all kinds of mixed motives, still he rejoiced because the Good News was going forth. It's obvious whose Kingdom Paul was fighting for—and it wasn't the Apostle Paul International Ministries empire. He was jealous *for* Jesus instead of being jealous *of* his brothers. Can we say the same?

Let this be our guide:

> Do nothing out of selfish ambition or vain conceit, but in humility consider others better than yourselves. (Phil. 2:3)

Overcome the evil of jealousy and envy with *love*—love for the Church, love for the lost, love for the Lord. If you are secure in your relationship with Him, if you know His smile, you will feel threatened by nothing and in competition with no one. Your only desire will be to see others blessed!

Remember the example of Jesus: Because He knew who He was, where He came from, and where He was going, He washed the disciples' feet (John 13). Establish your heart in God, then serve and promote others!

5) A religious hypocrite is highly critical. That is a natural consequence of dead religion or a dry, worn-out walk. Religious hypocrites are not truly happy, so they don't like to see others happy. They can't accept the fact that people are being blessed. Miserable people make others miserable too! And because they do not walk by faith and experience the riches of God's grace in their own lives, their outlook is al-most always negative. If there is a down side to the service and a weak point in the minister, they'll find it. And they'll play it for all it's worth, with bulldog tenacity. A minor flaw becomes a major failing.

These people don't glow; they glare. No one is truly free in their presence. Somehow there is always the feeling that you are being judged, watched, scrutinized, critiqued. Their ever-watchful eye searches you out with a quick, self-righteous glance, making you know you just don't measure up. Their haughty holiness hems you in; their pseudo-spiritual smug-ness smothers you. They do not advance the work of God.

Faultfinding, stiff traditionalists always manage to find something bad to say about those the Lord is using. When John the Baptist came, he was criticized for his lifestyle of extreme self-denial. When Jesus came, the same people criti-cized Him for eating and drinking (Matt. 11). Why? Their purpose was not to know the truth. Their purpose was to prove the "competition" wrong. That is how religious hypo-crites operate. They are so petty! Are we?

When Jesus healed on the Sabbath, the hypocrites didn't rejoice. They were indignant because He violated one of their minuscule, man-made rules. When the crowds—including little children—shouted praises as the Son of God entered Je-rusalem, the hypocrites didn't add their voices too. They were upset because it was so noisy and out of order. But Je-sus said we would know a tree by its fruit. What kind of fruit do these hypocrites bear? What kind of disciples do they pro-duce? Where is the proof of their piety? Where is the proof of *our* piety?

Some things are really very simple. Criticism will not produce compassion, and faultfinding will not produce faith.

It's easy to sit back and tear down, but what have we built up? How many people have we strongly influenced that are now doing the work of God effectively? Are we producing life or death, hope or despair, an attitude of love or a fault-finding spirit? Why don't we stop attacking our fellow soldiers who are on the front lines and instead go out and join them? Maybe we'll find out that they're doing a better job than we could ever dream of doing! And if we see that they are, in fact, doing something wrong, we're in a position now where we can help them, not hurt them.

There is a place for bringing correction. Exercising discernment is necessary. Some things *are* wrong—and some are pretty obvious too. But correction brings life and improvement, and discernment produces growth and progress. Both are motivated by love—for the Lord, for His people, and for those in error. This is not the case with a negative, complaining, censorious spirit. It never bears lasting, good fruit. It is fueled by self-righteousness more than by compassion and truth.

It's one thing for an experienced, zealous, active soul winner—who happens also to be a seminary professor—to sit down with a young evangelist and point out to him his error and fault. It's another thing for some highbrow theologian who almost never reaches out to the lost to sit back and tear down every modern evangelistic ministry for being too "shallow." If he's got the goods, let him lead the way!

Enough with our sideline sarcasm and armchair arrogance. Let's take up our cross and put down our criticism. It's impossible to carry both.

Very often the man who first appears as a heretic turns out to be the one who was recalling Christendom to a long-neglected truth. He may have shouted a little too loudly as the only way of getting a hearing, but had he not shouted, had he not rocked the boat, his fellow-Christians might not have become aware that they were heading for dangerous shoals. Protestantism has an obligation to "suffer fools gladly" lest it stifle the message of one who is "a fool for Christ."

Robert McAfee Brown, The Spirit of Protestantism

Persons are very ready to be suspicious of what they have not felt themselves. It is to be feared many good men have been guilty of this error.... These persons that thus make their own experience their rule of judgment, instead of bowing to the wisdom of God, and yielding to His Word as an infallible rule, are guilty of casting a great reflection upon the understanding of the Most High.

Jonathan Edwards, Jonathan Edwards on Revival

Kindly reflections on the present religious movement: Part one, questionable procedure. Part two, probable evil results.

Pamphlets posted on public buildings in 1874
by leading ministers in Sunderland, England,
warning against the meetings
of Moody and Sankey.

Solo singing is not worship. It's a parade of human conceit. It's distracting, irreverent.... [His melodeon is] a devilish pump machine that wheezes out blasphemy.

Objections raised to Sankey's music
ministry in England and Scotland

We know we're doing right. These men are two centuries behind Boston. Pity them and keep on singing, Sankey.

Moody's response to the
criticism in Sunderland

Chapter Five

The Hypocrite's Checklist (II)

In the last chapter, we looked at five signs of hypocritical religion. Did you examine yourself, did you explain yourself, or did you simply excuse yourself? Did you find traces of religious hypocrisy? Are you being honest? Or, to ask the same question a little differently, how would your friendly critics score you? (*That* is something worth thinking about!) Well, there's more to come. Now we go to the very heart of religious hypocrisy: outward religion.

6) A religious hypocrite wants his spirituality to be seen. Underlying the actions of the hypocrite is the desire to be highly thought of by other people. (Why else would someone put on an act?) How blinding pride is! It leads the hypocrite to put on an outward show so as to receive the favor of man, while all along, God knows the bankruptcy of the heart. What a pitiful way to live.

> *Everything they do is done for men to see*: They make their phylacteries wide and the tassels on their garments long; they love the place of honor at banquets and the most important seats in the synagogues; they love to be greeted in the marketplaces and to have men call them "Rabbi" [or, "Pastor" or

"Evangelist" or "Prophet" or "Bishop" or "Doctor"…]. (Matt. 23:5-7)

We love to "wear" our spirituality too, always making sure everyone knows how close we are to the Lord. Our public prayers are long, loud, and powerful (while our private prayers are almost nonexistent). Our praise in the midst of the assembly is so demonstrative—hands raised high, a glowing smile on our face, a neat little dance step in the aisle—and we're not even thinking about God! For whom are we performing?

Years after the event took place, John G. Lake, an early twentieth-century missionary to South Africa, related this account:

> Close to a South African city in which I was ministering, there were hills with outcroppings of rocks—like a series of cliffs, one above another. I would go up into these hills to be alone and rest. One day I observed a lady bringing a young child and setting him on one of the shelves above a small cliff. She left the child some food and water. It seemed a dangerous thing to do, since the child might fall and hurt himself. However, I observed that the child was crippled and could not move around.
>
> After his mother left, I went over to him, laid my hands on him, and prayed. Immediately the child bounded off down the hill to catch his mother. Not caring to meet anyone, I moved around the hill out of sight.[1]

What would we have done? "Get the cameras! Let's get a testimony and some good pictures. We'll put this in our newsletter. It will really generate some bucks. And it will make people think the world of us." Too few of our media-trained American ministers would have had the purity of heart to say, "Let's get some pictures to encourage our friends and coworkers. It will bless them to see how the Lord has moved"—with no ulterior, flesh-exalting motivation, with no publicity gimmicks in mind. Too few of us would have been able to go to the mother of the healed child and say, "Jesus did this!"—without stealing a little of the glory for ourselves.

We've taken the words of Jesus, "Everything they do is done for men to see," and almost turned them into a marketing suggestion. Whatever happened to secret devotion, secret obedience, and secret exploits? Whatever happened to entering our prayer closets and letting God Himself reward us openly? Why must we be so self-congratulating? There is a time for public testimony, but much of our timing leaves a lot to be desired.

Just think: In today's Christian circles, we award the anointing and boast about our "big" men and women of God. "Who is the Christian man or woman of the year? Who is the Christian singer of the decade?" Nineteen centuries ago, it would have been quite a battle: "And now, the awards for the apostle of the year. Our nominees are Paul for his ministry to the Gentiles, and Peter for his work among the Jews." Or how about today, in the lands where being a Christian still costs a lot: "Meet Reverend Lee, the persecuted saint of the year. He was tortured for ten years in solitary confinement and didn't crack." Will we give him a plaque? Or a ring?

I'll tell you the truth. I often wonder if we know even *one* of the top hundred leaders in the Church today. I wonder how many of them have ever seen a TV, let alone appeared on the tube. I wonder how many of the leading saints of this generation are even "in the ministry"—as we define it. What a day it will be when the first will be last and the last first. What a miserable letdown it will be for those to whom the Master says, "You had your reward in full." How pathetic that "reward" will look on that day!

7) A religious hypocrite is cynical and skeptical. When Jesus hung on the cross, Mark records that:

> ...the chief priests and the teachers of the law mocked Him among themselves. "He saved others," they said, "but He can't save Himself! Let this Christ, this King of Israel, come down now from the cross, that we may see and believe." (Mark 15:31-32a)

Yet some of these men had already seen Jesus perform every imaginable healing and deliverance, and still they didn't believe. The Bible way is *believe* and you will *see* (John 11:40). Faith is not an option! And for those who are true seekers, when they do see God's power, they *will* believe (see John 4:46-53).

Of course, there are many children of God today who love the power of the Holy Spirit, who embrace His ministry in full, who flow in His gifts and anointing, who believe in signs and wonders, but who are anything but naive. They have had their fill of contemporary charismatic nonsense, and they know that gullibility is not a virtue. They have seen more than enough Holy Ghost hype and they've had it with "Spirit-filled" flakes. In their eyes, only a fool would believe everyone who says, "God told me" or "Jesus healed my hangnail."[2]

But there are others who are so wary that they must weary God. They are so uncharismatic that for all practical purposes they might as well be anti-charismatic. (In fact, some of them are proud to call themselves anti-charismatic. Others simply glory in their "balance.") They're not just hesitant about the supernatural workings of God, they often hinder and hold back His hand. Yet they claim to be champions of the Word! They are tireless crusaders for total dependence on the Scriptures—and on the Scriptures alone.

But something doesn't line up. They claim to believe in all the miracles of the Bible, but the moment a modern miracle is reported, they're totally skeptical that such a thing could possibly occur. They claim to believe God spoke to His people "way back then," but let someone say the Lord spoke to them today in a vision or by voice, and the religious SWAT team (Self-appointed Watchdogs And Truth-sentries) gets into action: "That stuff isn't for this age!"

Somehow I wonder how these spiritual experts would have fared during the exodus from Egypt (mass hysteria and hallucination?) or during the ministry of Elijah (coincidental lightning mistaken for fire?) or after Jesus' resurrection (the women who saw Him suffered from cognitive dissonance?) or in the days of the Book of Acts (none of the prophets—not even Moses—ever spoke in tongues, and they certainly had the Spirit; there was no doctor present to confirm that Dorcas had really died; Paul was obviously under emotional duress as well as suffering from fatigue and dehydration when he claimed that an angel appeared to him on the boat). Some of us would not have believed back then!

The religious hypocrites said, "...If we had lived in the days of our forefathers, we would not have taken part with them in shedding the blood of the prophets" (Matt. 23:30). Yet they rejected John the Baptist and handed Jesus over to be crucified. They were just like their fathers—hostile to the prophetic voice.

Some of us do the same thing. We say, "Oh, for the days of the Great Awakening, or the Welsh Revival, or Azusa Street"—whatever our preference may be. *Those days would have been wonderful.*" But as soon as God begins to do something even vaguely similar in this day, we react immediately, "That can't be the Spirit!"

A noncharismatic pastor once described his denomination to me by saying, "If it's not in the Book, we don't believe it." I was tempted to reply, "My approach is a little different. If it *is* in the Bible, I *do* believe it!" There's quite a contrast there.

It is one thing to exercise wisdom, to test sensational sounding testimonies and to investigate extraordinary claims. But a skeptical, religious attitude is completely contrary to the spirit of the Bible, a book of the impossible, a book of the supernatural, a book of miracles and wonder. In fact, you could sum up the spirit of the New Testament age with the words: "Everything is possible for him who believes" (Mark 9:23)—not him who belittles. Beware of a skeptical heart.

8) A religious hypocrite produces bondage instead of freedom. The religion of the hypocrite is one of externals, not one of the heart. The hypocrite becomes more "spiritual" by making more rules. His religion is filled with lists of "do this" and "don't do that," and he measures himself (and others) by outward performance and arbitrary standards. He tells people what to do without bringing them into contact with the only One who can give them the power to do it. That is not the gospel!

Instead of encouraging believers to serve the Lord out of love and devotion, hypocritical religion brings God's children under bondage to fear. And it is *not* the fear of the Lord, that healthy awe and respect for an all-holy God who has the power to save or destroy. Instead, it is the fear that a slave has for an unpredictable, harsh master. One wrong move and you're finished!

It was to the Galatians in particular that Paul wrote about the problem of legalism. He wanted them to fully understand that "because you are sons, God sent the Spirit of His Son into our hearts, the Spirit who calls out, 'Abba, Father.' So you are no longer a slave, but a son; and since you are a son, God has made you also an heir" (Gal. 4:6-7). We are children in God's great family!

The religious hypocrite cannot grasp this. He insists on loading his convictions and customs on the backs of other believers. He puts a heavy yoke on their shoulders. It is a man-made yoke, instead of one that is born of God, and it crushes those who wear it.

Matthew knew what it was like to deal with hypocritical leaders, and he made things crystal clear in his Gospel. At the end of chapter 11, he records these beautiful words of the Lord:

> Come to Me, all you who are weary and burdened, and I will give you rest. Take My yoke upon you and learn from Me, for I am gentle and humble in heart, and you will find rest for your souls. For My yoke is easy and My burden is light. (Matt. 11:28-30)

But notice what follows at the beginning of chapter 12:

> At that time Jesus went through the grainfields on the Sabbath. His disciples were hungry and began to pick some heads of grain and eat them. When the Pharisees saw this, they said to Him, "Look! Your disciples are doing what is unlawful on the Sabbath." (Matt. 12:1-2)

These Pharisees had a different yoke! They were not carrying the Lord's burden. They were weighed down with their own regulations and scandalized by the true liberty that Jesus and His disciples enjoyed. And they wanted to bring everyone else into bondage along with them.

Jesus offered rest; they offered rules. He lifted the burdens of the weary; they loaded more burdens on. Jesus was gentle and humble in heart; they were judgmental and harsh. Jesus worked on men from the inside out; they started from the outside and never got in. Only grace can truly change the heart!

And when your heart is set free, when you are carrying the burden of the Lord, you can joyfully serve and sacrifice and suffer. You'll do anything, anytime for Jesus. You can work day and night and still be at rest. As John said, "His commands are not burdensome" (1 John 5:3)—even if it means laying down our lives. But the hypocrite is never at true rest. His religion is oppressive and heavy. He is wearing the wrong yoke.

What about you? Whose burden are you carrying? Whose yoke are you wearing? To all those weary and burdened, Jesus still says, "Come to Me."

9) A religious hypocrite is more concerned with outward forms and traditions than with the power of God, mercy, and compassion. He displaces the Word and the Spirit with human traditions. Jesus addressed this head on:

> …"Isaiah was right when he prophesied about you hypocrites; as it is written: 'These people honor Me with their lips, but their hearts are far from Me. They worship Me in vain; their teachings are but rules taught by men.' You have let go of the commands of God and are holding on to the traditions of men." And He said to them: "You have a fine way of setting aside the commands of God in order to observe your own traditions!" (Mark 7:6-9)

What this really means is that we esteem our wisdom (traditions) as of greater worth than God's wisdom (the Word). Heed well what Augustine said: "If you believe what you like in the Gospel and reject what you do not like, it is not the Gospel you believe, but yourself."[3]

This arrogant attitude leads people to exalt *form* over *substance*. It says, "We don't care about the manifestation of God's power and grace. Those upstarts didn't do it our way. They broke with our traditions!" In other words, they broke with our rigid, stiff, and inflexible order of service; they went against our fixed rules and spiritual presuppositions that determine exactly when and through whom God is allowed to move; they left out the liturgy; they raised their voices above the level we consider acceptable (or maybe they weren't loud enough); they allowed new believers to exercise charismatic gifts; they didn't come to the city under our denominational covering; they stopped preaching in the middle of the message and gave an altar call for the lost; they even dared to express their enthusiasm with the dance. Worst of all, many were genuinely healed and saved through the meetings!

And did it ever occur to us that the reason they were able to do what they did was precisely *because* they broke with those Spirit-stifling customs and laws? How have our dead traditions advanced the gospel, encouraged holy living, demonstrated God's power, or increased absolute faith in the living Word? Oh what death our traditions have wrought! The picture of the hypocrite is pathetic.

Here is a Muslim terrorist torturing his prisoner. Suddenly he stops. Why? It's time to say his prayers! What a hypocrite! Or consider the unethical Jew who steals people blind in his business but would rather starve than eat a non-Kosher food product. What a hypocrite!

In John 18, the religious leaders who were handing Jesus over to be crucified wouldn't venture into Pilate's quarters because they didn't want to become ceremonially unclean. What hypocrites! But we do similar things.

There are believers who will watch unclean movies, excusing themselves as being weak, yet be indignant when their pastor misquotes a Scripture. Others do not lift a finger for world evangelism but will fight to the death over a minor doctrinal issue, while still others criticize those who sing modern gospel choruses instead of the great, old hymns, but they don't enter into worship at all. What hypocrites!

> Woe to you, teachers of the law and Pharisees, you hypocrites! You give a tenth of your spices—mint, dill and cummin. But you have neglected the more important matters of the law— justice, mercy and faithfulness. You should have practiced the latter, without neglecting the former. You blind guides! You strain out a gnat but swallow a camel. (Matt. 23:23-24)

May God make us broad-hearted and kind, giving our lives for justice, mercy, and faithfulness, following in the footsteps of the Master, walking in love and compassion, ministering grace, and living to bless. May God deliver us from hypocritical religion. If there's anything the Church doesn't need, it's one more hypocrite.

10) A religious hypocrite is narrowly nationalistic and dangerously denominational. Jonah had no problem prophesying that the borders of Israel would be increased (see 2 Kings 14:25). But to go to the heathen, the enemies of his nation, and give them a chance to hear the Word of the Lord, that's a different matter!

Paul was able to get the attention of his angry fellow Jews in Acts 22 by speaking to them in their native tongue. They had believed the rumors they heard and somehow thought he was not one of them. But when he spoke to them in Aramaic (or, possibly, Hebrew), they listened carefully to his dramatic testimony until he said, "Then the Lord said to me, 'Go; I will send you far away to the Gentiles' " (Acts 22:21).

This was too much! They went crazy, "shouting and throwing off their cloaks and flinging dust into the air" (22:23). Yes, "they raised their voices and shouted, 'Rid the earth of him! He's not fit to live!' " (22:22) "He's going to the Gentiles! One of *us* is going to *them*. Impossible! Kill him! Eliminate him!" Such is the spirit of religious hypocrisy!

Do you know what made it totally clear to many white Christians that the Azusa Street outpouring was not from God? Blacks and whites were worshiping together! Even worse, the whites were going to the black church. Never! (Today there is a sinister rise of black racism in the church. It is as ugly and demonic as the white racism of 100 years ago, a racism that still lingers in certain circles. Look out!)

Religious hypocrites—or shall I say *religious racists?*—are dangerously close-minded. If the spiritual emphasis doesn't originate with their group, they categorically reject it. If the revival doesn't reflect their particular way of doing things, it can't be from heaven. And they will even persecute the new thing God is doing in the earth. As Paul said, "...the son born in the ordinary way persecuted the son born by the power of the Spirit..." (Gal. 4:29).

How sad that history often repeats itself. The early Methodists were persecuted and put out of churches by the hypocritical ministers of their day. Why? The Methodists broke with all rules and church precedents by preaching the new birth on the streets and in the city squares. But one century later, it was the traditional Methodist ministers who persecuted the newly formed Salvation Army. Why? The Salvation Army preached the new birth on the streets and in the city squares!

We start in the Spirit with zealous faith, following God at any cost. Then, if we're not careful, our success leads us to become complacent, compromised, and self-satisfied. Soon enough, we fight against those who want to get back to the Spirit, zealous faith, and radical obedience. Now they are threatening us. "Nothing new here, please!"

Of course, that doesn't mean that every group that is being persecuted is from God, nor does it mean that we can't reject messages, messengers, and movements that claim to be sent from heaven but in reality are not. There are some things we *should* oppose. What I'm talking about is a narrow, biased attitude.

Ask yourself a question: Do you tolerate one kind of behavior in your own group yet reject that same behavior in groups whose doctrine you reject? Do you condemn leaders outside your group for falling short of certain principles, but excuse your own leaders when they fall short of those very same principles? Do you reject a so-called revival because it has some fleshly manifestations and flaky extremes, even though similar manifestations and extremes could be found in the revival that helped birth your group or denomination?

"But it's different!" you say—as if God treats sin, or the flesh, or failures, or errors in your camp more lightly than He treats them in the camp of those with whom you disagree. No, it's denominationalism and sectarianism. It's using unequal weights and measures, holding double standards of judgment. It's pride; it's inexcusable; and it reflects a desire to always be in control.

The disciples of Jesus ran into this constantly. In fact, the religious leaders were sure that Jesus was not the Messiah because He didn't belong to their group. They mocked the temple guards who were impressed with the Lord, asking,

"Has any of the rulers or of the Pharisees believed in Him? No! But this mob that knows nothing of the law—there is a curse on them" (John 7:48-49). "It's only these illiterate fools who could be duped by such a deceiver! We know better."

Soon enough, this kind of spirit can turn militant and even violent. A hypocritical spirit is hateful, and hatred is murderous:

> Going on from that place, He went into their synagogue, and a man with a shriveled hand was there. Looking for a reason to accuse Jesus, they asked Him, "Is it lawful to heal on the Sabbath?" He said to them, "If any of you has a sheep and it falls into a pit on the Sabbath, will you not take hold of it and lift it out? How much more valuable is a man than a sheep! Therefore it is lawful to do good on the Sabbath." Then He said to the man, "Stretch out your hand." So he stretched it out and it was completely restored, just as sound as the other. *But the Pharisees went out and plotted how they might kill Jesus.* (Matt. 12:9-14)

> Meanwhile a large crowd of Jews found out that Jesus was there and came, not only because of Him but also to see Lazarus, whom He had raised from the dead. *So the chief priests made plans to kill Lazarus as well*, for on account of him many of the Jews were going over to Jesus and putting their faith in Him. (John 12:9-11)

These are frightening verses, aren't they? "We'll put to death everything that's alive and threatens our group. If we can't beat 'em, we'll murder 'em!"

We should search our hearts and see if we have even a trace of such a close-minded, narrow, and hostile spirit. That kind of attitude will miss God's visitation every time.

But thank God, when He comes, "the humble will hear and be glad." They will receive the blessing from heaven. Just think of the spirit that prevailed during the Welsh Revival in

1904, when all the pastors in Pentre *exchanged pulpits* for one day in a display of unity. Hypocrisy was defeated![4]

And as it happened that day, it will happen again. God's Spirit will sweep through the earth. The valleys will be exalted. The meek will inherit the land. God will use the foolish things to confound the wise and the weak things to bring down the mighty. He will make somebodies out of nobodies. He will use the unusable!

So,

Humble yourselves before the Lord, and He will lift you up. … [For] God opposes the proud but gives grace to the humble. (James 4:10,6b)

Lord, give us more grace!

They went across the lake to the region of the Gerasenes. When Jesus got out of the boat, a man with an evil spirit came from the tombs to meet Him. This man lived in the tombs, and no one could bind him any more, not even with a chain. For he had often been chained hand and foot, but he tore the chains apart and broke the irons on his feet. No one was strong enough to subdue him. Night and day among the tombs and in the hills he would cry out and cut himself with stones. When he saw Jesus from a distance, he ran and fell on his knees in front of Him. He shouted at the top of his voice, "What do you want with me, Jesus, Son of the Most High God? Swear to God that you won't torture me!" For Jesus had said to him, "Come out of this man, you evil spirit!" Then Jesus asked him, "What is your name?" "My name is Legion," he replied, "for we are many." And he begged Jesus again and again not to send them out of the area. A large herd of pigs was feeding on the nearby hillside. The demons begged Jesus, "Send us among the pigs; allow us to go into them." He gave them permission, and the evil spirits came out and went into the pigs. The herd, about two thousand in number, rushed down the steep bank into the lake and were drowned. Those tending the pigs ran off and reported this in the town and countryside, and the people went out to see what had happened. When they came to Jesus, they saw the man who had been possessed by the legion of demons, sitting there, dressed and in his right mind; and they were afraid. Those who had seen it told the people what had happened to the demon-possessed man—and told about the pigs as well. *Then the people began to plead with Jesus to leave their region.*

Mark 5:1-17

The greatest sin of the evangelical church is that we want to put God in a little box.

D. Martyn Lloyd-Jones

Chapter Six

The Disruptive Messiah

The entrance of the Messiah into the world was traumatic—for the world, that is. It is the same when He comes to take residence in an individual life. Everything must change!

Think of the great crisis Joseph went through as a result of Mary's pregnancy. Think of his personal anguish and inner battle when he found out his espoused wife was pregnant. (Yes! The woman he was about to wed was already pregnant—and not by him.) How long was it before the angel spoke to him? What did Mary try to tell him? And what kind of trauma did she experience? How costly it is to give birth to the Son of God! When the Lord comes into the world (and our lives), He comes with upheaval.

The people of the Gerasenes begged Jesus to leave their region. His visit was more than they could handle! Two thousand pigs committing suicide; their owners left without income; the whole town talking; the supernatural deliverance of a demonized man: "It's too much! We like things the old way. We prefer the simple pattern of everyday life. Jesus, please leave!"

The Savior came, but the lost didn't want Him. The Creator came, but His creation had no room for Him. The Deliverer came, but many captives preferred their bondage. Jesus is not always a welcome guest!

This attitude runs deep. Could it be that people would rather have a raving, demon-possessed man on the outskirts of their city than come face to face with God's life-changing power? Is it possible that an evil presence—even in its raw, ugly form—is more to be tolerated than a holy presence? Is the world more comfortable with the devil's insanity than with God's order?

Would people rather let gross sinners remain in bondage—providing themselves with a subtle excuse for their own wretched condition—than realize that total deliverance is possible, thereby challenging their own lives? And do the extreme forms of degeneracy serve to legitimize our less extreme forms of depravity? Do triple-X movies provide the perfect foil for our R-rated excursions? (Anything so we can say, "I'm not so bad!") But if God can make that demonized man whole and holy, what does that say to us?

Revival is an encounter with God the Holy One, disclosed and made known. Revival removes the veil and makes things clear. Revival is stark and absolute, uncovering the nature of man and revealing the glory of God. In the end, it boils down to this: *Do we really want God to live in our midst?* (Don't answer that question too quickly. Mull it over and ask for insight. The picture is bigger than you may realize!) Not everyone was thrilled when the long-awaited Messiah arrived.

Consider the synagogue in Capernaum. Everything was so peaceful there. The services were so predictable, so reverent, so orderly. Then Jesus came. It was a madhouse! One of the nicest men in the community fell on the ground shouting. It was so distracting—let alone distasteful and somewhat disgraceful. It disrupted the prayers, and there wasn't even time for the sermon. How nice it was before Jesus came to our synagogue! Then we could do things our way. Then things were comfortable.

Jesus upsets our routine, and His very presence brings to light the hidden attitudes of the heart, as Simeon prophesied: "...This child is destined to cause the falling and rising of many in Israel, and to be a sign that will be spoken against, *so that the thoughts of many hearts will be revealed...*" (Luke 2:34-35).

When people speak against Jesus, the sinful condition of their hearts is made known. How striking that, for the most part, it was nice, religious, law-abiding people who called the Son of God demon-possessed, raving mad, Beelzebub, and illegitimate. His coming uncovered their souls!

> At these words the Jews were again divided. Many of them said, "He is demon-possessed and raving mad. Why listen to Him?" But others said, "These are not the sayings of a man possessed by a demon. Can a demon open the eyes of the blind?" (John 10:19-21)

> [Jesus said:] "He who belongs to God hears what God says. The reason you do not hear is that you do not belong to God." The Jews answered Him, "Aren't we right in saying that you are a Samaritan and demon-possessed?" (John 8:47-48)

Why did they hate Him so? The Lord Himself gave the reason: "The world cannot hate you, but it hates Me because I testify that what it does is evil" (John 7:7).

And that is exactly what happens in times of revival. Jesus is again glorified in the midst of His Church, and He rebukes evil and iniquity and reveals coldness and lethargy. We find out what's really in people's hearts! And as it was with the Savior, so it is with revival. Both will be spoken against. As Arthur Wallis wrote: "If we find a revival that is not spoken against, we had better look again to ensure that it is a revival.[1]

Of course, excesses and errors should be spoken against. But more often than not when there is a true move of God, it is proud religionists who will oppose and malign it; it uncovers the condition of their hearts.

We are accustomed to hearing the wonderful reports of the Welsh Revival earlier this century. We know how Evan Roberts was deeply loved and respected by so many of his countrymen. But not everyone loved him! In the words of psychiatrist Dr. Forbes Winslow, "I would have men like Evan Roberts locked up as common felons, and their meetings prohibited like those of socialists and anarchists as being dangerous to the public."[2]

Revival brings things to light. Deep sentiments surface with a vengeance. It is difficult to remain neutral when God is visiting His own!

Revival is often the making or breaking point of many a church and minister. It forces us to deal with the most fundamental of all spiritual issues: What will we do with Jesus? How will we respond to the Lord? Here He is in our midst! How is it possible that everything will *not* be radically affected?

The world itself has not been the same since Jesus arrived on the scene. The Jewish people have not been the same (consider what they have suffered in rejecting Him and how divided they have been over Him). History has not been the same (most nations date events from His birth). Religion has not been the same. Everything has changed and been disrupted. And when He visits His Church, serious shaking will take place. He demands a lot of room!

Jesus, the Messiah, the Son of God, the Lord, has become the dividing line of human experience, and He will be the plumb line by which every life is measured:

> There will be trouble and distress for every human being who does evil: first for the Jew, then for the Gentile; but glory, honor and peace for everyone who does good: first for the Jew, then for the Gentile. ... *This will take place on the day when God will judge men's secrets through Jesus Christ, as my gospel declares.* (Rom. 2:9-10,16)

> In the past God overlooked such ignorance, but now He commands all people everywhere to repent. *For He has set a day when He will judge the world with justice by the man He has appointed.* He has given proof of this to all men by raising Him from the dead. (Acts 17:30-31)

God now calls all men to account.

This is a picture of revival too. He brings judgment, not just joy. He comes with claims, not just charisma. He is demanding, not just delightful. He is the Lord of all, not just lovely and adorable. He refuses to merely "fit in." When did He ever make a deal with someone? When did He say, "Choose your terms"? When did He tell a potential disciple, "Surrender half—that's enough," or "Three-quarters is sufficient"? Absolutely not. He died for us all, and He died for *all* of each of us. He expects all in return.

Encountering the Son of God is radical. Surrender is total and absolute. What general would accept a partial surrender?

Yet we often drift from this truth. We serve God out of habit and worship Him by rote. We divide our life into little compartments. We give Jesus a nice compartment of His own! But when He comes in revival power, when He is glorified in the midst of His people, then He stakes His claims and renews His rights over the flock He purchased with His blood. He is still the Head of the Body, and He takes that headship seriously!

We don't just add Him in for thrills—along with some neat manifestations of the Spirit for an added attraction. We don't simply invite Him to show up for a few hours each night and then leave Him at the church building. He is the fullness of God in bodily form (Col. 2:9), the all-consuming fire, the Lord of glory. And when we cry, "Come, Lord! Consume me!" He just might do that very thing.

Do we grasp the meaning of those words? "Come Lord"—the King in His majesty; the Creator in His splendor; the Master in His holiness; the Son of God in His might. Do we really want *Him* to come? "Consume me"—in fire, in flames, in a blaze of purity; until my carnal flesh is burned beyond recognition and a new creature shines forth; until my will is totally absorbed in my Maker's; until the unseen is far more real than the seen; until I am utterly dominated by my God. Is that what we want, or are we merely seeking a little brushfire to warm and cheer us, or a Holy Ghost cookout that will satisfy our cravings? Once you pray, "Consume me, Lord," you can't negotiate with the flames.

Notice again Mark 5:15:

> When they came to Jesus, they saw the man who had been possessed by the legion of demons, sitting there, dressed and in his right mind; and *they were afraid.*

The Lord's life-transforming power can actually be fearful. It's overwhelming to see just what He can do. This thing is real, my friends.

How often have you encountered the stark, utter power of God? It can be a little frightening!

A furious squall came up, and the waves broke over the boat, so that it was nearly swamped. Jesus was in the stern, sleeping on a cushion. The disciples woke Him and said to Him, "Teacher, don't you care if we drown?" He got up, rebuked the wind and said to the waves, "Quiet! Be still!" Then the wind died down and it was completely calm. He said to His disciples, "Why are you so afraid? Do you still have no faith?" They were terrified and asked each other, "Who is this? Even the wind and the waves obey Him!" (Mark 4:37-41)

"Who are You, Lord?" is a common question during revival. We see Jesus as He really is. For some, this is quite a shock!

Revival is always more than we asked for and reckoned for. That's why lots of people check out. They prefer to maintain their rights. They like their seat on the throne. It's easier to strut than surrender!

The same holds true for pastors and leaders: By nature, we like to run the show. We like to know what's going to happen, when it's going to happen, who is going to be involved, and how long it's going to take. And we like to start it and stop it at will. Such are the ways of man.

Leaders in particular need to ask themselves some hard questions: Am I willing to relinquish control? Am I willing to let God take over? Whose church (or flock, or ministry, or work) is it anyway? Whose reputation is at stake, mine or His? Whose kingdom am I building? Am I looking for the Spirit or for safety? For sweeping revival or for secure religion? For the Holy Ghost from heaven or for high grades from headquarters? Do I *really* want revival?

These questions demand an honest response. It's easy to fool ourselves, and so the cycle is repeated. We beseech Jesus to come, then beg Him to go. We pray that He'll visit us, then plead that He'll leave us. We ask Him to draw near us, then urge Him to depart from us. Do we want the biblical Lord, or would we prefer a make-believe savior created in our own image? Do we want the One who made time itself, or would we rather have a run-by-the-clock visitation? Are we hungry or in a hurry? The crucified life is not a quick fix.

Why are we so hasty and rushed when at last He graces us with His manifest Presence? Why do we run from meeting with the Lord at the altar—after all, it's getting late!—only to spend hours meeting with one another at the restaurant? (To paraphrase Leonard Ravenhill, we're more at home in the supper room than the upper room!) Isn't the Lord more wonderful than flesh and blood? Isn't He sweeter than any dessert? Why can't we stop, be still, and let God be God? (You're right. It does mean death to the flesh!)

This is the sentiment that has cut short many a revival: "We like things the way they used to be!"—to which God may say, "Fine! Have it your way." But the results will be catastrophic. For where God's Spirit is not valued, His manifest Presence will soon vanish. When we refuse to give Him glory and be thankful (Rom. 1), He will give us over to our own lusts—spiritual or otherwise—to do what our carnal minds think best. But make no mistake: It is an act of judgment.

May it not happen to this generation! May we not retreat into our religious safety zones, where the Presence of God is all but shut out. No! We must invite the Lord to come and do His thing—with humble, dependent hearts. We must receive Him, not resist Him, and run to Him, not repulse Him.

And may we no longer grieve the Spirit by making Him into a commercial commodity. May we cease to cheapen the meaning of true visitation by calling every little trickle a mighty flood. May we not give way any longer to foolishness and carnality in the name of revival, making superstars and idols according to our liking, exhibiting manifestations instead of exalting the Master. The Lord will not put up with this for long. And if He chooses to withdraw, what then can we do? What hope would we have? Where could we turn?

How well I remember the anguish and fear that gripped me when I realized the Lord was about to remove His outpouring from a fellowship that was ashamed to give Him glory. ("As quickly as I came, I'll go," the Spirit spoke to my heart.) I was overcome by the burden of the Lord and seized with pangs of intercession. No prospect could have been more devastating. Spiritual food had finally come for a starving people, and we were in danger of losing it all!

We cannot afford the consequences of spurned revival in this day. I tremble to think of what that could mean for America and the world. God's people have been praying and fasting for years, crying out to the Lord of the rain clouds to inundate us with His showers. There is now a window of opportunity for our nation. But when the torrents come, will we say, "It's too wet! It's too stormy! I liked the dry weather better"? May it not be!

We need the floodgates of heaven to burst open so the divine tidal wave will come. Let it flush out what it must. Let it wash away everything that is not built on the Rock. Let it bring to the surface all the muck and mire. Whatever the consequences, we need the floods! We need the glorious Lord glorified in our midst again. "Come, Lord, consume us with Your flames! We mean it with all our hearts."

But some will say, "What do I do? I fear I have already grieved the Lord. I ignored Him in the past. I failed to welcome Him when He came. I practically spurned Him when He drew me and rejected Him when He called me. I feel like the people at the Gerasenes. Is it all over for me?"

Look back to the Gospel of Mark. There's more to the story than we've told! There is good news for some of those people who at first drove the Savior away.

Do you remember what happened to the man who was delivered? He wanted to go along with Jesus. (Just think, everyone was begging the Lord. The demons begged Him to let them go into the pigs; the people begged Him to leave their region; and the formerly demon-possessed man begged Him to take him along.) But Jesus said to him:

> ..."Go home to your family and tell them how much the Lord has done for you, and how He has had mercy on you." So the man went away and began to tell in the Decapolis how much Jesus had done for him. And all the people were amazed. (Mark 5:19-20)

Since the Lord could not stay, He sent this man out as an ambassador, and this brand new evangelist must have done a good job spreading the news. Soon some of them were asking for Jesus to help them (see Mark 7:31-37), and He responded to their cries. As a result, "People were overwhelmed with amazement. 'He has done everything well,' they said. 'He even makes the deaf hear and the mute speak' " (Mark 7:37).

He was willing to give them another chance. (How many chances has He already given us as a nation?) In fact, He took the initiative to return to that region, and when He arrived, things were different. This time they begged Him to heal! For them, there was still time for mercy. For them, there was another chapter to be written. The same holds true for you as an individual.

Maybe you really didn't understand the wooing of the Lord. Maybe you were afraid of His powerful moving. Maybe you were immature or even rebellious. Maybe you did grievously sin. The real question is: Is He drawing you again even now? Are you longing for Him at this moment? Is the Spirit at work once more in your heart? Then turn to Him without delay! Soften your heart, renew your faith, resist the enemy's lies, and pour out your soul to the One who died for you. Ask for mercy and restoration. Ask for refreshing rain!

Let this be your hope: When His people are sincere, having learned well from their mistakes, He may well return in even greater power. It's not too late to ask! Only cry out to Him *today*. Tomorrow may never come. This is the hour you've been waiting for. Don't let it pass you by. Jesus is still seeking willing vessels. Will you have Him as Lord? It's time for some disruption.

Where is the blessedness I knew
When first I saw the Lord?
Where is the soul-refreshing view
Of Jesus, and His word?

What peaceful hours I once enjoy'd!
How sweet their mem'ry still!
But they have left an aching void,
The world can never fill.

Return, O holy Dove, return,
Sweet messenger of rest,
I hate the sins that made Thee mourn,
And drove Thee from my breast.

The dearest idol I have known,
Whate'er that idol be,
Help me to tear it from its throne,
And worship only Thee.

William Cowper

Lord, engage my heart today
With zeal that will not pass away.
Now torch it with Thy holy fire
That never more shall time's desire
Invade or quench the Heaven born power.
I would be trapped within Thy holy will,
Thine every holy purpose to fulfill
That every effort of my life shall bring
Rapturous praise to my Eternal King.
I pledge from this day to the grave
To be Thine own unquestioning slave.

Leonard Ravenhill, completed at 2:30 a.m.,
February 12, 1994, at the age of 86

Chapter Seven

God Wants All of Me

What is God after in revival? What is His goal? Of course, we know that the Father delights in glorifying His Son, and we understand that the great harvest of souls is always near His heart. But there is something else He is after—me! He is jealous for my total loyalty, my unreserved dedication, my unblemished love, my unswerving commitment. Almighty God wants all of you and all of me! That is the root of revival. The Lord lays absolute claim on His own.

Unfortunately, as intense as revival can be, it is possible to get caught up in the externals, in things "outside" of us. We can witness God touching people dramatically, watching them weep and seeing them swoon, marvelling at the manifestations. And all the while, we can be little more than spectators. We can talk about the sin of our nation, grieving over moral decline and racial division, agonizing over the endless abortions and unspeakable immorality, sickened by the pervasive drug abuse and ghastly murders. And still, the focus is outside of us. America—not me—is in a mess. We can even lament over the backslidden state of the Church, over our powerless words and feeble deeds. And yet the emphasis is more on "them" than on "us." The problem lies with this abstract "Body" of which we are merely a part. But that is not the heart of revival. No. God is probing deeper! He is putting His finger on *me*.

We need revival because *I* have sinned, because *my* heart has grown cold, because *my* life has become compromised. God wants to light the fire again *in me*. He wants to rekindle the passion *in me*. That is the root of revival. The Lord is purifying His Bride. The Lord is reclaiming His Church—one member at a time. It is awesome to be dealt with by God! His very nature is jealous, as He said to Moses, "Do not worship any other god, for the LORD, whose name is Jealous, is a jealous God" (Ex. 34:14). Putting anything or anyone before Him is idolatry.

Idolatry? Yes. It means allegiance to other gods, and if such a thought is repulsive to us, remember: It is much more repulsive to our Lord, who spilled His blood that we might be His. It's time to smash the idols! It's time to live for God and God alone. It's time to be consumed in our commitment and radical in our relationship. Does He deserve anything less?

In the world some of us partied with abandon, not even thinking about the consequences. We gave our bodies and minds to sin, embracing lust and licence with delight. But now things have changed—for the worse. Some of us lost our health for the devil. Now we won't lose our reputation for the Lord! Some of us went to jail for the enemy. Now we won't even go to prayer meetings for our Friend. Some of us were brash for Satan. Now we're bashful for Jesus! Some of us were on fire for hell. Now we're lukewarm for heaven. It just doesn't make sense.

We once gave ourselves freely for that which cost us everything and profited us nothing. Now we hold ourselves back from that which cost *God* everything—the death of His

Son!—and profits us everything. How can this be? Revival makes things right. God desires nothing less than all of us, and when we are revived, we desire nothing less than all of Him. It is a marriage made in heaven. Revival articulates the cry of Song of Songs 8:6-7:

> Place me like a seal over your heart, like a seal on your arm; for love is as strong as death, its jealousy unyielding as the grave. It burns like blazing fire, like a mighty flame. Many waters cannot quench love; rivers cannot wash it away. If one were to give all the wealth of his house for love, it would be utterly scorned.

Revival is all about the claims of love. Husbands, how strong is your love for your wives? Wives, how deep is your love for your husbands? Parents, how intense if your love for your children? God's love for you is infinitely stronger, deeper, and more intense. He aches for you! He longs for you! How do you feel towards Him? Is the cry of your heart the same as David's?

> O God, You are my God, earnestly I seek You; my soul thirsts for You, my body longs for You, in a dry and weary land where there is no water. I have seen You in the sanctuary and beheld Your power and Your glory. Because Your love is better than life, my lips will glorify You. (Ps. 63:1-3)

It is that earnest seeking of God, that desperate thirst and driving hunger that is so characteristic of revival. It leads to an encounter that is so dramatic that we can only say, "Your love is better than life!" What more can we want than Him? And what more does He want than you and me?

Listen to the searching words of Duncan Campbell:

> Is my sense of need, and your sense of need, the very ground on which God can work? Oh, how true it is that hunger, real hunger, creates a capacity for God.... And the

reason why we are not filled is simply because we are not hungering after God....

The crisis of conversion is ever to be regarded as a conviction of guilt, but the crisis of sanctification is a conviction of want. You have it expressed in the words of the hymn:

> "Oh, when shall my soul find her rest,
> My strugglings and wrestlings be o'er,
> My heart by my Savior be possessed,
> Be fearing and sinning no more?"

There you have the cry of want; there you have hunger expressing itself; there you have a true longing after God; there you have a vessel into which God wills to pour Himself.[1]

Do you desire Him more than anyone or anything else? Be assured that God desires you too—and His desire is as infinite as He is. He proved it by giving His Son. (What more could He do?) And just as Jesus held back nothing from us—laying down His very life—He expects the same devotion from us. In fact, you can mark this down as a rule of the Spirit: If you hold back nothing from God, He will hold nothing back from you. Simply yield to Him every area of your life you want Him to bless. The problem is never with what He gives but with what we give. He will smile on what He owns.

Does He own all of you? Every last part? Now is not the time to hold back! Total obedience is not optional; it is required. God *demands* your all. Does this trouble you?

Please listen clearly (especially if you are a full-time Christian "worker"—although, in a sense, all of us are full-time workers). God is not primarily interested in your talents. He is not just after your time. He wants you. His claim is total. It goes beyond "the ministry." (Eventually, ministry can become nothing more than a performance. Some people perform better than others.) God's claim goes deeper than your public life. (Have you ever heard of people—even Christians—leading a double life? Are *you* leading a double life?) The Lord is even looking for something more than your private life. (Some of us are habitual Christians. Our actions are upright and our devotions always on schedule. But something major is missing.) *God wants your heart.*

How this cuts to the core! How this slices through the sham! How this flushes out the fake! My motivations, my thoughts, my ambitions, my desires, my innermost being— God wants all of it. I am not my own.

So wrote Paul to the Corinthians:

Do you not know that your body is a temple of the Holy Spirit, who is in you, whom you have received from God? You are not your own; you were bought at a price. Therefore honor God with your body. (1 Cor. 6:19-20)

So he wrote to the Colossians:

Since, then, you have been raised with Christ, set your hearts on things above, where Christ is seated at the right hand of God. Set your minds on things above, not on earthly things. For you died, and your life is now hidden with Christ in God. When Christ, who is your life, appears, then you also will appear with Him in glory. (Col. 3:1-4)

Brothers and sisters, you died! Jesus is now your life.

So Peter wrote to his readers:

Therefore, since Christ suffered in His body, arm yourselves also with the same attitude, because he who has suffered in his body is done with sin. As a result, he does not live the rest of his earthly life for evil human desires, but rather for the will of God. For you have spent enough time in the past doing what pagans choose to do—living in debauchery, lust, drunkenness, orgies, carousing and detestable idolatry. (1 Pet. 4:1-3)

Now is the time to do the will of God!

It was for such a purpose that Jesus shed His blood: "And He died for all, that those who live should no longer live for themselves but for Him who died for them and was raised again" (2 Cor. 5:15). He died for us so that we might live for Him. This is really the most basic of the basics, "Christianity 101," so to say. Tragically, for much of the contemporary Church of America—and that means many of us—it seems like a lofty and even unattainable goal. For the revived saint, it is as normal as eating and drinking. Jesus is our all in all, and our life is all *in Him.*

The fiery Irish evangelist W.P. Nicholson was known for two themes in particular: "God's love" and "God's hell." He preached both with overwhelming conviction. But his preaching flowed from his prayer life (he generally rose at 6:00 a.m. and refused to be disturbed by anyone until noon, giving his mornings to wrestling in prayer), and his prayer life flowed from his devotion to the Lord.

Perhaps the sweetest fruit of Nicholson's prayer life was the deep familiarity that was produced between himself and the person of Christ. In Nicholson's book, *On Towards the Goal,* he writes, "I do not know anyone in the Lord that I know better than the Lord. I do not know my wife or my mother the way I know the Lord. I do not know the best friends I ever had the way I know the Lord. We walk together, my Lord and I, because we are in fellowship, and there is nothing that I have but is His." Truly this is the essence and heart of revival, an intimate visitation and fellowship with Jesus Christ....[2]

Do you know Him like that? He is inviting you to come deeper! He is calling you to His side. He wants you—not just your words, your deeds, and your possessions, but you—to come to Him. He calls you to be wholly holy, and the essence of holiness is a life surrendered to God.

Of course, it's easy to think of holiness as merely a question of external standards. But Andrew Murray approached the heart of the matter when he wrote,

> Our work in becoming holy is the bringing of our whole life, and every part of it, into subjection to the rule of this holy God, putting every member and every power upon His altar.... Holiness is what there is of God in us.... Holiness is the losing of self and being clothed with the spirit and likeness of Jesus.[3]

Holiness is God in me and I in Him. It is a life lost in His love. Holiness is being wholly His—and His being wholly mine. Dare we desire anything less than whole-hearted holiness? Dare we strive for anything other than complete devotion?

"But it's so hard!" you say with tears. I know. I've been there too. It's hard to pull yourself up by your own bootstraps. It's hard to overcome chronic sins. It's hard to teach a discouraged, old Christian new tricks. It's hard to believe again when your hopes have been dashed to the ground so many times before. But there is an answer! What you need is a fresh infusion of divine life. What you need is more of the personal, intimate knowledge of God. What you need He is! And He is very near. His revival presence is in the air. Now is the time to believe!

Seek Him with all your heart. Cry out to your Savior and Friend. He will not ignore your tears. He will not refuse your plea. All your years of frustration and longing have been deposited in your heavenly account. Now your spiritual investment has come to maturity. That which you longed for is here! Tell Him that you want nothing less than all of Him, and ask Him to take all of you. You are praying an irresistible prayer, and it will bring undeniable results. Don't stop until the answer comes. The Lord is at the door.

Let the words of hymn writer and biblical scholar Edwin Hatch be yours this hour:

> Breathe on me, breath of God
> Fill me with life anew
> That I may love what Thou dost love
> And do what Thou wouldst do.
>
> Breathe on me, breath of God
> Until my heart is pure
> Until with Thee I have one will
> To do and to endure.
>
> Breathe on me, breath of God
> Till I am wholly Thine
> Until this earthly part of me
> Glows with Thy fire divine.

Can you ask for anything less?

Revival is always a revival of holiness. And it begins with a terrible conviction of sin. It is often the form that this conviction of sin takes that troubles those who read of revival. Sometimes the experience is crushing. People weep uncontrollably, and worse! But there is no such thing as a revival without tears of conviction and sorrow.... Revival in China in 1906 was "marked by a wholly unusual conviction of sin." In 1921, in the revival that began in the East Anglian fishing ports of Lowestoft and Great Yarmouth, strong fishermen were literally thrown to the floor under conviction, until one eyewitness reported: "The ground around me was like a battlefield with souls crying to God for mercy."

Brian Edwards,
Revival: A People Saturated With God

There has never been a spiritual revival which did not begin with an acute sense of sin.

W. Graham Scroggie

Chapter Eight

Conviction!

"If this is conviction, what is hell?" These were the words exclaimed by a shaken evangelist on a frigid, snowy night in Reading, Pennsylvania, in the winter of 1829. Although he was a skilled soul winner and had seen many come under deep conviction of sin—even to the point of shrieking and crying out while he was preaching—this was more intense than anything he had ever witnessed.

He had received an urgent call at midnight. A strong-willed, muscular, unsaved man was overcome by guilt after attending a gospel service. When he got home, he began to contort and groan under the enormous weight of his sin. His family called the evangelist to come at once, fearing that he would die if he could not get relief. And so it was that Charles Finney made his way over to the home of Amos Buck, in spite of a severe blizzard.

Buck was married to a believer but showed no interest at all in the Lord. On this particular night, he attended a gospel meeting, and as Finney described, "The sermon had torn him to pieces."

Finney approached the house. "I could hear his moanings," he recalled, "or I should almost say howlings" from a distance of several hundred feet. Still, he was not prepared for what was coming:

> When I entered I found him sitting on the floor, his wife, I believe, supporting his head,—and what a look on his face! It was indescribable. Used as I was to seeing persons under great convictions, I must confess that his appearance gave me a tremendous shock. He was writhing in agony, grinding his teeth, and literally gnawing his tongue for pain. He cried out to me, "O Mr. Finney! I am lost! I am a lost soul!" and added several things that still increased the shock upon my nerves. I recollect exclaiming, "If this is conviction, what is hell?"

After some effort, Finney was able to reach him: "His burden was soon removed. He was persuaded to trust the Savior, and he came out free and joyful in hope." And so Amos Buck was born from above, the first convert in Finney's meetings in Reading, serving the Lord as an exemplary Christian until his death at age 60 in 1841.[1]

A moving story? Yes. A totally unusual story? Not really! Such scenes are typical in times of revival. After all, what type of reaction can be expected when a rebel comes face to face with the King against whom he has been fighting—and sees that he is absolutely undone and within inches of eternal destruction? What kind of response would be considered normal when an unholy sinner encounters the Holy One— and finds himself utterly and completely without excuse? Or when an unclean transgressor stumbles into the blinding light of the pure and spotless One—and discovers his nakedness, his pollution, his filthy stains? Or when a child molester beholds the face of the heavenly Father? Or when a murderer sees the Giver of life? Or when a lawbreaker stands before the Judge of all the earth? Oh, what intense conviction will come! It is a work of the Spirit and the Word.

This overwhelming sense of God, bringing deep conviction of sin, is perhaps the outstanding feature of true revival.... To cleansed hearts it is heaven, to convicted hearts it is hell, when God is in the midst.[2]

How we need this again in our day! How we need the convicting, converting sword of the Lord, the flaming arrows shot from heaven, the fresh word from the throne that hits home. How we need preaching that brings grown men to their knees, that causes proud sinners to writhe in agony, that shatters the delusions of the rich and famous, that breaks the spell cast over drug-crazed teens, that opens spiritually blind eyes with a jolt, that uncovers that which is hidden and discloses that which has been concealed.

Duncan Campbell relates,

[Another] main feature [of the 1949 Hebrides revival] has been deep conviction of sin—at times leading almost to despair. I have known occasions when it was necessary to stop preaching because of the distress manifested by the anxious, and many would find expression for the feeling in their hearts and the burden of their guilty conscience, in the words of John Newton:

> My conscience felt and owned its guilt,
>   And plunged me in despair;
> I saw my sins His blood had spilt
>   And helped to nail Him there.

[In the parish of Uig] all lorries and vans available were put into service to convey the people to the place of worship, yet many were forced to walk miles; but distance did not matter, and at any rate they knew that the meetings would continue: if they were not in time for the first, they would be sure of getting the second or the third. So they came across the moors and over the hills, young men and maidens, their torches flashing in the darkness, intent upon one thing, to get peace from a guilty conscience, and refuge from the storm in their bosom, in the shelter of the Rock of Ages.[3]

Heavy conviction of sin is a cornerstone of revival. An observer of the 1859 revivals in Ireland and Glasgow explains:

"When the Comforter is come," said our Lord, "He will convince the world of sin." This is the only way to give true comfort to sinners. No preaching of "Peace, peace," will do. The prodigal must be brought to himself, and see his want and misery, ere he will determine to return to his father. The whole need not a physician, but they who are sick. The Lord begins His great work, then, by sending home arrows of conviction to the heart. Thus those long careless and stout of heart fall wounded before Him. They awake out of their long sleep of carnal security, to see themselves posting on to hell. They feel as if ready to be swallowed up by the pit of destruction. The terrible sense of the awful guilt of their sin presses upon their awakened consciences. They can no longer resist the strivings of God's Spirit. They can no longer close their eyes to the momentous concerns of eternity.[4]

Someone mucking out stalls at a stable might not feel too dirty in the presence of the horses, riders, and other stable hands, in spite of all the manure. But put that same person at a wedding reception, and suddenly, "I'm a filthy mess!" In the same way, the "average" lusting, lying, greedy, godless sinner might not feel too evil in the presence of fellow sinners. In fact, Proverbs says that every way of a man is right in his own eyes (see Prov. 16:2). But put that same person before the judgment seat of Almighty God, and suddenly, "It's all over! I am undone! I am lost! Have mercy on me before it's too late!"

Spirit-filled preachers can turn a simple sermon into a preview of the Judgment Day. Everything comes to light! And where there is light, there is heat. A friend of Evan

Roberts described the preaching of W.W. Lewis shortly before the Welsh Revival broke in 1904:

> This mighty man of God was clothed with power from on high, and we were summoned to a scrupulous assize...each one became a terror unto himself. We saw ourselves in the light of the last judgment.[5]

But where are the Spirit-filled preachers today? (Not just screamers or shouters, but Spirit-filled preachers.) Where are the brokenhearted revivalists? (Not showmen or performers, but revivalists with broken hearts.) Where is the message (and messenger) on fire? Where is the living and active Word of God? Something that ought to be common is all too scarce.

It's not that everyone who gets saved has to writhe and groan. It's not that everyone has to stay convicted for days and weeks. But we hardly even see sinners convicted for *minutes* anymore. How the pendulum has swung!

Rarely has there been so much talk of anointing *by* our leaders and so little evidence of anointing *on* our leaders. Rarely has the gospel message been so tame, so tepid, so toothless. Rarely have there been such dull swords or such harmless "truths." It's bad enough that we barely threaten the devil, but we hardly even challenge the saints, let alone confront the sinners.

How desperately we need unction in our pulpits today. Holy Ghost unction in our pulpits will create a whole lot of action in our pews—and in our communities too. If the preacher is moved, the people will be motivated. Fire is "contagious." But as Matthew Henry noted, "Those words are not likely to thaw the hearer's hearts that freeze between the speaker's lips."[6]

God give us some heat! And take out Your hammer, Master! Unsheathe Your blade, O Lord!

"Is not My word like fire," declares the LORD, "and like a hammer that breaks a rock in pieces?" (Jer. 23:29)

For the word of God is living and active. Sharper than any double-edged sword, it penetrates even to dividing soul and spirit, joints and marrow; it judges the thoughts and attitudes of the heart. Nothing in all creation is hidden from God's sight. Everything is uncovered and laid bare before the eyes of Him to whom we must give account. (Heb. 4:12-13)

Just think: If a sharpened, double-edged sword cuts and carves, slices and slashes, ruthlessly reaching its mark, what does God's Word do? It is sharper than any double-edged sword and infinitely more penetrating. Talk about being cut to the quick!

Oh that preachers would meet with God, experience His burden, and then go for the heart, searching out the motives of the soul and piercing the hard crust of our humanistic, pleasure-saturated society. Then sinners would stagger under the revelation of "forever" and saints would be stirred by everlasting truths.

Where are the holy vessels? Where are those gripped by God? Where are the servants who preach with surgical precision? After hearing Gilbert Tennent speak during the days of America's Great Awakening, George Whitefield said, "I never before heard such a searching sermon.... He has learned...to dissect the heart of a natural man. Hypocrites must either soon be converted or enraged at his preaching."[7]

Of Howell Harris, a Welsh contemporary of Whitefield and John Wesley, it was said that "he used to speak of hell as though he had been there himself."[8] That is preaching with conviction! God's man and God's message are one. How different this is from a hollow, taught-by-flesh-and-blood word.

The world is cursed with holiness preachers who have never trembled under awesome Sinai, or lain prostrate in shame before Calvary and had the vile ownership of themselves strangled to death in the rare air heights of Pentecost. Testify to what the Lord has done for you, but at the peril of being cast away as reprobate silver, presume to preach or teach what you have not bought by suffering.[9]

Real people recognize the real thing, and we can only arouse others if we have been aroused ourselves. Those alarmed with the urgency of the hour know how to sound the trumpet blast.

Sometimes revival preaching suddenly awakens the sinner to the awful reality of eternal damnation. In the words of Matthew Henry, "The damnation of Hell (as our Saviour calls it) is the fire of God's anger fastening itself upon the guilty conscience of a sinner to its inexpressible and everlasting torment."[10]

What an awful thought! The sinner looks up and suddenly—oh no! An avalanche of sins comes tumbling down upon him and a torrent of crimes against God and man floods his whole conscious being. They are *his* sins and *his* crimes! He's guilty, guilty, guilty before the One he ignored, mocked, and disdained. And there's no one else to blame, no one to share the guilt, no one to argue his case. Wrath and judgment await him—with no way out and no turning back. That is conviction in God's court.

How precious does that grace appear the hour we first believe! Who could imagine that the Son of God would die for us? As Charles Wesley expressed in song:

> Five bleeding wounds He bears,
> received on Calvary.
> They pour effectual prayers;
> they strongly plead for me.

> Forgive him, oh, forgive they cry,
> Nor let that ransomed sinner die.[11]

Jesus intercedes on the rebel's behalf! He interposes Himself between His Father and the pervert, the terrorist, the rapist, the atheist, the idolater, the hypocrite, the mass murderer. And He pays for all their sins! He receives the judgment due them. Then He offers them entry into His Kingdom, adoption into His family, and a share in His righteousness, peace, and joy. Wonderful grace of God! Awesome salvation of the Lord! No wonder true conversion goes down deep.

David Berkowitz, the infamous Son of Sam, the most notorious serial killer in New York City's history, is now a fully repentant, joy-filled child of God. Jesus' blood can make the foulest sinner clean! And it can happen in an instant of time. From Son of Sam to Son of God! As Berkowitz read a Bible in prison, for the first time in his life it came alive, and the words jumped off the pages at him, striking him in his heart. The poison drained out; the grace poured in. A fellow prisoner of Berkowitz (and a former murderer too) felt himself surrounded by the flames of God for one whole day—and cried out for mercy in his cell. He is now a heaven-bound saint!

Lord, give us such radical conversions every hour—in our neighborhoods and our schools; on our jobs and college campuses; in Hollywood and the world of sports. Transformed lives every day! The fruit of an encounter with the Lord.

Reverend Barbour Johnstone, who traveled into Belfast to investigate the revival it was experiencing in 1859, was stirred by the reports of a man who had seen many careless sinners come under conviction:

> He said it was as if a man were stripped naked, and laid upon red-hot bars of iron. The stricken one seemed as if in

hell, writhing in agony, blind to the outer world, and utterly helpless, until God granted deliverance. He said, "You could never forget such a sight, and could only stand by in silent awe, wondering at God's work."[12]

One young woman, who had opened her heart to the Lord a few weeks earlier, then fell heavily into sin, was gripped at the end of a prayer meeting:

> Just as we were about to close, a young woman burst out into a loud and bitter cry. She threw up her arms wildly, and then tore her hair. They carried her out into the vestry. She was in utter despair and could not pray…. Her sin had found her out, and now, under all its terrors, she was driven distracted. She would receive no consolation. The invitations of Jesus, she said, were not for *her*. She tried sometimes to pray, but could not finish one cry for mercy. The thought of her sin arose, and with a wild cry, and every muscle quivering, she sunk again into despair. It took four people to keep her from doing herself bodily harm. It was a terrible sight. "I never saw before," said one of our young preachers who was present, "what it is to be under the conviction of sin without hope."[13]

When hope finally dawned for this poor soul, it was glorious. She knew the meaning of *relief*.

Another young woman was literally struck down in one of the meetings and carried into a separate room:

> She was lying on the floor, dreadfully convulsed—torn with the alarms of an awakened conscience. She seemed in the deepest despair and darkness. Speaking to her was useless. Her one cry was, "*Lord Jesus, have mercy upon my soul this night!*" wailed forth in deep agony, as if she felt herself sinking into *hell*, and saw that none could help her but *Jesus*.[14]

Such are the deep dealings of the searching Spirit! Such is the searing pain felt by an awakened conscience. For the first time, it sees sin from God's perspective. But where is this level of conviction in our contemporary meetings?

If anything indicates the shallowness of our modern message and the superficiality of many of our conversions it is this painfully obvious lack of conviction. Hearts have grown so hard and preaching has become so soft! Two young men murder their parents and then go out for ice cream. Pedophiliacs form organizations to promote adult sex with children. Abortion doctors put in long, grueling days to generate big bucks by slaughtering the unborn. Little kids watch gory mutilation movies and get bored. And all the while, in the deepest moral crisis our nation has ever known, so many of our preachers entertain!

Who can imagine what will happen when the Spirit punctures this armor of insensitivity and stabs through this shield of callousness? Who can fathom the depth of anguish many of the unsaved will experience when their muddled consciences are finally roused? What will happen when they face God—and their sins—in this world? It will be an unforgettable scene. And the radical change that will be wrought in their lives will not be quickly forgotten either. Oh for revival conviction!

The revival in Indonesia in the 1960's and 1970's was marked by absolutely amazing demonstrations of the power of God, even if some of the extraordinary stories told were exaggerated. Still, one experienced missionary to Indonesia said, "I think the greatest thing that I have heard and that I have seen is people being convicted of sin and of the need of a Savior."[15]

Good things often take time. Must we always be in such a hurry? Why not let conviction do its work? It is one thing to be urgent, pressed, consumed, and constrained. It is another thing to be premature. The deeper the spiritual planting, the more lasting the spiritual harvest. God can get to the heart!

No matter who the sinner is, no matter what his background, conviction can find him out. Even "good, moral, decent" people become undone when their innermost being is brought into the glaring light. In fact, for those raised in the faith, it sometimes gets really intense. The Lord doesn't let them go so easily! Much has been given to them, much is required from them, and, thank God, much is done for them.

Charles Spurgeon was reading about the Puritans when he was just six. His favorite book was *Pilgrim's Progress*, and he loved the Bible and respected his elders deeply. As a sinner, he was far more godly than many saints. But for years, especially as a young, clean-living teenager, he was deeply aware of the fact that he was breaking the law of God. He needed to be born again! Arnold Dallimore relates:

> Finally he told himself, "I must feel something: I must do something." He wished he might give his back to be scourged or that he might make some difficult pilgrimage, if by such efforts he might be saved. Yet he admitted, "That simplest of all matters—believing in Christ crucified, accepting His finished salvation, being nothing and letting Him be everything, doing nothing, but trusting to what He has done—I could not get hold of it."

At last it became unbearable: "I thought I would rather have been a frog or a toad than have been made a man. I reckoned that the most defiled creature...was a better thing than myself, for I had sinned against Almighty God."[16]

In fact, he recounted in later years: "I had rather pass through seven years of the most languishing sickness, than I would ever again pass through the terrible discovery of the evil of sin."[17]

When Spurgeon's yoke fell off, just like the load fell from Pilgrim's back when he received a revelation of the cross, he knew he was forgiven. But as Dallimore notes:

> The suffering through which he passed...had a lasting effect upon him. A recognition of the awful evil of sin was deeply ingrained upon his mind and made him loathe iniquity and love all that was holy. The failure of preachers he had heard to present the gospel, and to do so in a plain, direct manner, caused him throughout his whole ministry to tell sinners in every sermon and in a most forthright and understandable way how to be saved.
>
> Moreover, those lessons were not something merely for the future. His love for Christ was such that, although as yet he was only fifteen, he could not wait to do something for Him but must find ways in which to serve Him and must do so right away.[18]

No wonder Spurgeon could extol the life-transforming power of convicting preaching. He said:

> A spiritual experience which is thoroughly flavored with a deep and bitter sense of sin is of great value to him that hath it. It is terrible in the drinking, but it is most wholesome in the bowels, and in the whole of the after life.
>
> Possibly, much of the flimsy piety of the present day arises from the ease with which men attain to peace and joy in these evangelistic days. We would not judge modern converts, but we certainly prefer that form of spiritual exercise which leads the soul by the way of Weeping-cross, and makes it see its blackness before assuring it that it is "clean every whit."
>
> Too many think lightly of sin, and therefore think lightly of the Savior. He who has stood before His God, convicted and condemned, and with the rope about his neck, is the man to weep for joy when he is pardoned, to hate the evil

which has been forgiven him, and to live to the honour of the Redeemer by whose blood he has been cleansed.[19]

That revelation of the totally undeserved love of God can melt the hardest heart. Robert Murray M'Cheyne relates these accounts from the 1839 revival in Dundee, Scotland:

> I have also, in some instances, heard individuals cry aloud as if they had been pierced through with a dart. These solemn scenes were witnessed under the preaching of different ministers and sometimes occurred under the most tender gospel invitations. On one occasion, for instance, when the minister was speaking tenderly on the words, HE IS ALTOGETHER LOVELY, almost every sentence was responded to by cries of the bitterest agony. At such times I have seen persons so overcome that they could not walk or stand alone.[20]

Beautiful Jesus! What convicting power there is in the love of God! It was a revelation of His goodness and my badness that set me free from shooting drugs in 1971, and I have been free indeed. There is grace available without measure!

Evangelists, go and proclaim liberty to the captives! Prophets, declare the shattering Word of the Lord! Pastors, get to the heart of your people! Convict, convert, console. Expose, exhort, equip. Reveal, revive, refresh. Don't draw back from the truth.

Make the saints firm and the sinners squirm. Build up the foundation of the meek and tear down the stronghold of the proud. Comfort the afflicted and afflict the comfortable. Minister the message of God in a manner worthy of His name. Preach the gospel, my friend. It is an awesome and glorious task.

Once again I hear heaven's call. Wanted: prophetic voices for a deaf generation. Wanted: sober watchmen for a blind people. Wanted: preachers who convict.

Out of death into life! All the old life behind and below! All the new life ahead and above! Inside the gate!...Such a scene no mortal ever saw!

The children clapped their hands in rapture. They shouted for joy. They sometimes rolled on the floor in unrestrained laughter and jumped and danced in great delight, while their faces were so transformed by this heavenly joy that the glory of the celestial city seemed to shine upon us.... This was a city of joy..."joy unspeakable and full of glory!"

H.A. Baker, recounting scenes from the
outpouring at the Adullam Rescue Mission
for young, male beggars in Yunnan, China

The history of the Moravians tells how the Holy Ghost came upon this movement one October morning in 1727. They were having communion. They went out joyful from that place, scarcely knowing whether they were on earth or had died and already gone to heaven. That joyfulness was characteristic of the Moravians for a hundred years. They were not just a happy people in the sense of working up their happiness—their joy came from within.

A.W. Tozer, *When He Is Come*

Joy is the most infallible sign of the presence of God.

Teilhard de Chardin

A life of intimacy with God is characterized by joy.

Oswald Chambers

Will You not revive us again, that Your people may rejoice in You?

Ps. 85:6

Thou longest to see thy children happy with the best happiness which centres in thyself; therefore revive us, for revival will bring the utmost joy.... A genuine revival without joy in the Lord is as impossible as spring without flowers, or day-dawn without light.

Charles Spurgeon, commenting on Ps. 85:6

Chapter Nine

Joy Unspeakable and Full of Glory

Why is there great joy in revival? Well, why is there water in the ocean? You can't have it any other way! Revival without joy would be unthinkable.

The psalmist said that in God's presence there is fullness of joy (Ps. 16:11). God is wonderfully resident in revival! His people are caught up in His glorious presence.

Jesus taught that when sinners repent, there is joy among the angels in heaven (Luke 15). During revival, sinners are repenting left and right! The angels are joyful; Jesus is joyful; we are joyful too!

The Word says that after weeping there is joy and after mourning there is comfort (Ps. 30; Matt. 5). In revival, the agony of conviction turns into the ecstasy of joy, and sorrowful mourning turns into melodious singing. God's people are clean, and a clean heart is a happy heart. Heavy burdens have been lifted, cumbersome weights have been removed, and there is the sound of freedom in the air. Liberation has come for the prisoners!

In that day you will say: "I will praise You, O LORD. Although You were angry with me, Your anger has turned away and You have comforted me. Surely God is my salvation; I will trust and not be afraid. The LORD, the LORD, is my strength and my song; He has become my salvation." *With joy you will draw water from the wells of salvation.* (Is. 12:1-3)

Why is there joy in revival? What a question! The Lord is doing great things in the midst of His people. The long-awaited visitation has come. Heaven is opened and blessings are being poured out. There is a deluge of grace on hungry and thirsty hearts. Families are being reconciled; lives are being transformed; prayers are being dramatically answered; the Spirit is displaying the wonders of the Son; the hope of eternal life is a present-tense reality—how could there not be joy?

The early believers were filled with joy: "While [Jesus] was blessing them, He left them and was taken up into heaven. Then they worshiped Him and returned to Jerusalem *with great joy*" (Luke 24:51-52).

What would you have done if you were there when Jesus ascended to heaven and you knew that this new faith of yours was not a dream? You would have rejoiced too!

For these believers in the days of Acts, just to be identified with Jesus became a source of joy. Being *flogged* for Him was a delight!

> …They called the apostles in and had them flogged. Then they ordered them not to speak in the name of Jesus, and let them go. The apostles left the Sanhedrin, *rejoicing* because they had been counted worthy of suffering disgrace for the Name. (Acts 5:40-41)

No wonder Paul and Silas could sing hymns and praise God at midnight, locked in a dungeon, and with open, bloody wounds from a fresh beating. They were suffering for the Lord! They were being treated just as He was, and Jesus said that when they persecute us for His name's sake, we should rejoice and leap for joy (Luke 6:23).

That joy can be contagious. Paul and Silas were so blessed in their suffering and pain that their victory led to the salvation of the jailer and his whole family—and these new believers also received the joy of the Lord: "The jailer brought [Paul and Silas] into his house and set a meal before them; he was *filled with joy* because he had come to believe in God—he and his whole family" (Acts 16:34). The Book of Acts, which is a picture of revival, is a book of joy:

> Philip went down to a city in Samaria and proclaimed the Christ there. When the crowds heard Philip and saw the miraculous signs he did, they all paid close attention to what he said. With shrieks, evil spirits came out of many, and many paralytics and cripples were healed. So there was *great joy* in that city. (Acts 8:5-8)

> When they came up out of the water, the Spirit of the Lord suddenly took Philip away, and the eunuch did not see him again, but went on his way *rejoicing*. (Acts 8:39)

> And the disciples were *filled with joy* and with the Holy Spirit. (Acts 13:52)

Is this any surprise? With Holy Spirit preaching and Holy Spirit miracles and Holy Spirit conversions, what else could we expect? The believers in Acts ministered the truth, and they got true results.

Often in revival, the intensity of the feeling of conviction of sin—which you know from the last chapter can get pretty intense—is surpassed by the overwhelming feeling of relief and joy when the sinner finds rest. The joy lasts much longer than the conviction too!

Speaking of revivals on college campuses, J. Edwin Orr stated:

> From the records of the past and the reports of the mid-twentieth century, it can be concluded that the misery of conviction and agony of confession have always been

followed by a sense of forgiveness and joy which completely eclipsed the travail of repentance. No one who was present at Bethel College in 1949 could ever forget the students standing in long lines at the cafeterias, swept by joy and singing the songs of deliverance in harmony "out of this world."[1]

If we could only learn to let the Lord fully do His work of probing, searching, uncovering, and sifting, we would see much greater joy among God's people once the work was done. If we could only learn to deal ruthlessly with sin, to cut it out from the roots, to get to the real cause of people's problems, to give up our quest for cheap solutions, then we would see deeper victory among the saved, and true, lasting conversions among the lost. As Orr noted, "the skipping of preparation and searching of heart often makes the...revival less thorough and less lasting.[2]

We often lack joy because we lack depth. The joy of the Lord is anything but shallow! In the midst of deep testing, it is there. When all hope seems lost, it is there. Why? We remember that God reigns and that He is for us, and we are overcome with joy. When we put no trust in the flesh, our eyes look up to our Deliverer—and He doesn't let us down. And so we rejoice in the Lord!

The joy of the Lord fills the emptied heart and inundates the poured out vessel. But God will not fill a self-satisfied sinner or saint. First, He will strip them bare of carnal security and fleshly pollution, then He will clothe them anew.

Don't be afraid of the weeping and wailing that often come before the joy. If the heart pain is the result of a message from God (rather than from a condemning word from man), it will not end in despair. It will end in delight! And don't be afraid of the dealings of the Spirit with your own soul. Don't faint when you see the junk He uncovers in your life. He knew it was there all along, and He still loved you. He will see you through!

Let Him do what He must do. Let Him bring you to the end of yourself. You'll find grace when you get there! And when your heart is purged you'll be ecstatic. You'll rejoice as if you were getting born again all over again. Revival joy comes from renewed lives. Obedience brings the overflow. We enjoy God as we obey Him.

Today, we want the time of dancing without the time of weeping. We want the comfort without the mourning, the birth without the travail, the release without the conviction. We want a cute Band-Aid with pretty colors to put on the chest of someone who needs a heart transplant. With our modern spiritual philosophy, we give a candy bar to a cancer victim and tell a funny story to a demonized sinner. It won't work!

But the Lord wants to give the real thing—even if it requires some surgery. The results are well worth the pain. The cure is worth the cutting! The healing will last forever.

Remember the calendar of Israel: The first day of the seventh month was the Day of the Trumpet Blast. It was a wake-up call! Then there were nine days of waiting leading up to the Day of Atonement on the tenth day of the month. In Jewish tradition, these became known as the Days of Awe, a time of soul searching and heart cleansing. Then came the Day of Atonement, simply called *the Day* by the rabbis, and it was set aside for fasting, for mourning over sins, for confession, for repentance, and for purging and purification before the Lord.

Then, just four days later, the Festival of Sukkot (Tabernacles) began. It was a time of rejoicing, and it lasted eight days.[3] One day of mourning followed by eight days of rejoicing! Do you see God's heart in this? True repenting will lead to true rejoicing.

Why bypass the wake-up call, the time of examination, and the day of repentance? The joy will last much longer if we do things God's way!

Of course, some sinners are instantly saved with little trace of conviction. They encounter the goodness of the Lord and immediately receive His grace. For them, joy comes without a long process of seeking, and the realization of the forgiveness of sin comes without a sense of deep conviction first. God can work like that if He chooses. Every life is different, and every salvation experience is unique. But we've taken the exception and turned it into the rule, and now we're paying the price. Our churches are full of bad fruit picked from trees before it was ripe.

Do you think Charles Finney knew something we don't know? It was his custom never to tell someone how to be saved—so as to lead them to the Lord at that moment—if they could still look him in the face. That was a sign to him that they were not sufficiently ashamed of their sins! Yet the sinners who stroll forward at our "altar calls" normally seem more casual than convicted, more antsy than ashamed, more eager to go home than to go to heaven. Is it any wonder that most of them don't go on with God? But revival will bring true conversions, and true conversions will bring joy.

The seventy-two returned *with joy* and said, "Lord, even the demons submit to us in Your name." He replied, "I saw Satan fall like lightning from heaven. I have given you authority to trample on snakes and scorpions and to overcome all the power of the enemy; nothing will harm you. However, do not rejoice that the spirits submit to you, but *rejoice that your names are written in heaven.*" At that time Jesus, *full of joy through the Holy Spirit*, said, "I praise You, Father, Lord of heaven and earth, because You have hidden these things from the wise and learned, and revealed them to little children. Yes, Father, for this was Your good pleasure." (Luke 10:17-21)

Let us glory in the joy of the Lord! Nothing fulfills like the joy of the Lord. Nothing refreshes like the joy of the Lord. Nothing renews like the joy of the Lord. The joy of the Lord is exhilarating! It is His own joy that we share: "I have told you this so that *My joy may be in you* and that your joy may be complete" (John 15:11).

Jesus wants us to live in that joy, and He wants us to have it to the fullest: "Until now you have not asked for anything in My name. Ask and you will receive, and *your joy will be complete*" (John 16:24). He wants that joy to last!

I tell you the truth, you will weep and mourn while the world rejoices. You will grieve, but your grief will turn to joy. A woman giving birth to a child has pain because her time has come; but when her baby is born she forgets the anguish because of her joy that a child is born into the world. So with you: Now is your time of grief, but I will see you again and *you will rejoice, and no one will take away your joy.* (John 16:20-22)

No one can steal our joy! It is not based on circumstances. It is not based on feelings and emotions. It is based on the goodness of God and our relationship with Him. Nothing external can change that! As William Vander Hoven said, "Joy is not the absence of trouble but the presence of Christ."[4] Or, in the words of Puritan minister Walter Cradock, "Take a saint, and put him in any condition, and he knows how to rejoice in the Lord."[5] Paul proved this out from his prison cell:

...The important thing is that in every way, whether from false motives or true, Christ is preached. And because of this *I rejoice. Yes, and I will continue to rejoice. ... But even if I am* being poured out like a drink offering on the sacrifice and service coming from your faith, *I am glad and rejoice* with all of you. (Phil. 1:18; 2:17)

And he commands us to rejoice with him: "Finally, my brothers, *rejoice in the Lord! ... Rejoice in the Lord always. I will say it again: Rejoice!*" (Phil. 3:1a; 4:4)

It is a joy that we do not work up, as A.W. Tozer said:

We do have many professing Christians in our day who are not joyful, but they spend time to work it up. Now, brethren, I say that when we give God His place in the church, when we recognize Christ as Lord high and lifted up, when we give the Holy Spirit His place, there will be joy that doesn't have to be worked up. It will be a joy that springs like a fountain. Jesus said that it should be a fountain, an artesian well, that springs from within. That's one characteristic of a Spirit-filled congregation. They will be a joyful people, and it will be easy to distinguish them from the children of the world.[6]

And that joy is our strength:

They read from the Book of the Law of God, making it clear and giving the meaning so that the people could understand what was being read. Then Nehemiah the governor, Ezra the priest and scribe, and the Levites who were instructing the people said to them all, "This day is sacred to the LORD your God. Do not mourn or weep." For all the people had been weeping as they listened to the words of the Law. Nehemiah said, "Go and enjoy choice food and sweet drinks, and send some to those who have nothing prepared. This day is sacred to our Lord. Do not grieve, for *the joy of the LORD* is your strength." (Neh. 8:8-10)

How can we fight the battles of the Lord if we are constantly downtrodden and discouraged? How can we be a light in the darkness if our own lamps have grown dim? How can we set the world on fire if we are cold and dry? We need joy and gladness in our hearts. We need a touch from heaven. We need to be glad in the Lord!

God Himself prefers the atmosphere of a joy-filled heart. As William Gurnall said, "Christ takes no more delight to dwell in a sad heart, than we do to live in a dark house."[7]

Away with sedate services! Enough with somber Sabbaths! An end to sleepy sermons! No more slumbering saints! Jesus has risen from the grave! Get out of your bed and rejoice!

How can you walk closely with the Lord and not have joy? Jesus was already bringing joy when He was still in His mother's womb! Elizabeth, the mother of John, said to the pregnant Mary, "As soon as the sound of your greeting reached my ears, the baby in my womb *leaped for joy*" (Luke 1:44).

When the angels announced His birth to the shepherds, they proclaimed, "Do not be afraid. I bring you *good news of great joy* that will be for all the people" (Luke 2:10b). Good news of great joy! That is the foundation of our faith. The time of redemption has come.

> The desert and the parched land *will be glad*; the wilderness *will rejoice* and blossom. Like the crocus, it will burst into bloom; it will *rejoice greatly* and *shout for joy*. The glory of Lebanon will be given to it, the splendor of Carmel and Sharon; they will see the glory of the Lord, the splendor of our God. ... Then will the eyes of the blind be opened and the ears of the deaf unstopped. Then will the lame leap like a deer, and the mute tongue shout for joy. Water will gush forth in the wilderness and streams in the desert. The burning sand will become a pool, the thirsty ground bubbling springs. In the haunts where jackals once lay, grass and reeds and papyrus will grow. (Is. 35:1-2,5-7)

Jesus Himself had a special anointing of joy: "You have loved righteousness and hated wickedness; therefore God, Your God, has set You above Your companions by anointing You with the *oil of joy*" (Heb. 1:9).

The Savior was not only "a man of sorrows, acquainted with grief." No, He endured the shame and suffering of the cross "for the joy set before Him" (Heb. 12:2), and now we rejoice in Him! "Though you have not seen Him, you love Him; and even though you do not see Him now, you believe in Him and are filled with an *inexpressible and glorious joy*" (1 Pet. 1:8).

Yes, there will be trials and tests. But they cannot ultimately keep down the overflowing river of joy:

> In this [salvation] you *greatly rejoice*, though now for a little while you may have had to suffer grief in all kinds of trials. These have come so that your faith—of greater worth than gold, which perishes even though refined by fire—may be proved genuine and may result in praise, glory and honor when Jesus Christ is revealed. (1 Pet. 1:6-7)

Consider it *pure joy*, my brothers, whenever you face trials of many kinds, because you know that the testing of your faith develops perseverance. (James 1:2-3)

The trials only serve to strengthen us, and the battles make our faith that much more bold. We come through the fires even more confident in the goodness of God, and that goodness makes us glad:

> Enter His gates with thanksgiving and His courts with praise; give thanks to Him and praise His name. For the LORD is good and His love endures forever; His faithfulness continues through all generations. (Ps. 100:4-5)

We have good reason to rejoice!

But what has become of your joy? A joyless life is an un-revived life. It's time to go back to the well!

Three hundred years ago, Richard Baxter gave a challenge:

I desire the dejected Christian to consider, that by his heavy and uncomfortable life, he seemeth to the world to accuse God and His service, as if he openly called Him a rigorous, hard, unacceptable Master, and His work a sad, unpleasant thing. I know this is not your thoughts: I know it is your-selves, and not God and His service that offendeth you; and that you walk heavily not because you are holy, but because you fear you are not holy, and because you are no more holy.... If you see a servant always sad, that was wont to be merry while he served another master, will you not think that he hath a master that displeaseth him? ... You are born and new born for God's honour; and will you thus dishon-our Him before the world? What do you (in their eyes) but dispraise Him by your very countenance and carriage?[8]

What does our life proclaim to the world? Real joy—not some worked-up, emotional frenzy—can distinguish us from other religions and faiths. Real joy stands out!

One sure sign that we need revival is that we cannot relate to the New Testament norm:

Speak to one another with psalms, hymns and spiritual songs. Sing and make music in your heart to the Lord, always giving thanks to God the Father for everything, in the name of our Lord Jesus Christ. (Eph. 5:19-20)

Let the word of Christ dwell in you richly as you teach and ad-monish one another with all wisdom, and as you sing psalms, hymns and spiritual songs with gratitude in your hearts to God. And whatever you do, whether in word or deed, do it all in the name of the Lord Jesus, giving thanks to God the Father through Him. (Col. 3:16-17)

Shall we call this the normal Christian life? Revival makes things normal again!

It is true that we can lose the joy of the Lord in many ways: through sin; through being out of His will; through lack of communion with the Lord; through unbelief; through materialism and love of this world; through discouragement in the midst of prolonged attack; through bitterness and pride; through a morbid view of the gospel; through a simple failure to ask God for His blessing; through legalism; through a faultfinding, critical spirit; through lack of fellowship with the saints; through lack of worship and thanksgiving; through overdependence on people and circumstances.

There are lots of ways to lose the joy! But one moment in the presence of God can restore that joy in full. Revival brings restoration; revival brings rejoicing; revival really revives! Jesus comes into clear focus, and He is wonderful to behold!

That is the secret of the joy of the Lord—focusing on Jesus the Lord. Otherwise, how could we have joy? It really is a mystery. There is so much suffering in the world today, so much hardship, so much pain. There are so many who reject and mock the Savior, so many who are lost in their sins. How can we rejoice?

We look to Jesus, that's how. We weep with Him, grieve with Him, intercede with Him, and share His burdens. We give ourselves to the sick and suffering, travailing in the pangs of labor to see their answer birthed. We don't look for a superficial fix. We face the problems head-on instead of trying to waltz our way through life. We are realists, we are sober, and we care. We know both the fellowship of Jesus' sufferings as well as the power of His resurrection, but that resurrection power conquers death!

Answers to prayer do come! Deliverance springs up and healing bursts forth. Every minute of every day foul sinners are being redeemed. There is the sound of victory, not defeat, in heaven. Our God is not depressed! And while revival stirs the whole range of emotions—the agony of conviction, the terror of damnation, the pangs of sorrow for the lost, the joy of fellowship restored—it is the joy that will endure forever. And when we get a glimpse of the glories of the world to come—of eternal, unbroken, perfect fellowship with our God and His family—our hearts are filled with joy. Do you have the joy of the Lord?

When Howell Harris was first used in revival in Wales in the 1700's, his message thundered with the terrors of hell. People were broken and shattered by his words, and there was deep repentance and grief. At that time too, many of the churches were deeply divided. There were breaches in the Body that displeased the Lord.

But then, the brokenness led to changed hearts, and there was a "Reunion" of the churches. This revival, Harris said, was characterized by the "spirit of singing, rejoicing and leaping for joy." How glorious is the refreshing of the Lord! "Oh, that salvation for Israel would come out of Zion! When the LORD restores the fortunes of His people, let Jacob rejoice and Israel be glad!" (Ps. 14:7)

If the Church experiences this today, Israel will certainly experience it tomorrow. And on that day, the Lord Himself will rejoice with exceeding joy:

Sing, O Daughter of Zion; shout aloud, O Israel! *Be glad and rejoice with all your heart*, O Daughter of Jerusalem! The LORD has taken away your punishment, He has turned back your enemy. The LORD, the King of Israel, is with you; never again will you fear any harm. On that day they will say to Jerusalem, "Do not fear, O Zion; do not let your hands hang limp. The LORD your God is with you, He is mighty to save. He will take great delight in you, He will quiet you with His love, *He will rejoice over you with singing.*" (Zeph. 3:14-17)

Oh that God would rejoice and sing in our midst!

He does, when His people are holy. He does when we walk with Him. He does when we are revived. Revival makes Him glad.

You English blame us, the Welsh, and speak against us and say "Jumpers! Jumpers!" But we, the Welsh, have something also to allege against you, and we most justly say of you, "Sleepers! Sleepers!"

Daniel Rowlands, the Welsh revivalist,
replying to the criticism of
John Thornton of England, in the early 1760's

It was a meeting characterized by a perpetual series of interruptions and disorderliness. It was a meeting characterized by a great continuity and an absolute order. You say, "How do you reconcile these things?" I do not reconcile them. They are both there…. I have never seen anything like it in my life; while a man praying is disturbed by the breaking out of song, there is no sense of disorder, and the prayer merges into song, and back into testimony, and back again into song for hour after hour, without guidance. These are the three occupations—singing, prayer, testimony.

G. Campbell Morgan, *Glory Filled the Land*

And as to the imprudences, irregularities, and mixture of delusion that has been observed; it is not at all to be wondered at that a reformation, after long continued and almost universal deadness, should at first, when the revival is new, be attended with such things.

Jonathan Edwards, *Jonathan Edwards on Revival*

Chapter Ten

Jerkers, Jumpers, and "Holy Disorder"

Jerkers? Jumpers? Holy disorder? These are just a few of the accompaniments of revival, some of them good, some bad, and some neutral. There are heavenly manifestations, hellish manifestations, and human manifestations. There is the presence of fresh fire, false fire, and fleshly fire. There is that which is from above, that which is from below, and that which is in between. Some bring about conversion; others bring about confusion. They need to be sorted out.

This much is sure: If you don't like excitement, revival is not for you. If you prefer the quiet of the graveyard, you will have a problem with the noise that often accompanies revival. Revival bursts with new life, and new life is exciting.

You don't like the emotional display? Then tell the father of the just-returned prodigal son in Luke 15 to calm down. The celebration and singing are unnecessary! Tell the just-healed lame man in Acts 3 to get control of himself. Leaping and jumping in the Temple are irreverent. Tell King David in Second Samuel 6 to quit putting on that ridiculous public show: dancing, twirling, spinning, making an absolute fool of himself. That's undignified for a king. (Come to think of it, someone did tell David that very thing. Her name was Michal, and as a result, she bore no children to the day of her death [2 Sam. 6:23].)

Howell Harris addressed this attitude more than 200 years ago:

> If a man was in…jail for debt, and never hoped to come from there, and beyond expectation a relative from the East Indies, hearing of his circumstances, would come and pay his debt and release him, would you blame him much if he could not contain himself for some time, but did leap as David before the Ark? Would you not excuse him? The case here is beyond this![1]

Yes, the case of revival is far beyond this. Sinners are being pardoned! Lifelong captives are being set free! God is visiting His people! That's what revival is all about.

No wonder, then, that revival is marked by all kinds of emotional displays. And much of it is fine. God gave us emotions, and we are called to love Him with heart and mind, to bless Him with all that is within us. Those who think that true worship is always a somber affair better read their Bibles again. (Or maybe they just need a touch from heaven!) Fervent praise looks and sounds a whole lot different than a funeral procession.

Unfortunately, as Baptist evangelist Vance Havner said, "The same church members who yell like Comanche Indians at a ball game on Saturday sit like wooden Indians in church on Sunday."[2]

It has nothing to do with being conservative. It has to do with the sad fact that most believers are more alive to the world than to the Lord.

In times of revival, things change radically. Believers act like believers, worship like believers, and respond like believers. After all, there's a lot more to shout about in the house of God than on the football field—if we really believe.

Is it any wonder that the early believers at Azusa Street, caught up with the awesome excitement of a new experience that they believed to be a modern Pentecost, were criticized for their emotional fervor? They were called Holy Rollers, Ranters, and Holy Kickers—among other things. Their enthusiastic religion was mocked and misunderstood, much like the early Methodists who were subjected to all kinds of ridicule for their enthusiasm (the old English way of saying fanaticism). But these people, both the illiterate and the highly cultured, were turned on, charged up, and plugged in. Their behavior was no surprise—even if it sometimes went to fleshly extremes that needed to be corrected.

But there is another factor at work in revival, beyond the response of the emotions. When the revelation of eternity suddenly strikes someone, when for the first time a person experiences the reality of God, there is hardly time to think through a proper response. The reaction, if it can be called a reaction, is spontaneous and inevitable. Does the studious man who unexpectedly steps on a razor-sharp nail carefully and quietly consider what has just transpired in the region of his foot, or does he automatically let out a cry—even if he's in a library? When a large, hairy spider pounces on the hand of a delicate young lady, does she rehearse in her mind the guidelines of proper etiquette, or does she jump up and shriek—even if she's at an important luncheon?

The realities of revival are far more gripping and intense than the pain caused by a nail or the disturbance caused by a spider. We're talking about people's souls, about heaven and hell. We're talking about God. How foolish to think we can put revival into a neat little package. How silly to think we can turn it on and off—and the congregation along with it—like a light switch on the wall. Those who think in such terms expose their ignorance of—not expertise in—the overwhelmingly powerful nature of revival. Maybe they do know how to turn it off. But they surely won't be able to turn it on again!

The plain fact is that many of us have become used to a bland religious experience. It's so predictable, so controlled (and I don't mean by the Spirit). You would hardly guess that our God was alive and active. Revival makes us uncomfortable, and that's good, because comfortable religion is worthless. You may well hear some new sounds (like the sobbing of the sorrowful, or the cry of the convicted, or the laughter of the liberated) and see some new sights (like the stagger of the stricken or the dance of the delivered). Get ready for revival!

When surprising, outward manifestations began to occur in the meetings of John Wesley, George Whitefield, who was the first among them to break with tradition and begin open-air preaching, heard about these strange occurrences and was critical. But, says Wesley,

> I had an opportunity to talk with him of those outward signs which had so often accompanied the inward work of God. I found his objections were chiefly founded on gross misrepresentations of matters of fact. But the next day he had an opportunity of informing himself better: for no sooner had he begun (in the application of his sermon) to invite all sinners to believe in Christ, than four persons sunk down close to him, almost in the same moment. One of them lay without either sense or motion; a second trembled exceedingly; the third had strong convulsions all over his body, but made no noise, unless by groans; the fourth, equally convulsed, called upon God, with strong cries and tears. From this time, I trust, we shall all suffer God to carry on His own work in the way that pleaseth Him.[3]

When similar things began to occur in Whitefield's meetings, he was inclined to silence the people or have them removed. But Lady Huntingdon, whom Whitefield greatly respected, saw things otherwise. This was the counsel she gave to the greatest preacher of that century: "You are making a mistake. Don't be wiser than God. Let them cry out; it will do a great deal more good than your preaching."[4] Are we also trying to be wiser than God, or can we trust Him to do His work in His way?

Sometimes the Lord sovereignly sweeps in and, emotions or no, reactions or no, the place shakes. All of us know Acts 4:31: "After they prayed, *the place where they were meeting was shaken.* And they were all filled with the Holy Spirit and spoke the word of God boldly." But do we believe it? It's not the hyped-up story of some high-powered TV preacher. It really happened 2,000 years ago, and it has happened since.

In one of the most famous accounts from the Hebrides Awakening, Duncan Campbell describes what took place during an all-night prayer meeting. He had just arrived to begin a series of meetings. Many of the believers had a great sense of expectation, but as a whole, the people in the area were resistant to the gospel. A deacon said to him that night, "Mr. Campbell, God is hovering over, and He is going to break through." Yet the meeting was completely ordinary. Still, the deacon was confident and said to Campbell, "Do not be discouraged. God is coming. Already I hear the rumblings of heaven's chariot wheels."[5]

Right! "The rumblings of heaven's chariot wheels." We've heard that one before! And did this deacon speak with Elijah too? But this was not a matter of religious talk. It was not another instance of some pseudo-spiritual mumbo jumbo. Not at all! God came in power that night.

The deacon suggested that they spend the night in prayer, and so about 30 of them gathered in a cottage to seek the Lord. They battled without a breakthrough, until Campbell felt led to ask the blacksmith to pray. After praying for 30 minutes (as Campbell noted, "in revival time doesn't matter"), the blacksmith closed with these bold words, "God, do You not know Your honour is at stake? You promised to pour floods on dry ground, and You are not doing it." He then stopped, waited, and concluded with these words, "God, Your honour is at stake, and I challenge You to keep Your covenant engagements."[6]

And how did God respond? "That whole granite house shook like a leaf," said Campbell. Some present thought there had actually been an earth tremor, but Campbell thought at once of Acts 4:31. He related:

> I saw about a dozen men and women prostrated upon the floor. They lay there speechless as God gave His witness to their hearts. He had taken the field. The forces of darkness were going to be driven back. Sinful men were going to be delivered. We knew that something had happened.

> And when we left that cottage at three o'clock in the morning we learned what it was. Everywhere men and women were seeking God. As I walked along the country road, I found three men on their faces, crying to God for mercy. There was a light in every home; no one seemed to be thinking of sleep.[7]

Yes, "the whole village [was] alive, ablaze with God." The fire fell and ignited men's hearts. The granite house shook, and people's galvanized hearts were shaken. The wind from heaven blew in! What response would have been proper? And would one of our modern religious Spirit-stiflers have rebuked the house for being too easily moved?

A minister who observed the 1860 Tinnevelly Revival wrote:

> Let us not put our views of decorum and of order above the mighty operations of the Spirit. When He comes forth in His glory, it is as it were a judgment day; there is an overwhelming revelation of sin and of danger; and we can no more expect men to act under such circumstances in accordance with ordinary rules of decorum, than we could expect men aroused from their beds by an earthquake to avoid every demonstration of a noisy or alarming character. Perhaps it behooves us all to surrender our very imperfect views of the power and majesty of the Holy Spirit, and prepare for something grander, more awful and more revolutionary than we have witnessed.[8]

How little we know of the height and depth and breadth and length of God's power. How little we know of revival!

Look over to the ocean shore, where a crowd of young people frolics in the pounding surf. Suddenly a huge wave sweeps in, and they are thrown like dolls. Why? They were hit by a ten-foot wave! Now look again. It's a church service in times of revival. There are all kinds of unusual manifestations. People are collapsing and crumbling; others lie flattened and motionless. Why? The Spirit struck them! The divine tide rolled in! They were overwhelmed by the Presence of the King.

Strange things can happen at such times! Sometimes the Lord will humble the proud in the most unexpected ways. He may do the opposite of that which our religious prejudices have led us to expect. In fact, most revivals come with some kind of religious stumbling blocks. There can be holy silence blanketing the services of the shouters, or loud shouts erupting in the services of the silent. There can be weeping for the laughers and laughter for the weepers. This can be a test from heaven! It is designed to upset our applecarts. (See my chapter entitled "Don't Put Out the Spirit's Fire" in *The End of the American Gospel Enterprise* for more on this.[9])

Sometimes the Lord will bring down the ungodly, openly. At other times He'll pour out an overflowing blessing that His people can hardly contain. And then there is the flesh. It wants to get involved too. Once the real manifestations start taking place (although not every true revival will have all of these outward signs), it's easy for people to start putting on a show.

During the Cane Ridge Revival at the turn of the nineteenth century in the Wild West of America, people began to get the jerks. Heads and necks would snap with a loud noise. The long, loose hair of the women would crack like a whip (really!). According to one account, a drunken mocker was seized with a case of the jerks during an outdoor meeting. Yet the more he jerked, the more he cursed God. He wanted to guzzle his alcohol, but he couldn't get it to his mouth! Finally, the bottle fell from his hands and broke, bringing on a torrent of blasphemy. He then jerked with such sudden force that he broke his neck and died.[10] Yes, that's a pretty wild story! But then, revival can get pretty wild.

How much of the jerking was from God (a stumbling block to confound the religious, or a divine act to loosen up—no pun intended!—the stiff and judge the unrepentant)? How much was an unconscious psychological reaction ("This is what happens when the Spirit falls, so the moment you feel something, jerk!")? How much was an intentional public display? How much was related to demons (either genuine deliverance, with spirits leaving people, or else demonic distractions to the true moving of God)? Who can give a definite answer from such a distance? It was probably a combination of all of the above.

During the Methodist awakenings in the 1760's, some Welsh believers began to get so excited that they would jump for joy, even becoming known as the Jumpers. (Remember the leaping lame man and dancing King David!) One meeting they had went on continuously for three days and nights. Was it just a move of God, or did the people go off the deep end? One minister made his opinions known: "It appears to all true and serious Christians that they [i.e., the Methodists] are stark mad, and given to a spirit of delusion, to the great disgrace and scandal of Christianity."[11]

Another minister saw it very differently!

When these powerful outpourings descended on several hundreds, if not thousands, throughout South Wales and Gwynedd, there arose much excitement and controversy concerning the matter; many were struck with amazement and said, "What can this mean?" "They are drunkards," said some. Others said, "They are mad," very like those [earlier scoffers] on the day of Pentecost long ago; but hardly anyone dared harm them, apart from making them a target for hostile tongues.[12]

Why such discrepancies? According to William Williams of Pantecelyn, one of the most respected national leaders at that time, "When our soul came to taste the feasts of Heaven, the flesh also insisted on having its share, and all the passions of nature aroused by grace were rioting tumultuously."[13] Spirit and soul, body and mind, emotions and will were all getting into the action, and, no doubt, there was a mixture.

The newspapers had a field day with the Azusa Street manifestations. Typical story lines included: "Humane Society Is to Tackle Jumpers"; "Whites and Blacks Mix in a Religious Frenzy"; "Disgusting Scenes at Azusa Street

Church"; "How Holy Roller Gets Religion"; "Holy Kickers Baptized 138"; "Holy Rollers' Meetings Verge on Riot"; "Gifts of Tongues Works Havoc Among Churches." On one occasion it was alleged that, following a baptism on the beach, one man "so lacerated his neck with his finger nails while in a violent spasm that he bled a great deal. When he was carried away to the bath house the sand was discolored with blood."[14]

The skeptical reporters considered it typical for the fervent at Azusa Street to have "cataleptic fits" during the course of a normal service. Yet it cannot be denied that modern Pentecostal denominations trace their origins to that very outpouring, an outpouring that was not free of both fleshly and false manifestations.

There is no way to totally avoid this, as much as we try. There will always be some mixture of the human and the divine elements in our meetings. No one on earth has yet graduated from the realm of feelings and emotions (although some believers have become so cerebral they could use a good pinch). No one is perfectly and completely filled with the Spirit (although some of today's teachers seem almost perfectly emptied of the Spirit). God has only earthen vessels through whom He can work, and it is earthen vessels He blesses and earthen vessels who can go berserk.

Often, to the outward eye, it's hard to figure out what's what. (I'm not talking about people stripping naked or destroying furniture or getting into fistfights "in the Spirit." It should be pretty easy to figure out what "spirit" is behind that!) Emyr Roberts explains,

> We have only laughter to express the most ribald revelry and the most godly joy; we have only tears to express the most selfish and worldly grief and the most godly sorrow.

Therefore we must not be unduly surprised that spiritual rejoicings are so similar in their manifestations of a very different kind.[15]

The problem is that so many get carried away, as if falling or jerking were the divine mark of blessing. For others, pandemonium actually becomes the purpose of the revival meeting. Here is another example from the 1740's in Wales: The powerful preacher, Daniel Rowland, was one of the most solid men of his generation, and his ministry stirred the hearts of the hearers. Still, it seems things were getting a little intense.

After Rowland's long, presermon prayer, people began to cry out praises at the top of their lungs, and it got so loud that, in the words of one observer:

> There was such a noise and confusion through the whole church that I had much ado, though I stood nigh the minister, to make sense of anything he said. His preaching, again, flung almost the whole society into the greatest agitation and confusion possible: some cried, others laughed, the women pulled one another by the caps, embraced each other, capered [cavorted] like, where there was any room.... Nay, I never saw greater instances of madness, even in Bedlam [a mental asylum] itself.[16]

Yes, people can get genuinely touched and then overreact. Others mistake the outward reaction for the inward reality. They want to fall, or cry, or laugh, or jerk. They think the emotional or physical display is an indication of spirituality. In their case, it's more of an indication of immaturity. We don't come to church to keel over or roll on the floor. We come to meet with God! And if that encounter knocks us down, shakes us up, and rolls us through the aisles and out the exit right to our car door, so be it. But we should never focus on the manifestations. We should pursue the Presence!

The question is not, "Did you get it?" but, "Do you know Him?"

This is where revivals often get sidetracked. Jerking or jumping becomes central, instead of Jesus being central. We look for laughter instead of looking for the Lord. We seek the sensational—after all, isn't that a great way to bring in the people?—instead of seeking the Spirit. That's just human nature: fallen, foolish, and frivolous. But let's not feed it!

These days, the filling has to be thrilling, and God's Presence must produce some kind of exciting spectacle. And if the Lord chooses not to move in that way—what then? Will we work it up?

In Numbers 11, the Israelites complained. They weren't satisfied with God's provision. They wanted meat, not manna. So the Lord sent quail to them in abundance, piled "three feet above the ground, as far as a day's walk in any direction" (11:31). What a blessing! What a miracle! What an answer!

> But while the meat was still between their teeth and before it could be consumed, the anger of the LORD burned against the people, and He struck them with a severe plague. Therefore the place was named Kibroth Hattaavah, because there they buried the people who had craved other food. (Num. 11:33-34)

We're still craving "other food." We're still not happy with the way of Gethsemane and Calvary, the way of self-denial, of death to the flesh, of godly character, of persevering in prayer, of sacrificial love. I wonder how much silliness there will be in our meetings when evangelist Ananias and prophetess Sapphira start dropping dead at our feet. They won't need any ushers to catch them. People of God, we had better wake up!

This thing is not a game. The eternal destiny of human souls is at stake. An almighty, holy King sits on His throne. And while He may laugh in scorn at those who seek to overthrow His rule (see Ps. 2), He certainly is not laughing about the perishing multitudes, about young lives being destroyed, about His people being in disarray, about the name of His Son being reproached. Yet some of us are only interested in spiritual feasting and revelry.

There are some amazing insights to be found in John 6. Jesus had miraculously fed the five thousand, and the next day the people came looking for Him, taking boats across the sea to find Him. When they arrived, Jesus said to them:

> ...I tell you the truth, you are looking for Me, not because you saw miraculous signs but because you ate the loaves and had your fill. Do not work for food that spoils, but for food that endures to eternal life, which the Son of Man will give you. On Him God the Father has placed His seal of approval. (John 6:26-27)

The miraculous signs should have drawn attention to Jesus. Instead, the people had something else in mind. Look at this carefully:

> Then they asked Him, "What must we do to do the works God requires?" Jesus answered, "The work of God is this: to believe in the One He has sent." So they asked Him, "What miraculous sign then will You give that we may see it and believe You? What will You do? Our forefathers ate the manna in the desert; as it is written: 'He gave them bread from heaven to eat.' " (John 6:28-31)

Do you see what they're saying? "Feed us again!" Only one day before, Jesus had worked an outstanding miracle right in front of their eyes. Why were they asking for another sign so "we may see it and believe You"? It's because they were hungry! Notice the hint at the kind of sign they were expecting: "What will You do? Our forefathers ate the manna in the desert; as it is written: 'He gave them bread from heaven to eat.' "

"Jesus, how about more food! How about another fish and bread miracle—maybe with some dessert too?" And they missed the Son of God! When His teaching got hard, they left Him that very hour. It's a tragic picture of just how superficial we can be, seeking the filling of our stomachs and the thrilling of our emotions, as if it is primarily for this that Jesus came. And when we're done feasting—who needs Him anymore!

Think of the great miracles and signs in the Book of Acts. They certainly drew the crowds. But as soon as the crowds came, the focus of the preaching turned to Jesus, the crucified and risen Son of God, the exalted Lord of all. The tongues of fire at Pentecost were incredible, but Peter stood up and preached Jesus, not tongues. It's true that he offered the promise of the Spirit to all who would repent and believe, but the heart and soul of his message that day focused on the person of Jesus—His death, His resurrection, His ascension, and His pouring out of the Spirit. He didn't say, "Great! Let's have a tongues meeting. Who wants to have this neat experience too?" No, tongues was not the central issue. The whole purpose of the baptism in the Spirit according to Acts 1:8 is that we receive power to be witnesses for the Lord around the world, not that we have an exciting experience.

It's the same with the healings in Acts. They were wonderful demonstrations of God's might and mercy. They were dramatic proofs that Jesus had risen from the dead. And they were attention-getters too! But once the disciples had the people's attention, they would immediately point to the Lord. The healings were platforms from which they declared the Good News. Yet it's so easy to get so caught up with manifestations—even wonderful workings of God like healing and deliverance—that we forget about the whole purpose of revival. It's so easy to get caught up in the current that we forget where we're going or even why we got into the boat.

And then, when carnal excesses become predominant, another problem arises. The frozen chosen who worship at the Frigidaire Fellowship are already scared off by the excitement and intensity of revival. They were the ones who needed a little excitement! But the behavior of the fanatical followers at the Church of Frenzy is so scandalous it further scandalizes the already scandalized. And so, the division which revival inevitably brings gets bigger than necessary. Instead of melting the cold hearts of the frigid, it confirms them in their icy faith. They become as hot as an arctic winter and as rejuvenated as a fossil in a petrified forest. As for the frenzied, instead of sobering them up, revival sends them sailing off into oblivion. Soon drooling at the mouth is considered a sure sign of the Spirit.

It is true that in past revivals people have actually growled and roared like lions, gotten down on all fours and barked like dogs, or gobbled like turkeys. Again, these could be explained as public acts of humbling and judgment, the results of emotional frenzy, part of the deliverance process, or mocking demonic distractions. But it would be absurd—not to say bizarre!—to actually seek after or cultivate such things. And it would be totally incomprehensible to gauge someone's spirituality by their barking, growling, or gobbling. That kind of nonsense can only bring reproach. And it deserves to be reproached!

When the believers in Los Angeles began to speak in tongues earlier this century, churches divided and split over the issue. That was bound to happen. But when these zealous Christians claimed that they could write in tongues, and that these tongues were all foreign languages which could be understood by the heathen in distant lands, this brought mockery to the things of the Spirit—especially when these alleged languages were publicly dismissed as meaningless gibberish by linguists.[17]

> Muttering an unintelligible jargon, men and women rolled on the floor, screeching at the top of their voices at times, and again giving utterances to cries which resembled those of animals in pain. There was a Babel of sound. Men and women embraced each other in the fanatical orgy.... Suddenly [a fashionably dressed, pretty, young woman] arose and began to cackle like a hen. Forth and back she walked in front of the company, wringing her hands and clucking something which no one could interpret. The leader explained that she was speaking a dialect of a Hindoo tribe. He said she would leave soon for India to teach the natives the gospel.[18]

The gulf brought about by tongues was made even wider by the extreme claims and actions of the recipients of this gift. Just think of how many more people could have been touched if there had been greater wisdom and sensitivity among the leaders, and if the serious and not the spurious had received greater emphasis.

It is essential that those ministering in revival keep things in proper perspective. We are called to devotion, not disorder. Christ, not chaos, is our goal. And we should never try to put stumbling blocks in people's paths (read 2 Cor. 6:3) or glory in the unusual and sensational. Things will get heavy enough anyway without us trying to work it up or put on a show. And when the miracles begin to explode all over, they will advertise themselves. Jesus sometimes had to tell people to keep quiet after they were healed. The crowds would have become totally unmanageable.

And when demons start manifesting, it can get distracting. No wonder Jesus rebuked them and ordered them to be silent. Who needs the testimony of demons anyway? Those with experience in deliverance ministry often remove from their public meetings people manifesting unclean spirits. It distracts from the Word of God.

What then should we do? Here are some simple guidelines (although all this is easier said than done): 1) Let the Spirit speak and act. (Remember Lady Huntingdon's counsel to Whitefield.) He knows what He's doing! 2) Let intentional, fleshly displays be set in order. People do get out of control. 3) Let demons be shut up. They've got nothing good to say. May God give us discernment. And if you're sure you've already got all the discernment you need, pray more. You're in for a suprise! As Oswald Chambers said, "When we are certain of the way God is going to work, He will never work in that way any more."[19]

In the early 1980's, I was involved in an outpouring that took place in one particular church. Strong messages of repentance were followed by people sobbing and getting right with God. Others for the first time began to speak in tongues, another screamed out and collapsed, another felt fire in his hands. God was at work, and no man was orchestrating it. But the only thing that mattered was the dramatic impact made on many in the body. That outpouring changed my life!

I think of a couple of the many instances of deliverance I've seen over the years: a man bound by drugs and alcohol, falling to the floor convulsing, with blood coming out of his mouth, without me ever touching him and without him knowing that I was ordering spirits to leave in Jesus' name.

Or there was the well-dressed woman in Italy, suddenly dropping to the ground, foaming at the mouth. Deliverance can be quite dramatic! But the only thing that really counts is whether or not these people went on with God. That's what matters to heaven.

Yet it's so easy to lose focus! And the moment we start seeking wild manifestations—looking for the outward things themselves—we're asking for trouble. The flesh can conjure it up, and the devil can counterfeit it.

Then should we still pray for the sick and look for healing? Absolutely! The ministry of healing is foundational to a true New Testament church. Asking God for healing is far different than looking for outward manifestations. Healing by its very nature brings divine life and the compassionate touch of heaven. But if, when we pray for the sick, they begin to shake, will we start holding "shaking meetings"? (Of course, the fact that no one gets healed doesn't faze us. Look at them shake!)

Should we drive out demons in Jesus' name? You better believe it. In fact, revival to demons is like light to roaches. It sends them scampering! Demons practically came out of the woodwork when Jesus was on the earth, and they'll turn up at the most unexpected times (and in the most unexpected people!) during revival. There are just as many demons around today as there were in Jesus' day. The only thing that has changed is that in most modern countries, few believers are interfering with their work. These unclean spirits control the lives of many of our politicians, actors, educators, and other "respectable" people, while preachers stand up and proclaim, "Driving out demons was only for the New Testament age." The devil loves that teaching!

Still, as important as true deliverance ministry is, our emphasis is never to be put on seeing people foaming with saliva (how gross!) but rather on seeing people filled with the Spirit. Am I speaking clearly enough?

What a shame that some Pentecostals seem more concerned with being "holy rollers" than with being wholly righteous. How pathetic that in this critical day and hour—with the Church and the world rapidly approaching the climax of the ages—some of us are still *focusing* on people being "slain in the Spirit." (There's more to say about this in the next chapter.) As John G. Lake wrote two generations ago:

> We have treated the precious Spirit of God as though He is a method of providing a means of spiritual entertainment for our souls. God's purpose is far mightier than that. God's purpose is that our spirit be tuned to heaven, our heart capable of hearing and realizing the songs of glory, appreciating the companionship with God and feeling flames of His divine love, expressing and revealing it to the hungry world that knows not God.[20]

It is true that the moving of the Holy Spirit can be accompanied by all kinds of manifestations. The Spirit fell on Saul's troops who were sent to capture David, and these hostile men began to prophesy. The soldiers who came into the garden to arrest Jesus fell backward to the ground when He said, "I am He." And when the Tabernacle was dedicated, not even Moses could enter in to minister, because of the cloud of glory literally filling the place. God's Presence changes things!

And let's not forget some of the other scenes from the Gospels and Acts: the tongues of fire, the screams of those being delivered from demons, the joyful dances of those just healed, the crying out of sinners under conviction, and the loud praises of those whose burdens were removed. These are the sights and sounds of revival.

But more important than any of these sights and sounds is the issue of substance. What is God doing in the midst of His people? There is nothing lightweight about the Lord, and if anyone means business, it is He. And so, while there may be jerkers and jumpers in revival, there must be no jokers. Revival is a matter of eternal life and death.

In a true revival, a real work of God, there is a burden. The prophets of old called their messages burdens. In the old-fashioned evangelism, God's people had an agony over lost souls. One could feel it in the very atmosphere. In our revival meetings in Europe, the people are groaning and weeping before the service has even started. Before I can begin preaching, I myself am weeping. Oh yes, that is the true way of revival....

Oh, that God would give us weeping prophets once again! Oh, that He would give us a new generation of young men and young women who have this agony and this burden for lost souls! I think of Paul who, in saying farewell to the elders of Ephesus, could remind his hearers that day and night, for many a long month, he had been weeping in their midst. As Mr. Whitefield used to say to his great congregations, "If you won't weep for yourselves, dear sinners on the way to hell, then I'll have to weep for you!" Then he would break out into uncontrollable weeping, both in his preaching and during the meeting period.

James A. Stewart, Evangelism

Chapter Eleven

Oh, They Perish!

In the year 1812, Adoniram Judson led the first team of missionaries to be sent overseas from the United States. He had been raised in a godly home, and his father was a minister. But when he entered college, he became friends with a young skeptic named Jacob Eames, and Eames won Judson's heart and mind. Soon Judson's own faith was shaken, and when he returned home, in spite of his father's theological reasonings and his mother's tearful pleadings, he turned his back on God.

He went to New York, seeking fame and fortune as an actor, but his hopes were quickly dashed. The world did not live up to his expectations! Soon he became discouraged and decided to travel back to his family, although still distant from God and intellectually hardened to the gospel. But the Spirit of the Lord was working, gradually breaking down his resistance.

Then came the fateful night that changed Judson's course forever. He checked into an obscure little inn that he had never seen before. The only bed available was in a room next to that of a gravely ill young man, and all night long, Judson heard him struggling for his life, his parents by his side. In the morning, Judson noticed that something seemed wrong, and so he asked the innkeeper about the young man in the adjoining room. The innkeeper was sorry to share the news: The young man was dead. Judson then asked, meaning only to be polite, "What was his name?" "Jacob Eames," came the reply. Yes, Jacob Eames!

Only one thought dominated Judson's mind as he rode those many miles back to his home: "Lost! Lost! Jacob Eames is lost!" Reality had taken hold of these two, gifted young men. For Eames, it was too late. For Judson, it was just the beginning. Heaven and hell were real!

Judson humbled himself, and with the help of some godly professors, he renewed his commitment to the Lord, ultimately giving his life for the people of Burma. His first and second wives died on the rugged mission field, along with his first three children, and he suffered incredible hardship and torturous imprisonment.[1] But in the light of eternity, it made perfect sense to give himself heart and soul, body and strength, life and limb, to win the lost and dying. It was the only reasonable thing he could do!

Yet so few of us are moved to give ourselves for souls. Our hearts are cold and our eyes are blind! Revival fires melt the icy hearts and open the sightless eyes. The veil is lifted, and eternal matters come pressing in. An acute, painful urgency for souls arises in the hearts of God's people. We return to the New Testament norm!

Of course, some saintly men and women experience this kind of spiritual hunger during their normal walk with the Lord, unrelated to any special times of revival. Take for an example this entry from the diary of young James B. Taylor:

> I fell before the throne, and had a longing for souls: I *thirsted* to bring souls to Christ; I *groaned* to win souls, and almost with agony pleaded to have souls for my hire. I

think I felt willing to lay out my *life* for souls. Money is not what I desire. Souls, souls, I want souls: "Give me children," was my cry; and I wept with desire to say at last, "Here I am, Lord, and the children thou hast given me."[2]

But this is not the everyday experience of most believers, especially in America at the end of the twentieth century. Heaven and hell seem like fairy tales! The sports world seems real; movies and TV shows seem real; money seems real; earthly pleasures seem real. But heaven and hell? Perishing souls? Final judgment?

We talk the right talk, but our tearless prayers, our wholehearted pursuit of the things of this world, our obsession with worthless entertainment, our idolization of sports, our lack of burden for the lost, our dwelling at ease while the world perishes—all this testifies against us. Revival will open our eyes! The spiritual becomes more real than the natural, and eternal matters become more urgent than temporal matters.

Here is a typical account, taken from the First Great Awakening in America. After a notorious, sinful young woman was gloriously converted, Jonathan Edwards relates:

A great and earnest concern about the great things of religion and the eternal world, became universal in all parts of the town, and among persons of all degrees and all ages; the noise among the dry bones waxed louder and louder; all other talk but about spiritual things, was soon thrown by. The minds of people were wonderfully taken off from the world; it was treated among us a thing of very little consequence. They seemed to follow their worldly business more as a part of their duty, than from any disposition they had to it. It was then a dreadful thing amongst us to lie out of Christ, in danger every day of dropping into hell; and what persons' minds were intent upon was, to escape for their lives, and to fly from the wrath to come....

[And so] the work of conversion was carried on in a most astonishing manner, and increased more and more. Souls did, as it were, come by flocks to Jesus Christ.[3]

Unseen things become dominant. Accounts like this are commonplace:

Here, for example, is a farmer returning from the market in Ballymena [Ireland, in 1859]. His mind is wholly intent upon the day's bargain. He pauses, takes out some money, and begins to count it. Suddenly an awful Presence envelops him. In a moment his only thought is that he is a sinner standing on the brink of hell. His silver is scattered, and he falls upon the dust of the highway, crying out for mercy.[4]

That is how revival affects the lost, bringing abrupt, unexpected awakening to their darkened souls. But what happens to the child of God who experiences personal revival? He finds out quickly that he is no longer his own, no longer free to pant after earthly treasures, no longer able to languish in luxuriant leisure. People are going to hell! His complacent existence is shattered by the cries of the perishing. The realities of the world to come are now here. H.A. Baker relates these scenes from the outpouring at his children's mission in China:

The children saw not only darkness in hell, but also the lake of fire which was always approached through a region of stygian darkness.... When the children were peering down into this pit in hell we saw them taking a firm hold on some piece of furniture or getting down on their hands and knees, cautiously bending forward to peer into the infernal regions. They looked a moment and then drew back, afraid lest they fall in. They were horrified at what they saw. Then very cautiously they looked again and drew back. Sometimes the children lay flat on their stomachs, lest they slip and fall while looking over the brink of the lake of fire.

The lost were seen going into hell. Some fell in, some walked over the brink, and some were bound by demon chains and cast into hell by demons. One boy saw groups of the wicked bound in bundles, ready to be cast into this furnace of fire.

When the fire abated and the smoke settled down the moans of the miserable could be heard. When the fire at intervals increased in intensity and the smoke lifted a little there were shrieks and wails of agony.[5]

Do you really want revival? Then get ready for the burden of the Lord. Get ready for a broken heart!

It is difficult enough to grasp the degree of suffering experienced by multitudes around the world, without even thinking about final judgment. My thoughts go to the tragedy in Rwanda in 1994. First, hundreds of thousands of Tutsi tribes people were mercilessly butchered by their Hutu neighbors. Even the rivers belched out the stench of rotting carcasses, while crocodiles gorged themselves on the helpless flesh. Then the Hutus had to flee from the new Tutsi government, and as two million refugees pressed into Zaire, a cholera epidemic broke out. Thousands more died. Little children cried by the sides of their dying mothers, trying somehow to bring them back, and whole families were wiped out in a matter of days.

But then—how painful to even consider!—there is the question of eternity. Were these people—all of them, most of them, even some of them—lost forever? Will they rise on the Day of Judgment to be condemned? Oh the agony! And what of the old, religious Jewish man in Israel, saying his prayers without fail virtually every day of his life, or the devoted Buddhist monk in Tibet, or the sincere Muslim woman in Egypt—are they all lost? Do they perish when they die? Or think of the inner-city, teenage girl, born out of wedlock, without the benefit of an earthly father, with a mother always high on drugs, and now herself dead from a botched abortion at age 16. What happens to her?

No doubt, many of us have wrestled with questions like these. We have a hard time believing that every single person who doesn't truly put his or her faith in Jesus is bound for hell, and we struggle with the issue of the eternal destiny of those who never heard the gospel. Because we are sometimes uncertain about these things, we can more easily live without a genuine burden. It's not just this material world that distracts us. Our questions also gnaw away at our faith, lessening our sense of urgency and pain. Add to this the fact that there is so little preaching today about hell and final judgment, and it's easy to understand why most of us are unmoved by the most important issue of all: Where will people spend eternity?

But if we will stop long enough to be honest with ourselves and are determined to be true to the Word, some things are inescapably clear: The bulk of this human race is lost, the road to destruction is broad and there are many who walk that road, and a large portion (if not the vast majority) of the people we have known through the years—friends, family, neighbors, coworkers—have not yet repented and believed. At this point, they are bound for hell. All this is simply overwhelming.

Father, the burden is too great! Lord, save a multitude no one can number. Redeem this perishing race. Have mercy before it's too late. Intervene before another soul slips into hell! God, my insides are exploding, and my heart is breaking. Oh they perish! Oh they perish! Oh they perish!

No wonder the revivalist is consumed. Who can look eternity in the eye and remain unmoved? How dare we try to serve God unscathed!

The winds of revival will carry us away—away from selfish living, away from loveless ministry, away from the idols of this world, away to the heart of God, a heart pounding with compassion for the work of His hands, beating with mercy for His foolish, lost sheep, throbbing with a love that will stop short of nothing to make a way for sinners to be saved and rebels redeemed.

Is there anything more important than that? Can we say we love God and not really care about those for whom His Son bled and died? How we need our hearts to be revived! Sometimes we don't really care much at all. Why not admit it? We need to buy the eye salve so we can see!

This example will help us put things in perspective. Raised in a godly home, Scottish evangelist James A. Stewart was truly converted at the age of 14, and immediately he began to testify on the streets. By the time he was 18, he reached a crisis. He found it impossible to continue in secular work, even though he was always witnessing on his job and preaching to the lost every night. Finally he said to his mother, "I want to go and preach the gospel. Oh Mother, I can't stand it any longer. I can't eat. I can't sleep. I can't work. I must go and tell the lost about Jesus."[6]

Soon he was released into full-time, faith ministry, and there his burden intensified. He worked with men of God who wept for souls *before* they preached and *while* they preached. They were not high-flying, professional evangelists. They were burdened and broken laborers, constrained by the love of Christ.

But this was nothing new for Stewart. He had already met two young, passionate servants of the Lord, Oswald from Latvia and Enoch from Norway. Their lives made an everlasting impression on the teenage Stewart. He relates:

One night as [Oswald and I] were sharing a room in the city of Perth, I was awakened by the sobbing of my Latvian brother. I asked him what was wrong. He replied, "Oh, Jimmy, nobody seems interested in my mission field of Lataglia and souls there are going to hell because they do not know the gospel!"[7]

On another occasion, while rooming with Enoch, Stewart woke up, hearing deep groanings beside him.

The whole bed was shaking. "Enoch," I said, "What's wrong?" "Oh Jimmy!" he cried and then could not say any more for he was choking with sobs. I sat up. I thought he was going to die, but I heard him say, "Oh the souls! The souls! There are so few in Lapland to tell them of Jesus!"[8]

Can we relate to such a scene? Does it seem to be from another world? We need revival to make things real again! Then we too will choke with sobs for this dying, sin-crazed generation.

In February of 1994, we led a team to Andra Pradesh, India, for three intensive weeks of ministry. While I taught believers and leaders during the day, the team would go into the villages and evangelize. At night, we would hold large rallies.

The previous year, we had seen the tremendous dedication of these precious Indian saints. This time, they had been interceding nonstop around the clock, at least three people praying three-hour shifts, with someone fasting every day—for five straight months. Even the orphans at the children's home fasted every Friday.

And now the hour had arrived. Our team of ten sat in the opening Sunday service in the home church which met in a long hut with a dirt floor. About 200 people were inside, with more than 70 children filling the first few rows. It was time to pray, and everyone got on their knees. We were going to intercede for the upcoming meetings in five different cities, for the churches to be revived, and for many lost to be saved.

Our team will never forget the sight. These dear children, ranging from three to fifteen years old, prayed with their eyes closed and their hands raised, and some had tears streaming down their cheeks. They were crying for their country. They were pleading for souls. They were beseeching God for revival. And they were just young children!

Two thoughts went through the minds of most the team members: "What in the world am I doing here?" and "Am I even saved?" What could we possibly offer them? (Thank God, we did have something to offer, and the Lord honored those children's tears.)

After the meeting was over, the brother who heads up the work said to us, "You can see them praying like that every morning at 4:30 a.m." That was normal for them! Nintendo wasn't competing for their time. Sports wasn't knocking down their doors. TV wasn't calling them by name. Fashion was an almost unknown concept. Becoming rich and famous was not in their thinking. Their simple lives were mixed with simple faith, and they really believed the gospel. Can we say the same for ourselves? We need to be revived!

I know it's easier to live in a cozy cocoon, enjoying our temporal blessings, oblivious to the perishing multitudes. It's easier to remain sheltered and shielded, calloused and cold, distant and detached. But to live like that is to be deceived. It is to deny the very heart of the gospel, to ignore the horrible fact of sin and the holy antidote to sin. It is to demean the reality of the final resurrection—to salvation or to damnation. It makes a mockery of our whole profession of faith.

We sing, we pray, we preach, we teach, yet we hardly believe. This world has played tricks on us! Its illusions have misled us, and its fantasies have deluded us. And sadly enough, more often than not, our church leaders haven't helped much along the way. They haven't disturbed us either. (Or maybe they can't disturb us, since they themselves are not stirred.)

If we're happy, they're happy. If we're comfortable, they're comfortable. And in the course of a year, if there is a special series of messages preached, it's more likely to deal with the subject of building rather than burning. We'll raise all kinds of funds to rennovate the parking lot but rarely take an offering to rescue the perishing. We pay more attention to sound systems than to saving souls. This is not the New Testament Church. We need to be revived!

When missionary Amy Carmichael wrote the heartrending tract, "Thy Brother's Blood Crieth," many church leaders in the West criticized her, claiming that the tract condemned them as if they were the worst of heathen. But if you read the tract, you will see that it does not condemn.[9] It tells the truth—the agonizing truth of a world dying without the Redeemer, of masses of people living in darkness and perishing in darkness. It disturbs our dream world with a shriek. We don't want to hear that cry!

Search your heart and soul. What if you could be transported to the final judgment scene and hear Jesus say to people you personally know: "...Depart from Me, you who are cursed, into the eternal fire prepared for the devil and his angels" (Matt. 25:41).

How would you relate to those people today? Would there be a change in your priorities? Would you still be concerned about how they could help you succeed in this world, or would you be consumed with how you could help them be saved in the world to come? Would you warn them? Would you pray for them? Would you fast for them? Would you show them the love of Jesus at any cost? What if some of those people were family members and close friends?

You say, "But I haven't been transported to that final day of judgment. I read about it in the Word, but it seems so distant." Revival will bring it near. Are you ready?

When Christians and ministers are not in sympathy with God, they are not in a state to distinguish between spurious and genuine revivals of religion. Hence they often go forward with a series of efforts until many supposed converts are numbered, when in reality there is not a genuine convert among them. The reason is those who have been laboring in the work have begotten children in their own likeness. Not having the spirit of Christ themselves—not being deeply imbued with the true spirit of revival, they mistake their own excitement and the excitement around them for true religion, when it is perhaps anything else than a real work of the Holy Spirit. Now the more such efforts are multiplied, the more spurious conversions there are, so much the more are revivals brought into contempt and so much the more deeply the cause of Christ is injured.

Now I wish I could succeed in making the impression and fastening it not only on my own mind, but upon the minds of all the brethren that we cannot expect to succeed in promoting true revivals of religion any farther than we are truly revived ourselves—truly and deeply spiritual, having a general and all-absorbing sympathy with God—any farther than we are full of prayer and faith and love and the power of the Holy Ghost.

Charles Finney, *Reflections on Revival*

For I am verily persuaded the generality of preachers talk of an unknown and unfelt Christ; and the reasons why congregations have been so dead is, because they have had dead men preaching to them. O that the Lord may quicken and revive them, for his own name's sake. For how can dead men beget living children?

George Whitefield, in John Gillies'
Historical Collections of Accounts of Revivals

Chapter Twelve

The Myth of the "Double Portion" (Or, You Can't Give What You Don't Have)

Everyone knows the account. The prophet Elijah is about to be taken up to heaven in a chariot of fire. Elisha, his closest disciple, stays by his master's side. He has a special request for Elijah: "Let me inherit a double portion of your spirit" (2 Kings 2:9b). " 'You have asked a difficult thing,' Elijah said, 'yet if you see me when I am taken from you, it will be yours—otherwise not' " (2 Kings 2:10). And so Elisha stayed with his teacher inch for inch, until Elijah's famous ascent to heaven.

What exactly was Elisha asking for? Did he want twice as much as Elijah had? Of course not! Who would even think of asking for such a thing? No, Elisha wanted twice as much as the other disciples would receive. He wanted the inheritance of the firstborn. According to Deuteronomy 21:15-17, if a man had two sons, instead of splitting the inheritance fifty-fifty, he had to divide it into three parts, giving two-thirds to the firstborn (the "double portion") and one-third to the second-born son. (The same Hebrew expression in Zechariah 13:8 is correctly translated "two-thirds": " 'In the whole land,' declares the LORD, 'two-thirds will be struck down and perish; yet one-third will be left in it.' ") The firstborn son got a double share of the inheritance. The same Hebrew expression is used in 2 Kings and in Deuteronomy as well as in Zechariah.[1] Most people have mistakenly believed that the double portion meant "twice as much"; it simply means "double share."

So what's the big deal? It is a matter of spiritual realism. We can't give something we don't have—naturally or spiritually. We can't impart "double anointings." If we think we can, we're dreaming. Yet on prayer line after prayer line, "double portions" are being handed out freely, indiscriminately, carelessly, haphazardly. Just come on up and get zapped. Then go out and zap the world! You don't even have to meet any conditions like Elisha did. And when Elijah said it was a difficult thing, he obviously didn't know what we know. It's so easy!

Let's use some "spiritual mathematics." I lay hands on Brother A and give him a double portion of my anointing. Now he has twice what I have. He lays hands on Brother B, who now has four times what I have. Brother B lays hands on Brother C (we're up to eight times my anointing now) who lays hands on Brother D (16 times and counting!) who lays hands on Brother E (32 times the power) who lays hands on Brother F (he's up to 64 times my "zapping" ability) who lays hands on Brother G (128) who lays hands on Brother H (256) who lays hands on Brother I (512 times what I have). Brother I now lays hands on me and—glory!—I've got 1,012 times the anointing I had just a few seconds ago. And we haven't even gotten halfway through the alphabet, let alone prayed for any of the women.

Just think of what the apostles could have done with a technique like this! If only Moody and Wigglesworth had gotten wind of this...

"But doesn't the Bible tell us that Elisha performed twice as many miracles as Elijah?" Yes, if you include the resurrection of the dead man who was thrown into Elisha's grave. But Elisha never called down fire from heaven (Elijah did this three times), nor was he taken to heaven in a whirlwind, nor did he appear on the Mount of Transfiguration with Moses and Jesus, nor is he spoken of as the key, end-time prophetic figure, the forerunner of the Messiah (fulfilled at least in part by John the Baptist, the New Testament figure closest to Elijah). Elisha definitely did not have twice what his teacher had.

But there's more. If we can so easily multiply the power, why can't we heal really sick people more effectively? Why can't we bring more conviction on sinners? Why can't we liberate more captives? Why can't we do a better job of crucifying the flesh? You would think that with double and quadruple anointings (I once heard a sincere brother pray that the anointing would increase one hundredfold!) we could do a better job.

Sorry, but it's not so simple. Remember the words of Peter: "What I have I give you" (Acts 3:6). He learned this from Jesus Himself: "Freely you have received, freely give" (Matt. 10:8b). And what you haven't received, you can't give!

I was once at an airport in California, waiting for my plane home to Maryland. I was fellowshiping with a brother I had met a few days before, when a deaf man came up to us, asking for a dollar donation in exchange for a sign language list. After determining that the man really was deaf, the brother suggested to me that we offer to pray for him. The deaf man accepted our offer, and right there in public, we prayed for his healing—but nothing happened. I said to my friend, "Well, since we didn't have the power (or faith) to heal him, let's give him a dollar." That was all we had! It would have been much better to have been able to say with Peter, "I don't have any money, but I do have faith for your healing!" Unfortunately, all we had was money.

But that was just one example involving lack of faith for healing. What about the general tone of your life and mine? What do we have to give? Putting aside for now the question of miracles and spiritual gifts, how is your walk with the Lord? Who are you in private, and what are you birthing in public?

We need to go deeper. We need more of God in our lives. We need to walk with Him more closely so we can manifest Him more clearly. We need to be of one heart with the Master, never leaving His side. We need to let the Holy Spirit and the Word of God penetrate to the very core of our being if we want to pierce the hearts of the carnal. When we are touched deep within, we in turn will touch the indifferent.

This has been a chief characteristic of men and women used in revival through the ages. They were not superficial. Listen to this description of past revivalists:

> They lived and laboured and preached like men on whose lips the immortality of thousands hung. Every thing they did and spoke bore the stamp of earnestness, and pro-claimed to all with whom they came into contact that the matters about which they had been sent to treat were of in-finite moment, admitting of no indifference; no postpone-ment even for a day.... They felt that as ministers of the

Gospel they dared not act otherwise; they dared not throw less than their whole soul into the conflict; they dared not take their ease or fold their arms; they dared not be indifferent to the issue when professing to lead on the hosts of the living God against the armies of the prince of darkness.[2]

These men and women of God knew nothing of microwave ministry or McDonald's manifestations. They put no stock in fast-food formulas or fleeting faith, nor were they out to produce biodegradable believers. They lived in the light of eternity, and they wanted their fruit to last forever.

What was their own method of personal renewal and refreshing?

They were men of prayer. It is true that they laboured much, visited much, studied much, but they also prayed much. In this they abounded. They were much alone with God, replenishing their own souls out of the living fountain that out of them might flow to their people rivers of living water.[3]

This was the life habit of godly Robert Murray M'Cheyne:

His heart was filled, and his lips then spoke what he felt within his heart. He gave out, not merely living water, but living water drawn at the springs that he himself drank of. From the first, he fed others by what he himself was feeding upon. His teaching was in a manner the development of his soul's expectations. *It was the giving out from the inward life.* He loved to come up from the pastures wherein the Chief Shepherd had met him—to lead the flock entrusted to his care to the spots where he had found nourishment.[4]

These men went to the Source, and out of that life-flow others were nourished. And they let God go down deep into their lives. They knew the dealings of the Lord!

Those who heard Gilbert Tennent preach during the Great Awakening frequently used the word *searching* when describing his messages. God had first searched him out:

> From the terrible and deep convictions he had passed through in his own soul, he seemed to have such a lively view of the Divine Majesty, the spirituality, purity, extensiveness, and strictness of his law; with his glorious holiness, and displeasure at sin, his justice, truth and power in punishing the damned, that the very terrors of God seemed to rise in his mind afresh, when he displayed and brandished them in the eyes of unreconciled sinners. And though some could not bear the representation, and avoided his preaching, yet the arrows of conviction by his ministry, seemed so deeply to pierce the hearts of others, and even some of the most stubborn sinners, as to make them fall down at the feet of Christ, and yield a lowly submission to him.[5]

Are we willing to let God search us out? Do we have any skeletons in our closets? Are we ready to reproduce disciples (and that means birthing spiritual sons and daughters in our own image)? Can we say with Paul:

> Whatever you have learned or received or heard from me, or seen in me—put it into practice. And the God of peace will be with you. (Phil. 4:9)

> Follow my example, as I follow the example of Christ. (1 Cor. 11:1)

> You...know all about my teaching, my way of life, my purpose, faith, patience, love, endurance, persecutions, sufferings.... (2 Tim. 3:10-11)

Even if we leave out the reference to persecutions and sufferings, how do we line up with the rest? Are we following fully and fully "followable"? Would we be willing to reach into the very depths of our heart and offer that treasure to the Church and the world? Or would we say, "Oh no! Not that. My heart is a cesspool, not a cistern. It's filled with stinking rot, not spiritual riches. It's a horror house, not a treasure trove. Inside I'm ragged, not revived. Before I can refresh others, I need some refreshing of my own!"

What would the church look like if it was filled with believers just like you (or me)—in terms of commitment, zeal, devotion, purity, character, power? Does this prospect excite you or frighten you? When Paul told King Agrippa, "...I pray God that not only you but all who are listening to me today may become what I am, except for these chains" (Acts 26:29), he was leaving out the only thing in his life that he didn't want to see duplicated in the lives of others—namely, his shackles. As for his faith and his relationship with God, he could honestly pray, "Lord, may they become what I am."

Basketball legend Michael Jordan earned millions of dollars through all kinds of ads featuring the message, "Be like Mike." Wear the sneakers he wears, eat the cereal he eats, dress like he dresses, yes, "Be like Mike." But all the sneakers, cereal, and cool clothes in the world will not make us play ball like Jordan. It was his athletic skills and inner drive that made him who he was. His ads couldn't reproduce himself.

Yet in the Kingdom of God, we *can* reproduce ourselves. I can say to people—if I dare—"Be like Mike" (Mike Brown that is), and they can follow my example in the Lord. The question is, Do I dare? How about you? Granting that each member of the Body has his or her unique call, could you say to a new believer, as far as the whole thrust and course of your walk is concerned, "Be like me"?

Some well-known sports figures have protested recently, saying, "I'm no role model. I'm just an athlete." But like it or not, young eyes are watching them. They put on their show before millions of people every year, knowing full well that all the kids will try to emulate their moves; they are completely aware that their hairstyles and physical mannerisms will be copied; and they advertise everything under the sun with their charismatic personalities and popularity. Then they turn around and say, "Don't follow my example!"

Yet some of us do the very same thing—especially those of us in leadership positions. "Let me teach you; let me counsel you; let me encourage, exhort, and even entertain you. Watch me perform from week to week—but don't follow my example!"

Recently, a large church in Colorado hired two new pastors—a practicing, overt homosexual couple. (It's hard to even write about something like this.) They portray themselves as normal, caring ministers (and I'm sure they do have some "good" qualities), except that they have a different sexual orientation. Not everyone has to be like them!

Well, let's stop and think. Would you want to send your sons to that congregation? Would you want your boys to go to them for counseling? (Of course, none of us in our right minds would ever attend such a "church" even for a minute. They have obviously departed far from the faith. But I'm trying to make a point here about personal example.) Would these "ministers" help someone break free from a gay lifestyle, or would the pattern of their own way of living encourage those in the chains of sexual perversion to remain bound? The answers are obvious.

We can't say to someone, "Come up here!" if we are living in a rut. We can't bring people up if we are always down (spiritually or emotionally). We can't effectively call people to thrive if we barely survive. Those who look to us will become like us. Even the quality of our inner lives will be imparted by invisible, spiritual means. Are we pure? Are we fervent? Are we zealous? The hour is late, and talk is cheaper than ever. Do we mean business with God?

Is He calling some of us to deeper, more frequent times of separation? How serious are we about this whole matter of revival? Really. Honestly. Truly. How much do our insides burn with a desire to see the glory of God? How jealous are we for the reputation of Jesus our Lord? How broken are we for the lost and dying—for real people suffering all kinds of anguish and pain?

When the Lord poured out His grace on the Native Americans in the 1740's through the persevering efforts of David Brainerd, it was no surprise. The showers of mercy that fell on them were probably the heavenly equivalent of the buckets of tears Brainerd shed for them. That young missionary, having long ago departed from this earth, still speaks: "No amount of scholastic attainment, of able and profound exposition, of brilliant and stirring eloquence can atone for the absence of a deep, impassioned sympathetic love for human souls."[6]

Are we lovers of human souls? Genuinely? If we are, our message will get through. Love never fails (see 1 Cor. 13). But we will never minister anything more than we have gained through our encounter with the Lord. It is out of that encounter that we can touch the world, and people will feel the force of our words. There will literally be something— and Someone—behind them.

Just how real are we? We can preach a gripping word if we ourselves have been gripped. We can confront others with the truth if the truth has confronted us. We can break people's hearts to the extent that we have been broken. We can call for weeping—and get true results—if we weep too.

It is an irreversible law of the Kingdom: Everything produces after its own kind. Tears beget tears. Passion begets passion. Coldness begets coldness. Superficiality begets superficiality. If you want to discover the problem with the fruits, check the roots. What are we begetting?

We can preach repentance with power if we have repented and changed. We can call for holiness of life if the Holy One lives through us. We can bring a word on fire if God's fire blazes within. There is no room for hypocrisy here. A sleeping watchman cannot arouse a slumbering nation! And where there is revival, there is awakening. It can be no other way.

Forget the fancy talk. Enough with techniques and fads. Do we know the Lord? Are we walking with Him? Can we truly introduce Him to others? Do we have something substantial to give, or are we light-weight saints, skimming along with a surface-level surrender? Let us rather be submerged in the sea of the Spirit! Let us soak ourselves in the service of the Savior. Let us dive in, take the plunge, and swim. Nothing held back! Nothing reserved! Total dedication to the Lamb! It's time to go deeper, and then deeper again. The superficial has failed, and the shallow is being exposed. It's time for the genuine thing.

This was God's Word to the downcast and defeated Jeremiah. It holds true for us in this day:

> ...If you repent, I will restore you that you may serve Me; if you utter worthy, not worthless, words, you will be My spokesman. Let this people turn to you, but you must not turn to them. (Jer. 15:19)

Are there any more spokesmen out there? The world is still waiting. And when we speak as Spirit-filled vessels, the people will respond. They will hear the voice of God.

I was once told that I would never be a very popular evangelist because I did not sufficiently "sell my personality." Oh, the shame! Our business is to magnify the Christ of God and not to fling about our personalities. Dr. Herbert Lockyer, in pointing out the peril of man-worship in evangelism, says, "If a man is somewhat attractive, blessed with a fascinating personality and with power to influence multitudes, that man is often sought after rather than the Master."

James A. Stewart, *Evangelism*

One of [Evan Roberts'] severest trials during the revival was his being the object of men's worship. A friend of his once told me of finding him lying on the floor crying to the Lord to bring this to naught so that all the glory should go to God alone.

I.V. Neprash, in Richard Owen Roberts' *Glory Filled the Land*

There are many great lessons for us in the worship and reverence of the heavenly seraphim Isaiah described in his vision. I notice that they covered their feet and they covered their faces. Because of the presence of the Holy God, they reverently covered their faces. Reverence is a beautiful thing, and it is so rare in this terrible day in which we live. *But a man who has passed the veil, and looked even briefly upon the holy face of Isaiah's God can never be irreverent again.* There will be a reverence in his spirit and instead of boasting, he will cover his feet modestly. Even if he's been somewhere, instead of coming home and bragging about it, chances are he'll cover his feet.

A.W. Tozer, in Gerald B. Smith's *The Tozer Pulpit*

I am only a wick. With many of us it takes a long time to learn this lesson. It is only when the wick is soaked in oil that it can burn. If you wish for the fullness of the Spirit in order that your church should be crowded or people flock to hear you, the Holy Spirit cannot work through you. If people begin to talk about the wick, there is generally something wrong with the burning.

D.H. Dolman, in James A. Stewart's *Evangelism*

Chapter Thirteen

Fit for the Master's Use: A Portrait of the Servant of God

In every revival, there are men and women God uses in special ways, both young and old, highly educated and illiterate, mature and inexperienced. They often become the center of attention. All eyes look to them. They seem to be the dispensers of the heavenly blessings, those with the keys to the divine treasure chests. How will they respond to the challenge? What will they do in the spotlight? Will the cheering congregations be more dangerous to them than the jeering crowds? Will sweet words hurt them more than smooth stones? May God help us to stay low.

Here are some qualities to look for:

1) The servant of the Lord is not a superstar. We might just as well talk about a "dear devil" as a "superstar servant." The words don't go together! Of course, many believers, in their immaturity and carnality, idolize and glorify the instruments God uses. That is a shame, but not a surprise (although after a wonderful piano concert, people have the common sense to praise the pianist, not the piano). But it is really surprising that many of these human instruments thrive on such adulation. Even worse, they actually cultivate it. What could possibly be more un-Christlike than that?

In the early 1970's, a pastor on the East Coast had an outpouring in his church. Soon he was drawing crowds from the neighboring towns and many were being saved. He decided to rent a big coliseum, seating more than 20,000 people. Posters were made, advertising these "heaven on earth" meetings. Jesus, pictured as prominent and powerful, stood exalted over the coliseum. A little picture of the pastor appeared below. And when the meetings were held, the coliseum was filled. It was a great success.

A leading "ministry" out West heard about this pastor and began to counsel him. They told him to name his daily radio broadcast after himself instead of using the church name, and they gave him some wonderful advertising suggestions, which he followed to a tee. The second year, the advertising posters had a great big picture of the pastor standing over the coliseum, with a little Jesus standing below. The third year, Jesus was nowhere to be found on the posters. (Come to think of it, by that point, Jesus may not have minded being left out!)

I kid you not. I saw all this with my own eyes. This man's "ministry" even sent out a little pendant you could wear—inscribed with this "man of God's" face.

Hype moved in, and the Holy Spirit moved out. Instead of preaching the Word clothed with humility, this pastor now preached the Word clothed in tuxedos. Some of the ladies on the worship team had some interesting slits up the sides of their dresses. (We've certainly come a long way from legalistic dress codes!) Oh yes, this thing was going to keep moving, with or without God. In fact, not even a jail sentence could stop the work. This poor man ended up serving time on tax charges, then returned to his church pulpit upon his release.

But there is something much more subtle. Listen to the words of A.G. Gardiner:

> When a prophet is accepted and deified, his message is lost. The prophet is only useful so long as he is stoned as a public nuisance, calling us to repentance, disturbing our comfortable routines, breaking our respectable idols, shattering our sacred conventions.[1]

Once he becomes accepted and glorified, he loses his cutting edge. How so? In the beginning, he had no strings attached: "Here's my message. I speak it in love and with a broken heart. I want you to receive it. But if you refuse, I'll follow God anyway. I won't stop preaching. I won't compromise one bit." He had nothing to lose!

But then he becomes popular. He establishes a huge following, enlarges his staff, expands his outreach, and greatly increases his income. Now he has a big budget! And now people are expecting something from him: "Serve us that meal we like so much!" Then God says to him, "It's time to change your emphasis. People are becoming comfortable with you. Your words are falling on deaf ears. And you're getting sterile in your message. Go back to the cross!"

So he obeys the Spirit and challenges the people, only now they don't want to hear. His TV ratings drop; the income falls; his ministry machine begins to sputter; his empire begins to crumble; his staff is not getting paid. Now he needs to spend all his time fund-raising. He's trapped! (Some of you reading this will say, "That's me!" Then get on your face, pour out your heart to God, and go back to your true call. You have no other option if you really love the Lord. He will give you grace. Better to get it right now and face the small bit of shame and misunderstanding that will come your way, than to take the road of fleshly convenience and face the Father's disappointment and displeasure on the day when you give account. Pastors, hear me too: Even if you have a 50-member church—let alone one with 5,000 members—you can fall into this very same trap.)

The ministry of the revivalist, much like the prophet, is not always popular. Yet we glamorize almost every "prophet" we get, and the more "anointed" the speaker, the more we exalt them. Then we polish them up and smooth off their rough spots (balance is the key!). We tone down their message just enough to make it enjoyably offensive ("Oh, he shoots straight! I like that."), then we put them on TV (with play-by-play highlights of their worldwide exploits at the beginning of every show), and we advertise them in brilliant full-color magazine ads (with their "humble-but-oh-so-anointed" picture gracing the page).

Don't tell me we don't have a celebrity cult in the Church today! Don't tell me we don't have superstars!

Oh yes, we go to the meetings and the big-name preacher says: "Don't look at me, look at Jesus." But dear brother, it's a little hard to do! There's so much glitz and glitter, so much posing and posturing, that we can't quite see the Lord. You've gotten so big that you're blocking Him out.

Once, when Jesus was in Galilee and a major holy day was about to be celebrated in Jerusalem, His unbelieving brothers said to Him:

> ...You ought to leave here and go to Judea, so that Your disciples may see the miracles You do. No one who wants to become a public figure acts in secret. Since You are doing these things, show Yourself to the world. (John 7:3-4)

They said this in mockery, trying to goad Him. Today this is the guiding philosophy of many a Christian ministry!

One well-known pastor came up with a striking logo. It was a drawing of the globe with a banner running across it, and on the banner was this man's name (we'll call it John Doe Ministries) encompassing the earth. How self-exalting can someone get? This was his justification: People have already heard about Jesus, and they're not interested. So he'll get people interested in his name, and then, when they are drawn to him, he can point them to Jesus. (Do I hear someone groaning?)

The words of Paul seem almost incredible in this media-soaked age of ours, where some high-pressure "ministers" join the ranks of sports stars, news anchormen, suave actors, and glamorous supermodels, raking in millions for their personal gain. Hear the apostle speak:

> To this very hour we go hungry and thirsty, we are in rags, we are brutally treated, we are homeless. We work hard with our own hands. When we are cursed, we bless; when we are persecuted, we endure it; when we are slandered, we answer kindly. Up to this moment we have become the scum of the earth, the refuse of the world. (1 Cor. 4:11-13)

And Paul was boasting about this; it was a mark of his apostleship. Today, we'd send him to a "Successful Christian Living" seminar to learn prosperity secrets. We'd straighten him out!

But Paul had something many of us lack. He was an intimate soul mate of the Master. He was a sold-out fellow-laborer with the Lord. Jesus was his all in all. He wasn't in it for the finances (although he knew how to abound when God blessed him with an overabundance, and he was always a good steward). He wasn't in it for the fame (what fame?). He wasn't in it for the following (unless people would follow the Lord). Glorifying His Savior and God was his call. Why not live as he lived?

Smith Wigglesworth knew what it was like to minister to huge crowds, but he was just as delighted—maybe more delighted—to pray for the sick in hospitals and homes after he finished preaching. He didn't need an entourage with "bodyguards." He was not too big for the people. He would minister to an old dying widow just as he would minister to a king, and he would respond to a handwritten plea to come and pray for a demon-possessed boy just as he would respond to a formal request to preach in the largest church in the land. If it was God's will, he would do it with joy. After all, his business was to do his Master's bidding—not be someone great in the eyes of man.

As James A. Stewart noted:

> The mightiest work the Holy Spirit did through Dwight L. Moody in Great Britain was in small groups of five or six hundred people, not in the large audiences of twenty and thirty thousand. One may well be afraid of the crowds. We cannot journey far with God unless we are saved from numbers. It is sadly possible to think more of numbers than of Christ, who in the days of His earthly ministry went, not only to the cities but to inconspicuous places, proclaiming the Word.[2]

Let us take heed to the words of the German pastor Helmut Thielecke who said that "the worship of success is generally the form of idol worship which the devil cultivates most assiduously."[3]

That worship of "success"—leading to the superstar syndrome—is often the servant's greatest stumbling block and most subtle snare. Beware!

2) The servant of the Lord is not an entertainer. When Scottish evangelist James Stewart was just a teenager, he was offered a golden opportunity to get his message out around the world. Columbia Recording Company had already discovered a "boy gospel singer" and they were beginning to widely distribute his gospel music. Now, they wanted Stewart to record his messages and be Columbia's "Boy Preacher." He would preach and Columbia would get the message out to the nations. Just think of how many people could be reached! Just think of the income that could be generated! But Stewart's mother feared he wanted to accept the offer for his own glory, and then the Lord dealt with him clearly.

Stewart came to a shocking conclusion: Satan was trying to make him into a professional evangelist.[4] That's right, a professional evangelist—the contemporary American norm! How interesting it is to see that, what many preachers would jump at today as a godsend, this young preacher recognized as a satanic trap. But for Stewart, God was killing ambition and the desire to be popular or make money through the Word. The Lord was preparing him for a true outpouring!

And so, shortly before World War II, when Stewart was barely 20 years old, he saw revival break out in Eastern Europe. He became deeply sensitive to the difference between modern, hyped-up meetings and true visitation, really putting his finger on the problem in his little book on "Hollywood Evangelism."

Speaking of our entertainment-oriented Christianity, he wrote: "The atmosphere of these meetings is so much like Hollywood that one might almost expect some comedian or film star to rush on the platform."[5] (Today, we do have comedians and film stars rushing to the platform; they really draw the masses.) For Stewart, this was a no-compromise area:

I refuse to entertain sinners on their way to hell.... I want to preach every time as though it were my last chance. I do not want souls to curse my name in the lake of fire and say, "Yes, I went to such-and-such a Gospel meeting, but that preacher Stewart only entertained and joked. He made Christianity a farce!"

The old-fashioned method of evangelism was to make people weep, but the modern "Hollywood" way is to make people laugh. Everybody has to have a jolly good time.... We must have plenty of jokes or it would not be a good meeting. That is why there is such a woeful lack of conviction of sin in modern evangelism. *The Holy Spirit cannot work in a frivolous atmosphere.*

Here is a solemn truth that very few of God's people seem to see: Everything depends on the atmosphere of the meeting.... For example, if you were saved in a jazzy sort of atmosphere, light and frivolous, with the song leader more like a clown and the preacher merely glorifying himself and using fleshly effort, you will also turn out to be a jazzy frivolous Christian with no depth in your spiritual life.[6]

Samuel Chadwick hit the nail on the head when he wrote, "The Church always fails at the point of self-confidence. When the Church is run along the same lines as a circus, there may be crowds, but there is no Shekinah."[7]

It is the Shekinah that we must have, the Lord dwelling in our midst, a continual visitation that doesn't quickly pass. As someone has said, the Kingdom of God will not be advanced by our churches being filled with people, but by people in our churches becoming filled with God.

There is a place for clowns and stunt men, but that place is not the Church of Jesus. Better to give your money to Ringling Brothers, Barnum and Bailey than to waste it on meetings at the First Church of the Three Ring.

Of course, true revival will also bring the crowds, but when they came flocking to Stewart's meetings in Europe, he did not take this as an automatic proof of blessing. Instead, he asked himself some questions:

> It is well known that a crowd brings a crowd. Is that the only reason the people are coming? I want to know what is the center of attraction. Is it, after all, my own personality? Am I a novelty because I am a foreigner? Or am I humorous and entertaining? I also want to know if Christ is the center of attraction. I could have thousands of professions of conversion, but if Christ be not the center of attraction for the multitudes, then the campaign is a spurious work of the devil and not a genuine work of God.[8]

Entertainment has nothing to do with evangelism, amusement has nothing to do with anointing, and reputation has nothing to do with revival.

Stewart continues:

> When I was a boy, evangelists were humble and modest. This is the way we advertised our special meetings: "Dearly beloved friends in the neighborhood, we are commencing a series of evangelistic services in our church. We have a wonderful Saviour to proclaim to you!" Then the leaflet went on to tell about the glories and the beauties which are to be found in the Lord Jesus. Because Christ was everything to the neighborhood, so we advertised a wonderful, glorious Saviour. Then we added that Brother So-and-so from Such-and-such would preach about this wonderful, majestic Lord Jesus Christ. Yes, it was the Lord Jesus who was the center of attraction and He was the One who was magnified. An insignificant, humble man of God was coming to talk about this wonderful Savior.[9]

It doesn't take much thinking to admit that if the glorious Lord Jesus were being exalted in our meetings through the agency of His mighty Holy Spirit, we wouldn't need pulpit

pranksters, Christian comedians, sensational singers, enter-
taining evangelists, or miraculous ministers (kind of like
gospel magicians). No tricks. No games. Just the Lord!

We wouldn't tickle ears. (Remember what the great ora-
tor Whitefield said, "I didn't come to tickle your ears; no, I
came to touch your hearts."[10]) We wouldn't calculate which
message would produce the biggest offering. We wouldn't
figure out which musical guest would attract the most people. We would put all our emphasis on exalting the Son of
God, on having His manifest presence, on preaching His
Word in truth and power. Isn't that enough? And when the
music and the message and the miracles magnify the Master,
that's glorious.

It is common to see big ads for major conferences featuring this exciting speaker and this glamorous minister,
offering special attractions for the whole family and accom-
modations fit for royalty, yet making no mention at all of the
Lord. Not even once! Not God the Father, not the Lord Jesus,
not the Holy Spirit. The other names are important. His name
is not! One "apostle" encouraged other leaders to attend his
conference with a pitch that went something like this: "Just
think of how it would feel to be around all the anointed, five-
fold ministers that will be there." Wow! As for me, I'd prefer
a small, unfurnished room alone with Jesus. How about you?

During the Hebrides Revival, an interesting phenomenon
occurred. Duncan Campbell pointed out that

> While the main emphasis on the revival has been on the se-
> verity of God, a very remarkable thing should be noted:
> eighty-three hymns have been written by the converts,
> some as fine as anything we have in our Gaelic literature.
> And without one exception every hymn has for its theme
> either The Love of Jesus, or The Wonder of the Saviour.[11]

If we speak the truth in love and compassion, if we bring people into genuine contact with the living God, there will be lasting fruit. Hollywood is hollow, and entertainment is empty. It is more of Jesus that we need. He alone is the solution to gospel meetings that resemble game shows and ministry scandals that look like soap operas. In our abasement, He is beautiful.

3) The servant of the Lord is Spirit-dependent, not flesh-dependent. How could it be any other way for a true servant of the Lord? Anything else would be an utter contradiction in terms. Would the favored daughter of a generous, billionaire father sell her body to a pimp to help earn money for college? Perish the thought! Then how can an anointed and called servant of the Most High God hire his ministry out to Hollywood-type, superslick promoters? How can a child of the King of all kings lean on the paltry resources of the world?

One internationally known preacher once said on TV, "Without money, you can do nothing." Saintly old Leonard Ravenhill heard this and replied, "I thought Jesus said, 'Without Me you can do nothing.' " What a contrast in attitudes!

God can supply, does supply, and will supply. We don't need to grovel, nor do we need to compete with the world. Neither poverty nor riches are our goal, but there is so much carnality and greed running rampant in the Body today—in the name of the gospel, no less.

As Stewart pointed out,

Never in the history of the church has so much money been spent on "promoting" Christian workers as in this modern hour. [Stewart wrote these words forty years ago!] One could scarcely imagine Paul or Jonathan Edwards paying publicity agents to keep them in the limelight before the church and the world.[12]

Name for me one moving of God, one revival, that ever came about as a direct result of marketing strategies, surveys, polls, or promotional efforts, and then tell me of one revival or moving of God that did not come about as a direct result of concerted, consistent, faithful, fervent prayer. So what should we be doing? As John Hyde wrote, "The disciples were then [i.e., at Pentecost] shut up to prayer, and can anyone say what would happen now if God's Church should give herself up to this same resource?"[13]

What would have happened if the 120 disciples, in their excitement and zeal after the Lord's resurrection, decided to implement a "take the world for Jesus" campaign before Pentecost? There would be no Church today! They might have said, "Let's get people's attention and draw a crowd. We'll pray for the sick and preach. It will be great!" Then they would have missed out on the crowd that God Himself drew to the upper room: Jews from all around the world (just think of it!), supernaturally brought in by the noise of the mighty wind and the sound of the foreign tongues of praise, all hearing the Good News at the same time. And the preaching was anointed by God! How can we even countenance doing things any other way? The true servant of the Lord is repulsed by such a thought.

Listen to the warnings of some wise men of God:

I believe that what the world needs just now is not so much the multiplication of organization as the baptism of the Holy Ghost. We have piles of organization, but they lie prone upon the earth, incorporated death. We have got organizations enough to revolutionize the race. It is not more schemes we want, more associations, more meetings; we want the breath and fire of the Holy Ghost. A small organization, with breath in it, can do the work of an army.... We may be so intent upon committees that we have not time for the upper room. We may be so public that we forget the secret place. We may be so absorbed in devising machinery and careless about the power which is to make it go. That is our peril. I know it; I feel it.[14]

The Church knows perfectly well what is the matter. It is sheer cant to seek the explanation in changed conditions. When were conditions ever anything else? The Church has lost the note of authority, the secret of wisdom, and the gift of power, through persistent and willful neglect of the Holy Spirit of God. Confusion and impotence are inevitable when the wisdom and resources of the world are substituted for the presence and power of the Spirit of God.

The human resources of the Church were never so great. The opportunities of the Church were never so glorious. The need for the work was never so urgent. The crisis is momentous; and the Church staggers helplessly amidst it all.[15]

It has been pointed out that the first-century Church did not have publishing houses, church buildings, printed hymnals or Bibles, mission boards, fund-raising consultants, mass media access, or legal standing in society, and look at what they accomplished! Yet we do have all these things in America, and still our accomplishments here are meager. What did the early Church have that we don't have?

One sold-out missionary said recently, "The easier it is to live somewhere, the harder it is to believe."[16] Where he ministers, if people become seriously ill, they have three choices: Go to the witch doctor, go to Jesus, or die. We have an almost infinite number of choices: every kind of pill and prescription; doctors, specialists, clinics, hospitals; nutritional approaches and holistic treatments. And if all these fail, there's always Jesus! Unfortunately, by the time we go to Him, the situation is already so desperate and our faith so drained that we rarely see the deliverance we had hoped for.

Of course, doctors and medicine can be a tremendous blessing to the world, but we can be tempted to put our unconditional trust in them. That belongs to the Lord alone.

It's the same in ministry. We have so many options today—so many fleshly devices, so many resources, so many technological advances. They can all compete for our attention and can subtly seduce us away from dependence on God. It is one thing to utilize the marvels of modern technology in our efforts to win the nations. It is another thing to lean on them. Computers don't make disciples; disciples make disciples! And God doesn't respond to faxes; He responds to faith!

Beware the snare of hi-tech Christianity. Avoid getting sidetracked on the "information highway." Stay clear of the muddle of media dependence. The Spirit is sufficient. He always has been, and He always will be. He hasn't changed at all in the years since G. Campbell Morgan wrote these words about the Welsh Revival in 1904:

> If you and I could stand above Wales, looking at it, you would see fire breaking out here and there, and yonder, and somewhere else, without any collusion or pre-arrangement. It is a divine visitation in which God—let me say this reverently—in which God is saying to us, "See what I can do without the things you are depending on"; "See what I can do in answer to a praying people"; "See what I can do through the simplest who are ready to fall in line and depend wholly and absolutely upon Me."[17]

He is still saying, "See what I can do!"

4) The servant of the Lord is identified with Jesus, in His life and death. Let Amy Carmichael, the lifelong missionary to India, teach us what this means:

> Hast thou no scar?
> No hidden scar on foot, or side, or hand?
> I hear thee sung as mighty in the land,
> I hear them hail thy bright ascendant star,
> Hast thou no scar?

Hast thou no wound?
Yet I was wounded by the archers, spent,
Leaned Me against a tree to die, and rent
By ravening beasts that
compassed Me, I swooned;
Hast thou no wound?

No wound, no scar?
Yet, as the Master shall the Servant be,
And, pierced are the feet that follow Me;
But thine are whole: can he have followed far
Who has no wound nor scar?[18]

Pause for a moment, and let those words sink in. Read them again slowly. Then ask yourself: Am I marked? Am I scarred? Am I branded? Have I taken up my cross—daily (Luke 9:23)? Can I say with Paul—in any sense of the word—"I bear on my body [or, my life] the marks of [the Lord] Jesus" (Gal. 6:17)?

The deeper the death we die, the more glorious will be the resurrection we enjoy. The more we know the cross, the more life we can offer to the world.

We always carry around in our body the death of Jesus, so that the life of Jesus may also be revealed in our body. For we who are alive are always being given over to death for Jesus' sake, so that His life may be revealed in our mortal body. So then, death is at work in us, but life is at work in you. (2 Cor. 4:10-12)

Listen to J.H. Jowett again (or, are these words too strong for us?):

The ministers of Calvary must supplicate in bloody sweat, and their intercession must often touch the point of agony. If we pray in cold blood we are no longer the ministers of the Cross. True intercession is a sacrifice, a bleeding sacrifice, a perpetuation of Calvary, a "filling up" of the sufferings of Christ.

My brethren, this is the ministry which the Master owns, the agonized yearnings which perfect the sufferings of His own intercession. Are we in the succession? Do our prayers bleed? Have we felt the painful fellowship of the pierced hand? I am so often ashamed of my prayers. They so frequently cost me nothing; they shed no blood. I am amazed at the grace and condescension of my Lord that He confers any fruitfulness upon my superficial pains.

As soon as we cease to bleed, we cease to bless.[19]

Resurrection power is glorious. It is aquired by death.

5) The servant of the Lord is highly flammable. Some things are combustible, other things are not. Dry wood burns; water puts the fire out. It's the same with electricity. Some things are good conductors; others are not. High-voltage wires can carry quite a shock; thick rubber will stop the watts in their tracks. So also in the Spirit: A pure heart is easily ignited; unbelief and sin will quickly quench the flames. A holy life will transmit the Spirit's jolt; the flesh will blunt the force. What about you? What is your spiritual composition?

Missionary Amy Carmichael had prayed, "Make me Thy fuel, Flame of God." Jim Elliot, martyred by the Auca Indians, expanded on this:

God makes His ministers a flame of fire. Am I ignitable? God, deliver me from the dread asbestos of "other things." Saturate me with the oil of Thy Spirit that I may be a flame. Make me Thy fuel, Flame of God.[20]

Are you combustible?

There had been months of prayer for revival in the parish of Barvas in the Hebrides. A group of men met three nights a week, praying until four or five in the morning. Still, ignition was not achieved until a young deacon stood up one night and read from Psalm 24:

Who shall ascend into the hill of the LORD? or who shall stand in His holy place? He that hath clean hands, and a pure heart; who hath not lifted up his soul unto vanity, nor sworn deceitfully. He shall receive the blessing from the LORD. (Ps. 24:3-5a, KJV)

Duncan Campbell describes what happened next:

He read the Psalm again, then faced his praying companions with these words: "Brethren, we have been praying for weeks, waiting upon God. Now I would like to ask, Are our hands clean? Are our hearts pure?"

In the wee hours of that morning, the Spirit of God swept into the barn. Had you gone there at four you would have found three of the men in a trance, prostrate on the floor. They had prayed until they passed out of consciousness.[21]

The revival had begun. The fire was beginning to burn. Combustion was realized! Sin had been removed. Are we ready to burn?

Speaking of His forerunner, Jesus said, "John was a lamp that burned and gave light, and you chose for a time to enjoy his light" (John 5:35). Speaking of us all, Wigglesworth exclaimed, "Oh, if God has His way, we should be like torches, purifying the very atmosphere wherever we go, moving back the forces of wickedness."[22]

Do our lives purify or pollute? Do we give off light or levity? Do we deepen the working of the Spirit or dampen His flames?

There is no shortage in God. He can work through us in ways that exceed our grandest dreams. The problem is not with heaven's fires, it is with our flesh. Isn't it time that each of us—especially those in the ministry—come to an absolute and firm determination to allow nothing in our lives to get in the way of God's Spirit? Isn't it time that we too become flames of fire? If not now, when? If not you and me, then who? Servants of the Lord come clean. The fires are ready to spread. Can you feel the heat?

We often settle for second best (or, more realistically, one hundredth best). We are discouraged from reaching for the high mark or shooting for the "impossible." We think things will just continue as they have always been—more of the mundane, a surplus of the same! But is that a New Testament way to live? Shoot higher, my friends! Why not set for yourself the same consecration goals set by young Robert Murray M'Cheyne?

> I am persuaded that I shall obtain the highest amount of present happiness, I shall do most for God's glory and the good of man, and I shall have the fullest reward in eternity, by maintaining a conscience always washed in Christ's blood, by being filled with the Holy Spirit at all times, and by attaining the most entire likeness to Christ in mind, will, and heart, that it is possible for a redeemed sinner to attain to in this world.[23]

The more we are like the Master, the more we will be ablaze!

> I turned around to see the voice that was speaking to me. And when I turned I saw seven golden lampstands, and among the lampstands was someone "like a son of man," dressed in a robe reaching down to His feet and with a golden sash around His chest. His head and hair were white like wool, as white as snow, and His eyes were like blazing fire. His feet were like bronze glowing in a furnace, and His voice was like the sound of rushing waters. In His right hand He held seven stars, and out of His mouth came a sharp double-edged sword. His face was like the sun shining in all its brilliance. (Rev. 1:12-16)

God Himself is a consuming fire. Those who live in His Presence become like Him. The hymn writers of old knew this:

O that in me the sacred fire
Might now begin to glow,
Burn up the dross of base desire,
And make the mountains flow![24]

This was also the foundation of the early Salvation Army:

To make my weak heart strong and brave,
Send the fire
To live a dying world to save, send the fire.
Oh, see me on Thy altar lay
My life, my all, this very day;
To crown the offering now, I pray:
Send the fire![25]

In the same way, when the saintly Methodist leader John Fletcher prayed for the fullness of the Holy Spirit, he prayed for fire:

Lord, I stand in need of oil. My lamp burns dimly. It is more like a smoking flax than a burning and shining light. Oh, quench it not, raise it to a flame!

I want a "power from on high"; I want penetrating, lasting "unction of the Holy One"; I want my vessel full of oil; I want a lamp of heavenly illumination, and a fire of divine love burning day and night in my heart; I want a full application of the blood which cleanseth from all sin, and a strong faith in thy sanctifying word....

I do now believe that thou canst and wilt thus baptise me with the Holy Ghost and with fire; help me against my unbelief; confirm and increase my faith. Lord I have need to be thus baptised by thee, and I am straitened till this baptism is accomplished.[26]

O Lord, send the fire! We're ready to burn.

Robert Ellis of Ysgoldy in Caernarfonshire [Wales] related how a group of men harvesting hay during the Beddgelert Revival of 1817 suddenly threw their rakes in the air, dancing and jumping for joy, after having begun to sing the Welsh hymn:

> He's altogether lovely,
> Yes, 'tis true;
> Than all the world more worthy,
> Yes, 'tis true;
> Then fare ye well, dumb idols!
> My heart is won by Jesus,
> His face so fair and gracious,
> Yes, 'tis true;
> An ocean wide of comforts
> Yes, 'tis true.

Emyr Roberts, *Revival and Its Fruit*

Revival, above everything else, is a glorification of the Lord Jesus Christ, the Son of God. It is the restoration of Him to the centre of the life of the Church.... It leads to our hymns, our anthems of praise: Christ the centre of the Church.

D. Martyn Lloyd-Jones, *Revival*

Revival is a new discovery of Jesus.

James S. Stewart, in Duncan Campbell's
The Lewis Awakening

There are occasions when for hours I lay prostrate before God without saying a word of prayer or a word of praise—I just gaze on Him and worship.

A.W. Tozer

Chapter Fourteen

Jesus, the Pearl of Great Price, the Center of Revival

The exaltation of Jesus is the heartbeat of revival, and no book on revival would really be complete without a chapter devoted to Him. So I now have the privilege and joy of boasting about Jesus, my best Friend, my Savior and Lord, my Master and King, the Christ, the Anointed One, the Messiah, the Son of the living God, the Alpha and the Omega, the Beginning and the End, the Author and Finisher of our faith, the Vine, the Bread of Life, the Water of Life, the Way, the Truth, and the Life, the only Gate, the Good Shepherd, the Great Shepherd, the Chief Shepherd, the Lily of the Valley, the Fairest of Ten Thousand, the Word of God, the I Am. There is none like my Lord!

He is the image of the invisible God, the Ruler of all Creation, the Firstborn from the dead, the King of kings and the Lord of lords, the One who holds all things together by His powerful word. He is Jesus, my closest and most wonderful friend. He alone is worthy of praise!

To this day, men and women gladly suffer for Him, surrender all for Him, even die for Him—joyfully!—because in

Him, they have everything they need; in Him, they have discovered perfect love; in Him, they have found what their souls longed for; in Him, they have met God! Why shouldn't they gladly leave homes, jobs, possessions, riches, and reputation in exchange for fellowship with Him? Why shouldn't they say with Paul, "...I consider everything a loss compared to the surpassing greatness of knowing Christ Jesus my Lord, for whose sake I have lost all things. I consider them rubbish, that I may gain Christ" (Phil. 3:8). Why shouldn't they follow the example of Moses, who "regarded disgrace for the sake of Christ as of greater value than the treasures of Egypt...[who] persevered because he saw Him who is invisible" (Heb. 11:26-27).

Why shouldn't they glow like Stephen—even with shattered bones and bloodied bodies—if they too can see Jesus standing at the right hand of the Father waiting to receive them?

A radical, sold-out missionary to the Mexican Indians told me this story in April of 1993. An Indian came home one day after working in the fields. When his wife offered him dinner, he told her he wasn't feeling well, then he collapsed in a chair and died. His wife rushed out and gathered together some other believers—including one of the town leaders, who was also a believer. When they prayed for her husband, he was raised back to life. The missionary, who has seen many people raised from the dead, went to talk with him about his experience.

The little Indian sat and quietly related what happened. Then my friend asked him—as he asks everyone who has been resurrected—"What did you see?" Suddenly, the man sprang to his feet and began to jump up and down exclaiming over and over and over: "I saw the I Am! I saw the I Am! I saw the I Am!" He *is* the Resurrection and the Life![1]

When you see the I Am—in all His glory and splendor and beauty and power—you will never be the same. When you come into intimate, personal contact with Him, you will be changed. He is Jesus. He wants to be your friend! He is a Lord like no other lord and a Master like no other master. Those who know Him love to do His will. They count suffering for Him to be a privilege, sacrificing for Him to be a joy, and dying for Him to be an honor. His yoke is easy, and His burden is light. His smile is better than a billion dollars. His favor is worth more than all the praises human lips can offer. Press in to Him, experience Him, embrace Him. He is your life and the very substance of your being.

Sometimes we put the cart before the horse. We preach against sin without preaching about the Son. We major on holiness but minor on Him. We preach death to the flesh but fail to present the One who is life to our souls. The two messages go hand in hand! In fact, when you really experience the Lord, repentance comes naturally, self-denial comes easily, sacrifice comes voluntarily. Seeking Him becomes a delight!

In the diary of 21-year-old Robert Murray M'Cheyne, this entry is found, dated February 23, 1834: "Rose early to seek God, and found Him whom my soul loveth. Who would not rise early to meet such company?"[2]

Would you rise early if you were sure you would find Him too? Can you live without His Presence and smile? The seventeenth-century Puritan, Samuel Rutherford, could not: "A long time out of Christ's glorious presence is two deaths and two hells for me. We must meet. I am not able to do without Him."[3]

Can you relate to Rutherford's words? Is communion with Jesus that precious to you, or can you go on living without Him and hardly even notice His absence? Then you need to meet Him more deeply and see Him more clearly. When you do, you will be transformed.

Remember, before we arrive at Matthew 16, where Jesus calls us to take up our cross and follow Him, we first read Matthew 1 through 15: The Lord's glorious birth in chapters 1–2, the Holy Spirit descending as a dove and the Father's voice from heaven at His baptism in chapter 3, His wilderness victory over Satan in chapter 4, His extraordinary teaching in chapters 5–7, His healings (and the healings by the disciples too!) in chapters 8–10, His invitation to "Come to Him" in chapter 11, His driving out demons in chapter 12, His incredible parables in chapter 13, His feeding the multitudes and walking on the water in chapter 14, and His confounding the religious hypocrites in chapter 15. No wonder the disciples could say to Him, "We have left everything to follow You!" (Mark 10:28) Who wouldn't leave everything for a Savior like that?

As long as you and I live, we must never forget His grace: It was while we were gross sinners, lost and dying, that the precious, priceless, perfect Son of God laid down His life for us. Yes, "God demonstrates His own love for us in this: While we were still sinners, Christ died for us" (Rom. 5:8).

As expressed by Richard Wurmbrand,

> Jesus teaches us not to give to poor men kept at the right distance, but to call the poor, the maimed, the lame, the blind, the most disgusting persons into our homes when we have a feast (Luke 14:13). He called you, a wretched sinner, to come to heaven.[4]

Our sin made us ugly; Jesus became ugly for us—beaten, despised, and naked. Our sin disfigured us; Jesus was disfigured too! "His appearance was so disfigured beyond that of any man and His form marred beyond human likeness" (Is. 52:14b).

Our sin brought us shame; Jesus was put to shame for us! After He was brutally flogged, the Roman soldiers

...stripped Him and put a scarlet robe on Him, and then twisted together a crown of thorns and set it on His head. They put a staff in His right hand and knelt in front of Him and mocked Him.... They spit on Him, and took the staff and struck Him on the head again and again. After they had mocked Him, they took off the robe and put His own clothes on Him. Then they led Him away to crucify Him. (Matt. 27:28-31)

He did all this for you and me!

As He hung on the cross, "those who passed by hurled insults at Him.... In the same way the chief priests, the teachers of the law and the elders mocked Him. ... In the same way the robbers who were crucified with Him also heaped insults on Him" (Matt. 27:39,41,44).

But He blessed in return! That's the Lord we serve, the One we love. He is worthy of your life! He is worthy of your all! You lose *nothing* good by losing all for Him. The exchange is life for death, righteousness for guilt, freedom for bondage, a heavenly Father for an infernal tyrant, salvation for sin. Why not embrace Him today?

A Romanian Christian pastor who was ultimately tortured to death by the Communists prayed this prayer when he was ordained: "Lord, take my heart and never give it back to me. Why was I born if not to love you passionately?"[5]

And why were you and I born? Can we pray the same prayer? What have we got to lose?

Stop for a moment and think. Have you ever regretted an hour you spent in prayer, or a day you spent in fasting, or a night you spent in worship, or a week you gave to the mission field? Never! But—it is so true—we all regret many hours spent on small talk instead of prayer, many days spent on feasting instead of fasting, many nights spent on TV instead of worship, many weeks spent in carnal pursuits instead of the pursuit of souls. Only serving God satisfies! Only serving God makes sense!

If you have a secular job, work it for the glory of God! If you have a family, raise it for the glory of God! If you have gifts in arts, sports, learning, whatever gifts you may have, use them for the glory of God! Don't subsist on a mere animal level—eating, drinking, working, sleeping, fulfilling the lusts and desires of the flesh and the mind. No! Live for Jesus! Become like Jesus! Tell others about Jesus! Help them to become like Him too! There is no higher call.

Great hymn writers like Fanny Crosby and beloved gospel singers like George Beverly Shea were not exaggerating when they wrote, "Jesus is all the world to me," and, "I'd rather have Jesus than anything this world affords to give." In fact, the story is told of a conversation between Fanny Crosby, blinded by a quack doctor's botched procedure when only a tiny girl, and a gentleman whose eyesight was fine. He talked to her about what she was missing: She had never seen a sunset or any of the beauties of nature. She replied, "Yes, but the first thing I will see is the face of Jesus!" Oh, what a sight! It was after that conversation that she wrote the classic hymn, "And I Shall See Him Face to Face."

On the Mount of Transfiguration the disciples had an awesome experience. They saw Jesus transfigured, saw the glory cloud come down, saw Moses and Elijah, heard the

Father's voice, and then, "they fell facedown to the ground, terrified." Jesus told them not to fear, and "when they looked up, they saw no one except Jesus" (Matt. 17:6,8). The mountaintop experiences do not last forever. The miraculous visitations do not occur every day. But when all is said and done, there is one thing that remains: *We see Jesus.* What more do we need? What more could we possibly ask for?

I often read the accounts of the suffering Church and of the missionaries and martyrs who have given their blood for the faith. I wonder, "Could I endure such treatment? Could I withstand such torture? Would I be willing to sacrifice so much for the gospel?" The answer is simple: Never! In fact, no human being could be expected to victoriously endure starvation, deprivation, inhuman torture and degradation, horrible mistreatment, day in and day out for weeks and months and years and even decades. But with Jesus, the impossible becomes possible, and the unbearable becomes bearable. When He is there with you, you can survive anything!

Richard Wurmbrand tells the story of Victor Belikh, a Ukranian Christian bishop who was kept in solitary confinement for 20 years, with only a straw mat put in his cell each night for seven hours. Every day, for 17 hours, he was made to walk around the cell continuously, like a horse in a circus.

> If he stopped or broke down, they threw buckets of water on him or beat him and he was forced to continue. After twenty years of such a regime, he was sent to forced labour in northern Siberia, where the ice never melts, for another four years.

> I asked him, "How could you bear this suffering after the years in solitary confinement and a starvation diet?"

> He replied by singing a song he composed: "With the flames of love's fire that Jesus kindled in my heart, I caused the ice of Siberia to melt. Hallelujah!"[6]

Better to be in a prison cell with Him than to live in a mansion without Him. Better to have Him plus nothing else in this world, than to have everything in this world without Him. Choose Jesus as your portion, and with Him and in Him, you will have everything you need.

Speaking of his awful imprisonment in Tibet, Sadhu Sundar Singh said, "Christ's presence has turned my prison into a blessed heaven. What will it be like in Heaven itself?"[7]

When He comes, complaining ceases, excuses evaporate, and depression disappears. He becomes the focus of attention, and human boasting abruptly halts.

Sometimes we like to exalt people. We glory in flesh and blood. But the saintly ones know better. In 1834, when William Carey, the father of modern missions, lay dying, he called fellow missionary Alexander Duff to his bedside and whispered, "Mr. Duff! You have been speaking about Dr. Carey, Dr. Carey; when I am gone, say nothing about Dr. Carey. Speak about Dr. Carey's Savior."[8]

Oh yes, thank God for missionaries like William Carey and for believers who remained faithful, even to the death, and respect those who have sacrificed for Him. But if you ask them who they glorify and adore, they will answer with one voice: "Praise to the Lamb! Worthy is the Lamb! Glory to the One who was slain and purchased us for God from every tribe and language and people and nation and made us into a kingdom of priests." We should add our voices too!

More than 100 years ago, a couple went to hear a famous preacher in London one Sunday morning. As they left the building, the husband exclaimed, "Oh, what a wonderful preacher!" That night, they went to hear Spurgeon. When they left that service, the husband exclaimed, "Oh, what a wonderful Savior!"[9] May all our teaching and preaching and living and giving and serving and doing draw people's attention to Him.

Decide today: "I will have Jesus! I must have Jesus! I'll no longer follow Him from a distance. I will make Him my closest friend." And He will be yours forever.

> Again, the kingdom of heaven is like a merchant looking for fine pearls. When he found one of great value, he went away and sold everything he had and bought it. (Matt. 13:45-46)

Jesus: the Pearl of great price, the Center of revival.

What the church has been used to, is not a rule by which we are to judge; because there may be new and extraordinary works of God, and he has heretofore evidently wrought in an extraordinary manner. He has brought to pass new things, strange works; and has wrought in such a manner as to surprise both men and angels. And as God has done thus in times past, so we have no reason to think but that he will do so still. The prophecies of Scripture give us reason to think that God has things to accomplish, which have never yet been seen. No deviation from what has hitherto been usual, let it be never so great, is an argument that a work is not from the Spirit of God, if it be no deviation from his prescribed rule. The Holy Spirit is sovereign in his operation; and we know that he uses a great variety; and we cannot tell how great a variety he may use, within the compass of the rules he himself has fixed. We ought not to limit God where he has not limited himself.

Jonathan Edwards, *Jonathan Edwards on Revival*

I hope that none dislike the work, because they have not been used as instruments in it.

William Cooper, Preface to
Jonathan Edwards *The Distinguishing
Marks of a Work of the Spirit of God*, 1741

...God mercifully meets and blesses those who seek Him with all their heart, despite their sometimes defective notions, for which of course it is often their teachers more than they who are responsible. We should be glad that our God is so good.

J.I. Packer, Foreword to J.C. Ryle's *Holiness*

Chapter Fifteen

To Judge or Not to Judge?

G. Campbell Morgan was one of the most respected Bible teachers of the early twentieth century. He had a tremendous amount of insight into the Word, and his sermons are still highly valued today. When he heard of the 1904 Welsh Revival, he visited Wales and came back with a glowing, first-hand report. But when he learned of the 1906 Azusa Street outpouring (note: he visited Wales but only *heard* about Azusa Street), his verdict was different. He described it as "the last vomit of Satan."

R.A. Torrey, a powerful preacher and teacher, the author of important books on prayer and the Holy Spirit, and an early president of Moody Bible Institute, also made his feelings known, declaring that this new Pentecostal movement was "emphatically not of God, and founded by a Sodomite" (referring to accusations brought against Charles Parham).

According to H.A. Ironside, another highly regarded, mature leader, both the modern holiness and Pentecostal movements were "disgusting...delusions and insanities." Writing in 1912, he characterized Pentecostal meetings as "pandemoniums where exhibitions worthy of a madhouse or a collection of howling dervishes," were causing a "heavy toll of lunacy and infidelity."

W.B. Godbey, a famous holiness preacher who also wrote a one-volume New Testament commentary widely used by the holiness people, decided to check out the Azusa Street meetings for himself. After preaching a message, Godbey was asked if he had received "the Baptism." When he quoted some Latin phrases, the zealous believers were sure he was speaking in tongues. This, coupled with the intense, seemingly disorganized atmosphere there, was more than enough to convince Godbey that the work was definitely not from above. He called the Azusa Street believers "Satan's preachers, jugglers, necromancers, enchanters, magicians, and all sorts of mendicants," claiming that the movement was the result of spiritualism.[1]

Clarence Larkin, well known among some students of prophecy for his interestingly illustrated (to say the least!) book, *Dispensational Truth* also made known his views there about modern tongue-speaking. Writing in 1918, he said:

Another of the "Signs of the Times" is the revival of what is called the "GIFT OF TONGUES," in which the recipient claims that he is taken possession of by the "Spirit of God" and empowered to speak in an "unknown" or "foreign tongue." But the conduct of those thus possessed, in which they fall to the ground and writhe in contortions, causing disarrangement of the clothing and disgraceful scenes, is more a characteristic of "demon possession," than a work of the Holy Spirit, for the Holy Spirit does not lend Himself to such vile impersonations.

From what has been said we see that we are living in "Perilous Times," and that all about us are "Seducing Spirits," and that they will become more active as the Dispensation draws to its close, and that we must exert the greatest care lest we be led astray.[2]

Larkin ended the page with a woodcut depicting three frogs, under which is the reference to Revelation 16:13-16. There was nothing subtle here! And Larkin wrote these words of warning so as to be faithful to the scriptural mandate to "test the spirits" and "believe not every spirit." Is there anything we can learn from all this?

What would Larkin, Godbey, Ironside, Torrey, and Morgan say if they could see that the very movement they denounced and attributed to the devil has been the source of a sweeping, worldwide move of God, ultimately responsible for the conversion of multiplied tens of millions? What would they say if they could see the vast army of Pentecostal missionaries that has gone around the globe, or if they could witness some of the awesome healings and miracles that have taken place this century by the power of the Spirit? It is clear that they were guilty of serious misjudgment!

"Well what about all the fleshly aberrations, doctrinal irregularities, and scandals that have plagued the Pentecostal and Charismatic movements?" What a shame! They need to be recognized, renounced, and repudiated. But that doesn't discredit the work as a whole. Just look at Presbyterian churches today that ordain homosexuals, Lutheran churches that deny the Virgin Birth, or Methodist churches that no longer believe in hell or soul winning. Do these churches discredit Calvin, Luther, and Wesley?

The point of all this is simple. We need to be careful! We shouldn't be so hasty to denounce a new spiritual movement within the Body. We should wait until we know the facts firsthand (repeated stories won't do), until we see the fruit, until we clearly understand what is being taught, until we talk to people on both sides of the issue. And we should humbly go to the Word and to the Lord. Even then, we still must be careful not to go too far in what we say—unless the Spirit gives us no choice. And we should always ask ourselves: Is it *necessary* to form a conclusion at this point? Is it *beneficial* to speak out? Are things *so bad* that we need to sound the alarm?

The remarks of these godly men just quoted now seem pathetic and pitiful, the kind of things we don't want to repeat. And yet almost every new generation faced with a new move of God makes the same mistake. The fires of Catholic persecution of the Reformers were still burning hot when the Reformers began to persecute those who differed with them. Calvin and Luther subjected the Anabaptists to violent reprisals because they held to the baptism of believers only, refusing to baptize infants. (That means most of the readers of this book would have been persecuted too!) The Puritans fled from the oppression and tyranny of the Church of England yet flogged Quakers for following the "inner light," even putting some of them to death. (That "inner light" would have gotten many of us in trouble as well!) Yes, we can be dangerously judgmental.

The Word makes it abundantly clear that critical judging is a serious sin. And it is foolish too! Just think of how ridiculous many of our judgments will look on that Day when everything is made known.

Of course, there are some things that God actually commands us to judge. Look at 1 Corinthians 5. We are to judge anyone who claims to be a brother or sister but who is living in gross, overt, unrepentant sin:

> But now I am writing you that you must not associate with anyone who calls himself a brother but is sexually immoral or greedy, an idolater or a slanderer, a drunkard or a swindler. With such a man do not even eat. What business is it of mine to judge those outside the church? Are you not to judge those

inside? God will judge those outside. "Expel the wicked man from among you." (1 Cor. 5:11-13)

Paul says judge them! Hold them to account. Contrary to what some believers might say, we *can* determine what greediness or sexual immorality or slander are, and we can discipline those who won't get right with God. If they will not receive correction, they are to be put out of the church:

Even though I am not physically present, I am with you in spirit. And I have already passed judgment on the one who did this, just as if I were present. (1 Cor. 5:3)

This kind of judgment is essential. It preserves the purity of the Church, protects the other believers from being polluted, enhances the reputation of Jesus, avoids grieving the Spirit, and serves as a wake-up call to the straying saint. The modern American church has gone soft here, and the results have been catastrophic. In recent years, pastors who were exposed in the midst of long-term adulterous affairs continued to preach without interruption. They told their boards that they had repented! There was no discipline, no godly judging, no bringing forth the fruits of repentance, and obviously no time for restoration. These leaders never made it to the operating table to get the spiritual cancer removed, so how could they have time to recover?

Paul says plainly, "Judge those inside the Church, but leave it to God to judge those outside the Church." The world is full of blatant, open adulterers, extortioners, homosexuals, murderers, and alcoholics. They don't claim to be disciples of Jesus, so we don't expect Christian conduct from them and we certainly can't require it of them. We can preach the Word to them, calling them to measure themselves by God's commandments and standards, but we leave them to the Lord to discipline and correct.

It's another story within the Body. We are to deal with persistent, definite, unrepentant sin with godly justice, always following the spirit of Galatians 6:1:

> Brothers, if someone is caught in a sin, you who are spiritual should restore him gently. But watch yourself, or you also may be tempted.

We don't judge the person's heart or motives (this is so important), we don't hopelessly condemn them, nor do we judge whether or not they will respond to discipline. But we—in this case, the leaders—are definitely called to act as judges.

Judgment like this brings life and health to the Church. In fact, it follows the Old Testament call to judge with justice, which means more than simply deciding cases fairly (see Ex. 23:1-9). It means fighting for justice for the downtrodden and helpless and delivering them from their oppressors. That's why the prophets said: "Judge the fatherless" (KJV)—correctly translated in the NIV as, "Defend the cause of the fatherless" (Is. 1:17). That's why honest, God-fearing, bribe-rejecting men were to be appointed as judges over the people (see Ex. 18:21; 2 Chron. 19:5-7). That's why true restoration for Jerusalem included this divine promise:

> "I will restore your judges as in days of old, your counselors as at the beginning. Afterward you will be called the City of Righteousness, the Faithful City." Zion will be redeemed with justice, her penitent ones with righteousness. (Is. 1:26-27)

Godly judgment is just and fair, righteous and liberating. Ungodly judgment is dishonest and deceitful, damaging and destructive. The Lord pronounces woes on those who call evil good and good evil (Is. 5:20), and He abhors unrighteous judges and judgments (read Amos 5). We should love justice as much as we hate evil. It is when we see how important righteous judgment is that we will flee from critical judgmentalism.

Throughout 1 Corinthians, Paul deals with the theme of judgment, explaining when it is right and when it is wrong. In 1 Corinthians 2:15 he says that, "The spiritual man makes judgments about all things,"—meaning that he examines and tests the value of all things—"but he himself is not subject to any man's judgment"—referring to the condemning judgment of the unspiritual and unsaved (see 2:14). In 6:1-5 he writes emphatically that we must serve as judges when disputes and differences arise in the Body. One day we will judge angels! What a reproach it is when we can't judge disputes among ourselves, deciding instead to go to secular courts. (This sin—and it is a sin!—is rampant in our generation.) Paul says it's better to be defrauded by your brother than to take him before the unsaved and stain the reputation of Jesus.

On two occasions Paul tells the Corinthians to "judge for themselves" (1 Cor. 10:15; 11:13)—in other words, "You should have no trouble making up your minds on this matter." Then, in dealing with the Lord's supper, he warns the believers that if they do not judge themselves before eating and drinking—searching their hearts and lives, dealing honestly with sin, recognizing the body and blood of the Lord—then they will bring judgment on themselves:

> For anyone who eats and drinks without recognizing the body of the Lord eats and drinks judgment on himself. That is why many among you are weak and sick, and a number of you have fallen asleep. But if we judged ourselves, we would not come under judgment. When we are judged by the Lord, we are being disciplined so that we will not be condemned with the world. (1 Cor. 11:29-32)

Then, in 1 Corinthians 14:24-25, Paul says that when the gift of prophecy is powerfully in operation during a service and an unbeliever comes in, "he will be convinced by all that he is a sinner and will be judged by all,"—meaning that his sinful life will be exposed and his guilt revealed.

But elsewhere in 1 Corinthians, Paul warns strongly against passing unjust judgments:

> I care very little if I am judged by you or by any human court; indeed, I do not even judge myself. My conscience is clear, but that does not make me innocent. It is the Lord who judges me. *Therefore judge nothing before the appointed time; wait till the Lord comes. He will bring to light what is hidden in darkness and will expose the motives of men's hearts. At that time each will receive his praise from God.* (1 Cor. 4:3-5)

We have no business judging the motives of people's hearts. ("He's just doing this to be seen"; "She's in it for the money.") We are not called to sit in judgment of other ministers. ("He's away from his family too much"; "She spends too much time with her children and not enough time in prayer.") We are not called to play God. ("You watch. The Lord will remove His anointing from that preacher because he doesn't agree with my doctrine.") We are called to walk in wisdom, faith, hope, trust *and* love. (There is a flip side to this too: Leaders and their spouses who harshly judge their congregants—as if *they* know it all, as if *they* as leaders are unbiased in their opinions, as if all *their* thoughts are Spirit-born revelations. Oh for trusting relationships! Just because someone has an honest question about our leadership style doesn't make them a child of the devil.)

Paul had no place for those who sat in judgment of him (see 1 Cor. 9:3-6), and he rebuked those who presumed to judge others:

> Who are you to judge someone else's servant? To his own
> master he stands or falls. And he will stand, for the Lord is
> able to make him stand. (Rom. 14:4)

(Those words *"Who are you"* should be underlined and underscored. Who do we think we are anyway?)

The Scripture here is speaking of a household slave. He gives account to his master, not to us. What if he had to work night and day for six months because his master was ill; and after that six months, he was given one month off and told by his master to relax and enjoy life? What if we saw him during that time of relaxation without knowing the rest of the facts? What would we think? "He's a lazy bum!" But his master would say, "No. He saved my life. He's the finest servant I have!" Who are we to judge?

Why must we require everyone to live the same way we do? Maybe the Lord demands more from us because we are more mature than others. Then how can we (who are so mature) demand something from the immature that *their Lord* does not demand? Or maybe God holds us to a certain standard because of our weakness in a particular area. Why then should we hold stronger believers—who don't have a problem in that area—to the same thing? Why make someone use a kid's bike with training wheels when they have no problem driving a motorcycle?

Of course, certain things *are* sinful, regardless of our standards and opinions. To give one true example, a German Christian told a good friend of mine that when he goes naked into a sauna—together with naked women!—he has no problem with lust and never has a lustful thought. If that's so, it's a result of the hardness of his heart and the perversion of his society, not a result of his holiness and purity. It's sin whether he thinks so or not. But many other issues *are* debatable.

My family doesn't have a TV, although we have a monitor that we use if we want to watch a select, clean video. We think it's good that believers get rid of their TVs too. But we have no right to judge another family as unspiritual just because they have a television. Maybe they never turn it on. Or maybe they never watch anything other than a rare news documentary on a station without commercials. Or maybe they are new believers who have just turned away from immorality, drug and alcohol addiction, cursing, lying, beating their children, and even smoking. Maybe the Spirit hasn't dealt with them yet about wasting their time with hours and hours of sports or polluting their minds with daytime talk shows. If they keep growing, He will keep speaking. Our intercession will be more effective than our accusation.

> You, then, why do you judge your brother? Or why do you look down on your brother? For we will all stand before God's judgment seat. It is written: " 'As surely as I live,' says the Lord, 'every knee will bow before Me; every tongue will confess to God.' " So then, each of us will give an account of himself to God. Therefore let us stop passing judgment on one another [in disputable matters]. Instead, make up your mind not to put any stumbling block or obstacle in your brother's way. (Rom. 14:10-13)

Once John Hyde was praying for a pastor in India. He addressed the Lord and was about to say, "You know how he has grown *cold*"—

> when suddenly a Hand seemed to be laid on his lips, and a Voice said to him in stern reproach, "He that toucheth him, toucheth the apple of Mine eye." A great horror came over him. He had been guilty before God of "accusing the brethren" [see Rev. 12:10—that is Satan's work!]. He had been "judging" his brother. He felt rebuked and humbled before God. It was he himself who first needed putting right. He claimed the precious Blood of Christ that cleanseth from

all sin!…Then he cried out, "Father, show me what things are lovely and of good report in my brother's life." Like a flash he remembered how that brother had given up all for Christ, enduring much suffering from relations whom he had given up. He was reminded of his years of hard work, of the tact with which he managed his difficult congregation, of the many quarrels he had healed, of what a model husband he was. One thing after another rose up before him and so all his prayer season was spent in praise for his brother instead of in prayer.

He could not recall a single petition, nothing but thanksgiving! God was opening his servant's eyes to the highest of ministries, that of praise…. When Mr. Hyde went down to the plains, he found that just then the brother had received a great spiritual uplift.[3]

And just think: If this was how God felt about Hyde's speaking against a brother *in secret prayer*, how must the Lord feel when we freely, casually, self-righteously speak against our spiritual family—people who are the children of God and the brothers and sisters of Jesus—openly and in public?

Hyde himself knew what it was like to be misunderstood, and this helped him to have mercy on others. Early in his ministry, some of his fellow missionaries were critical of his prayer life. He spent too much time on his knees and not enough time out winning souls! But the missionaries later realized that the more he prayed, the more the work was blessed; and the less he prayed, the less souls were saved. Did Hyde know of the feelings of those missionaries? He said, "Oh, yes, I knew it, but they did not understand me, that was all; they never intended to be unkind."[4]

That's what you call walking in love! If Hyde could do it with the Spirit's help, so can we. We simply have no business flinging around our critical judgments. To paraphrase Smith Wigglesworth: If those of us who claim to have the gift of discernment would exercise it on ourselves for the next six months, we would never "discern" anything negative about anyone else again!

Jesus plainly rebuked those who chose to pass judgment based on appearances. "Stop judging by mere appearances," He said, "and make a right judgment" (John 7:24). Things are not always what they seem to be!

The story is told about a wealthy, old Jewish man who was known as a notorious miser. When a poor person would come to his house asking for aid, he would gruffly send the man away, telling him to go to the synagogue for help. He did this for years and gained a horrible reputation in the process. But when he died, the townspeople were shocked. The poor continued to go to the synagogue for help, but the synagogue ran out of money! You see, this so-called miser anonymously donated large sums of money to secretly help the poor, but turned them away from his door so they would never think he did it. He didn't want his deeds of kindness to be displayed before man, so he intentionally gave the opposite impression. He did what he did before the Lord.

Everyone thought he was stingy. Instead, he was saintly. How deceiving outward appearances can be! The Israelites wrongfully entered into a covenant with the Gibeonites—for all generations—because they judged by what they saw without consulting with the Lord (read Joshua 9, especially verse 14). Contrast this with the righteous judgment of the Messiah:

> The Spirit of the LORD will rest on Him—the Spirit of wisdom and of understanding, the Spirit of counsel and of power, the Spirit of knowledge and of the fear of the LORD—and He will

delight in the fear of the LORD. *He will not judge by what He sees with His eyes, or decide by what He hears with His ears; but with righteousness He will judge the needy, with justice He will give decisions for the poor of the earth.* He will strike the earth with the rod of His mouth; with the breath of His lips He will slay the wicked. Righteousness will be His belt and faithfulness the sash around His waist. (Is. 11:2-5)

If I were to be totally honest with myself, I would have to admit that I have judged people—at least in my thoughts, even if it was only momentarily—because I didn't like their hairdo or their clothes, or because I didn't like the sound of their voice, or because the car they drove was too nice (or not nice enough), or because they were too heavy (or too skinny), or because they wore a ministerial collar, or because they *seemed* proud (when it turned out they were actually shy). How would I like it if others judged me the same way? How do *I* seem to be in other people's eyes?

A missionary recently told me that he had been upset with a man in the States who promised to make a large contribution to his work. Two years went by, but the American never came through. The missionary was so offended that he decided not even to call when he visited the man's home state. The next year, the missionary was convicted about his attitude and called the brother to confess his sin to him. That's when he found out that the American man had come through a serious battle with cancer, and that he was planning on giving his friend the promised gift that very year! The cancer had incapacitated him so much that he had fallen behind on everything. Still, he wanted to make good on his word. If only the missionary had known the facts, he would have given himself to fasting instead of faultfinding, and to caring instead of criticizing.

If you want to build a case against someone or something, you can. If you want to quote someone out of context to make him look bad, you can. In fact, you can quote the Bible out of context and make it look foolish if you want to. An attacking spirit will never see the truth. Pride has blinded its eyes. If we really treated others the way we wanted to be treated, there would be a lot more blessing and glory and a lot less blood and gore.

Are you *sure* you know what you're talking about when you speak against that minister, ministry, or movement? Are you *positive* you haven't simply fed your negative suspicions ("I knew it!") by receiving reports from people who have an ax to grind and are themselves critical and judgmental (or just plain ignorant)? Couldn't people make a case against you just as easily? Aren't there people who have it in for you who would gladly give their side of the story to anyone who will listen? Aren't there things about you that could easily be misunderstood by those who didn't really know you? And wouldn't you become indignant if you heard that people were talking behind your back, sharing malicious rumors and misleading innuendoes as if they were facts? But we do the same thing!

> You, therefore, have no excuse, you who pass judgment on someone else, for at whatever point you judge the other, you are condemning yourself, because you who pass judgment do the same things. (Rom. 2:1)

As Oswald Chambers noted: "It is easy to see the specks and the wrong in others, because we see in others that of which we are guilty ourselves."[5] All of us would do well to pray: "Lord, help me to hate sin in myself as violently—and mercilessly—as I judge it in the lives of others." That would set us straight.

Just look at how much God hates the sin of bearing false and evil reports:

> If a malicious witness takes the stand to accuse a man of a crime, the two men involved in the dispute must stand in the presence of the LORD before the priests and the judges who are in office at the time. The judges must make a thorough investigation, *and if the witness proves to be a liar, giving false testimony against his brother, then do to him as he intended to do to his brother.* You must purge the evil from among you. The rest of the people will hear of this and be afraid, and never again will such an evil thing be done among you. Show no pity: life for life, eye for eye, tooth for tooth, hand for hand, foot for foot. (Deut. 19:16-21)

Are you *sure* you are not being a false witness against your brother? That violates one of the Ten Commandments! We cannot be too careful when it comes to passing judgment.

Jesus said:

> Do not judge, or you too will be judged. For in the same way you judge others, you will be judged, and with the measure you use, it will be measured to you. Why do you look at the speck of sawdust in your brother's eye and pay no attention to the plank in your own eye? How can you say to your brother, "Let me take the speck out of your eye," when all the time there is a plank in your own eye? *You hypocrite*, first take the plank out of your own eye, and then you will see clearly to remove the speck from your brother's eye. (Matt. 7:1-5)

It is pitiful but true: We often judge others most harshly in the very area where we are the weakest. But we let ourselves off the hook while nailing them to the wall. We see a father or mother yelling at their kids, and we judge them for being harsh, undisciplined, and out of control. Yet if we yell at our kids, we were just having a bad day, plus we were tired and the kids were really being ornery. We condemn others but excuse ourselves.

We notice someone glancing lustfully at an attractive member of the opposite sex. *What an unclean wretch,* we think. But if we cast that same glance...*Lord, You know my heart. You know I didnt really mean to do that. You know I want to be pure.* How interesting! And need I even mention how we feel when someone cuts us off on the road (we, of course, have *the right* to angrily honk our horns at them, since they could have killed us), but when someone honks at us after we *accidentally* swerve into their lane, we wonder what they're getting so excited about. We even get mad at them!

How tragic that we behave the same way in the Church! *The Body is continually damaged and defiled by this destructive, judgmental spirit.* Even the "super saints" often fall here, somehow believing they are *allowed* to judge because they are so close to the Lord, or else deceiving themselves into thinking that they *never* make judgments since God tells them everything directly. How many lives have been destroyed by the sinful judgments of those who say, "God told me all about you. I've heard from heaven." Let me say it once more: We need to be careful!

> Brothers, do not slander one another. Anyone who speaks against his brother or judges him speaks against the law and judges it. When you judge the law, you are not keeping it, but sitting in judgment on it. There is only one Lawgiver and Judge, the one who is able to save and destroy. But you—who are you to judge your neighbor? (James 4:11-12)

There are those words again: "*Who are you* to judge?" This is something God *is* telling us directly! Don't slander. Don't judge. Don't speak against your brother. You are not the judge! Nor are you—or I—the jury or the law. This is to be our rule of living:

> Do to others as you would have them do to you. ... Be merciful, just as your Father is merciful. Do not judge, and you will

not be judged. Do not condemn, and you will not be condemned. Forgive, and you will be forgiven. (Luke 6:31,36-37)

We of all people should be the society of the forgiving, filled with grace and graciousness. Caustic criticism and opinionated arrogance should stand out like an elephant in a ballet.

In some of His last words before His death, Jesus said to His disciples:

A new command I give you: Love one another. As I have loved you, so you must love one another. By this all men will know that you are My disciples, if you love one another. (John 13:34-35)

Isn't it time that we honor the Lord and show the world that we are His disciples, by loving one another the way He loved us? Isn't it time that we demonstrate our respect for the commands of our Redeemer? And shouldn't we be zealous to see His holy intercession come to pass? Listen to His great high priestly prayer:

My prayer is not for [the first disciples] alone. I pray also for those who will believe in Me through their message, that all of them may be one, Father, just as you are in Me and I am in You. May they also be in Us so that the world may believe that You have sent Me. I have given them the glory that You gave Me, that they may be one as We are one: I in them and You in Me. May they be brought to complete unity to let the world know that You sent Me and have loved them even as You have loved Me. (John 17:20-23)

How important this is to the Lord! Love like this can—and will—change the world. Without it we are doomed to spiritual palsy.

Enough with our psychoanalyzing games, reading our meanings into other people's words. Enough with our mudslinging accusations. Have we nothing good to say about one another? We will have our differences. But must we damn one another in the process? Must we consign to hell those with whom we disagree?

Someone has said that heaven will be a great eye-opener and a great mouth-closer. In fact, some people will be just as surprised to see you there as you will be to see them there! How our immaturity and lack of love must wound the Lord! It's time we step up higher.

And why is all this so crucial during times of revival? It is because revival, by its very nature, generates controversy and division, testing our love, testing our humility, testing our devotion to Jesus. On the one hand, we will be tempted to compromise for the sake of unity—but compromise kills. May we never betray the Lord for the supposed sake of the brotherhood! On the other hand, we will be tempted to become judgmental, either rejecting those God is using or scorning those who reject us. And almost nothing will cut short a move of God like a critical, censorious spirit sweeping through the Church. Almost nothing will put out the Spirit's fire like a harsh, judgmental attitude infecting the Body.

We either walk in love or we pay the price—and it is an awful price to pay. Who can calculate the eternal consequences of a revival cut short? Who can compute the loss? We dare not forfeit a visitation because of our foolish pride. We must walk in love. Now would be a perfect time to start. Have you any repenting to do?

It is too much for the clay to assume to itself the judgment of how it befits the potter to work. If the careless are brought to repentance,—the profane to holiness,—the unclean to purity;—if the old man with his deeds is put off, and the new man, which after God is created in righteousness and true holiness, is put on, that is the work of the Spirit of God—the fruit of the truth as it is in Jesus. The manner in which these things may be wrought in us or in others may be designed by God to try even his own people as to whether they will know his hand, amid the imperfection with which every work of God is marred when it passes through the hands of men.

John Bonar, "The Nature of Religious Revival"

Almost every major revival recorded…has been surrounded by an aura of irregular religious activity and has also been centrally affected by elements of weakness and sin. As a result, successive eras of church leaders have found it easy to immunize themselves and their followers against awakening movements by applying caricatures stressing the worst features of past revivals.

Richard Lovelace, *Dynamics of Spiritual Life*

Chapter Sixteen

The Proof of the Revival Is in the Living

With every revival there is one basic question: Is it of God? Are people being deceived, or is the Spirit genuinely moving? Will I miss out if I stand back and wait, or will I get messed up if I dive in? I don't want to resist the Lord, but I don't want to open myself to human suggestion or demonic influence either. So how can I be sure? How can I know whether or not this is true revival?

Until Jesus returns, questions like these will arise. That's the way it has always been! When Jesus ministered on the earth, some said it was the Holy Spirit at work through Him while others said it was the devil. At Pentecost, the crowd was divided over the issue of tongues: Were these men divinely inspired, or were they drunk? So also in virtually every great outpouring and spiritual movement in history, there has been great division!

There was controversy over the Reformation, controversy over the Puritan and Methodist revivals, controversy over the Great Awakening, controversy over the modern Pentecostal outpouring, controversy over the ministry of Finney, controversy over the ministry of Evan Roberts, controversy over the ministry of Spurgeon, controversy over the ministry of Moody. In fact, there was controversy over every move of God and every man and woman of God referred to throughout this book, including the prophets of Israel and the Lord Jesus Himself.

Controversy over what God is or isn't doing is to be expected, but that doesn't leave us in the dark! The fact that some have opposed the mighty work of the Spirit, at times even labeling it demonic, while others have been totally deceived by a false work, even to the point of mass suicide, does not mean that we are doomed to repeat the same mistakes. We don't have to be stubborn *or* silly, critical *or* credulous. If our hearts are humble and pure before God, if we really want everything He has for us, if we remain faithful to the clear testimony of the Scriptures, if we are open to correction and willing to be surprised, we can recognize and embrace revival when it comes and reject spurious movements when they arise. There are principles which we can use.

But first, we must be honest. We're not as smart as we think! What we call spiritual perception is often sinful prejudice. What we call insight is often ignorance. We are more influenced by our upbringing and environment than we would like to admit. Our church traditions—yes, *every church* has its traditions—often make us small-minded and narrow. Anything different or new tends to strike us as wrong.

Actually, believers and spiritual change are like me and new foods. You see, my mom was a very picky eater, and I have followed in her steps. There are only a few foods I like to eat (yes, missions trips can be interesting for me!), and I'm satisfied to eat the same foods every day—for years. When someone asks me if I like a particular food, I often say, "No,"—to which my wife replies, "In other words, he's never tasted it!" And that's how we are in the Spirit. When we say, "I don't believe in that," we often mean, "I've never experienced it myself," or, "That's not how they do it in my church," or, "I've never studied it out in the Scriptures." Yet we'll stubbornly defend our position for years, even if those being touched in this new way are sincere, godly, humble, sound, and dedicated believers. If it's new and different, it's wrong!

How small-minded we can be! There is a big Body out there, and the God we serve is a big God, full of variety and surprise. There are cultural differences in His Church, as well as differences of doctrinal emphasis, differences of call and anointing, and differences of burden. One style of worship may be wonderful to one group and woeful to another. A turned-on, black Pentecostal service may be glorious to some and gross to others, while a quiet Presbyterian service may be delightful to some and deathly to others. Yet both may be blessed by God! What is awesome to one group may seem awful to another.

The first time my wife and I were in a worship service in India, we thought the music was demonic. The only time we had ever heard such sounds and tones before was in the context of Hinduism. Yet the songs were powerful Christian songs, and the worship leader was a truly godly man, anointed by the Lord. We simply made a judgment based on previous cultural experience. It's so easy to do!

Pride can also affect our perception. Jealousy and envy can cloud our vision. Financial pressures can warp our thinking. Discouragement and disappointment can cause us to question whether others are really being blessed. We can jump to premature conclusions very quickly, because it's human nature to form an opinion, hold to that opinion, and stick to that opinion no matter what. We would do well to remember the wisdom of Proverbs:

> A fool finds no pleasure in understanding but delights in airing his own opinions. (Prov. 18:2)

> Even a fool is thought wise if he keeps silent, and discerning if he holds his tongue. (Prov. 17:28)

> Do you see a man who speaks in haste? There is more hope for a fool than for him. (Prov. 29:20)

When it comes to life-and-death spiritual matters, who cares about our opinions anyway? Certainly not God! He hasn't asked me for any advice yet (nor do I expect Him to consult with me any time in the future). Has He consulted with you lately?

But controversy about revival is not just limited to our own views. What happens when godly leaders come to opposite conclusions and make their conclusions known publicly? Then who do we follow? How do we know who's right?

Take, for example, the experiences of two missionaries, one in China and the other in Latin America. Both of them were in a Pentecostal service, both were exposed to fervent speaking in tongues, and both came to definite conclusions—diametrically opposed to each other!

This is the account of Raymond Frame, a missionary to China, who opened himself up to speaking in tongues when his coworker began getting excited in the service:

> I didn't want to be left out of the blessing that he was receiving. I let my mind become quite blank and began yielding myself to the external power outside myself that seemed to be pleading for full control of me.

At once a feeling of paralysis began to numb my feet. It soon affected my legs. I knew that before long I too would be lying helpless on the floor as were several others in the crowd. At the instant the numbness reached my knees, I became alarmed. "This thing is coming upon me, not from heaven, but from beneath. This is the wrong direction," I thought to myself. Without a moment's hesitation, I cried out: "May the blood of Christ protect me from this thing!"

At once it vanished and I was normal again.

A month later I met that co-worker of mine at another place. He appeared to be a sober and chastened man. "You know, Ray, that thing that happened to me that night wasn't of God. It was of the devil." ...my friend then described the spiritual darkness into which he was plunged, following that ecstatic experience.[1]

And so Frame concluded that the Pentecostal experience was of the devil. How different this was from the experience of the missionary in Colombia!

One time I was praying in a meeting. I believed very little in this matter of tongues and had doubts. But on May 20, 1967, in a prayer meeting in church, as I was praying in a very concentrated way, all of a sudden I felt as if someone had turned a very strong searchlight on me and I was burning. I was going to speak in Spanish, but couldn't. I couldn't see anything but flames of fire all around me, and I felt as if I were burning. Then I began to speak in tongues—I was conscious, but I was in ecstasy.[2]

For one man, tongues were ghastly; for another they were glorious. Personal experiences may differ! And in this case, obviously both of these men could not be right.

"Then," someone will say, "we must go to the Word of God!" I agree wholeheartedly, and I have searched the Scriptures intensively for the last 25 years, learning the biblical and ancient languages, studying the historical and cultural background, gaining an understanding of the theological controversies, and above all, lying on my face with the Word of God open, asking the Lord for insight by His Spirit, asking Him to speak to me and lead me, asking for an obedient heart. But it is impossible to *prove* from the Scriptures who was right and who was wrong in the two accounts just cited. Maybe the brother in China resisted the Holy Spirit; maybe the brother in Colombia opened himself up to demons. Using the Bible alone as a guide, it is impossible to draw any definite conclusions here. In fact, regarding the modern experience of speaking in tongues as a whole, it is impossible to prove *from the Scriptures alone* that twentieth-century tongues are or are not from God. Sorry, but it's not so simple. (And I write this as a fervent speaker of tongues.)

Someone might say, "Then I'll rely on my discernment!" But that's exactly what these two men did, and they ended up discerning differently. What makes you so sure that you're right and that the others are wrong? What do they discern about you?

Of course, the Holy Spirit living within us and the basic truths of the Word will keep us from gross error and major deception. And it is true that there may be times when you have to say, "I can't explain it, but I know that this is not from God." You have to follow that conviction! Ultimately, where the Word does not speak directly to a particular situation, you must follow the inner witness of the Spirit or even your own common sense. Many times this is the very thing that will save us from destruction. God knows how to warn His people, and He knows how to provide us with wise counselors and dependable guides.

The problem is that revival can be so overwhelming and intense, it can happen so rapidly and across such a wide spectrum, it can be so full of new experiences and surprises, it can stir up so much competition and pride, it can be accompanied by so many inaccurate and even false reports, it can be so challenging and unsettling, it can come through such imperfect vessels (actually, do you know any perfect vessels?), it can offer so much promise and hope, and it can defy our expectations in so many ways, that it is all too easy to draw the wrong conclusions.

On the one hand, we can be so hasty in our judgments, so narrow in our thinking, so prideful in our hearts, and so compromised in our lifestyles, that we turn our backs on a heavenly visitation. On the other hand, we can be so quick to follow anything exciting and new, so gullible and naive, and so curious to a dangerous fault, that we throw ourselves into a phony flood.

"But I have real discernment!" you say. That's what everybody thinks. Instead, let's consider some solid and sound principles that will help us to discern. There is wisdom available for the honest seeker.

All too often we are premature in rejecting the new things the Spirit does in the Church and too opinionated about our outlook and experience. Because of this, we should look carefully at these principles developed by Jonathan Edwards during the early days of the Great Awakening. How could the contemporaries of Edwards tell us if this was real revival? There was no doubt that many lives had been transformed dramatically, but a lot of new things were happening. Unusual manifestations were occurring, people were getting very emotional, and one man who had been prone to depression in the past actually committed suicide as a result of his spiritual struggles. Was the overall work from God, the devil, or the flesh?

First, Edwards gave distinguishing marks of revival which did not disqualify the work in general from being of God.[3] In other words, based on these things happening, you cannot say, "This proves that it is not sent from heaven!"

> I. Nothing can be certainly concluded from this, That a work is carried on in a way very unusual and extraordinary; provided the variety or difference be such, as may still be comprehended within the limits of Scripture rules.

Generally speaking, if something is unfamiliar to us, we don't like it. We get used to one way of doing things, and right or wrong, that's what we tend to stay with. That which is ordinary becomes the equivalent of that which is spiritual. But revival is anything but ordinary! The point Edwards is making is simple: Just because something is new and intense doesn't mean it's not from God, unless it clearly violates Scripture.

> II. A work is not to be judged of by any effects on the bodies of men; such as tears, trembling, groans, loud outcries, agonies of body, or the failing of bodily strength.

Physical manifestations like these neither prove nor disprove that the work is from God. On the one hand, when the Spirit is moving deeply on people's hearts and minds, it makes perfect sense that there would be some kind of outward effect or external release. On the other hand, someone could get worked up into an emotional frenzy and have the same kind of manifestations. So these things themselves prove nothing either way. Plus, the Bible does not give us the right to pass judgment based on physical manifestations. I know that there are Charismatics who think that someone falling or shaking like a leaf is proof that the Holy Spirit is moving powerfully, while to some Evangelicals, falling or shaking is proof that the people are in the flesh. But the Word of God gives us no right to make sweeping judgments based on these things alone.

> III. It is no argument that an operation on the minds of people is not the work of the Spirit of God that it occasions a great deal of noise about religion.

Yes, revival will draw a crowd, and it will get people talking. Even the secular world will be stirred, and the media will report both the good, the bad, and the ugly sides of the work. But that doesn't mean that God is not moving in the midst of it all and that He is not the author of the spiritual excitement. It is impossible to have a quiet, unheralded revival!

> IV. It is no argument that an operation on the minds of a people is not the work of the Spirit of God that many who are the subjects of it have great impressions made on their imaginations.

Could you picture a sweeping, radical outpouring that impacted countless thousands of saints and sinners without having some kind of impact on the imaginations? And Edwards is quick to point out that God actually uses this faculty for His purposes. (Maybe some heresy hunter can attack Edwards here too! This looks awfully close to the dread sin of "visualizing.") The Bible is full of images—about heaven, hell, and our intimate relationship with God—and these images stir our imaginations. Have you ever meditated on Psalm 23 or Revelation 21 through 22? Have spiritual truths like the armor of God in Ephesians 6 ever become especially vivid to you? Doesn't this involve the imagination? In any case, Edwards was certainly right when he said, "That persons have many impressions on their imaginations does not prove that they have nothing else." Just because their imaginations were touched doesn't mean that the whole work was a fantasy!

V. It is no sign that a work is not from the Spirit of God that example is a great means of it.

It is easy to say that people are weeping, or collapsing, or shaking, or laughing just because they have seen other people do the same. But Edwards claims that learning by example is both reasonable and scriptural—if the work is from God. Again, you can't prove anything either way from this.

VI. It is no sign that a work is not from the Spirit of God that many who seem to be the subjects of it are guilty of great imprudences and irregularities in their conduct.

Now we're getting down to business! Edwards says that God's purpose in sending revival is to make men holy, not to make them politicians. (Yes, that's what he wrote 250 years ago!) People who have been touched will make mistakes and will at times act foolishly. We are human before revival, during revival, and after revival. Heavenly perfection is not quite here yet! And so Edwards was not exaggerating when he said that, "if we see great imprudences, and even sinful irregularities, in some who are great instruments to carry on the work, it will not prove it not to be the work of God."

Have you ever heard of the church of Corinth—empowered by the Spirit but guilty of foolishness and sin? Do the excesses, problems, and even moral failures in that church prove that the gifts of the Holy Spirit are not good? Then in our day, how can we point at an immature revival minister or some congregations that have gone off the deep end and conclude that the work as a whole is not from the Lord?

VII. Nor are many errors in judgment, and some delusions of Satan intermixed with the work, any argument that the work in general is not of the Spirit of God.

Leaders today do not have apostolic authority to set forth church doctrine (i.e., by their own teaching as opposed to by the Scriptures), nor do they have the right to make church-wide, binding prophetic pronouncements. Their words are not infallible, and they will not be led perfectly in everything they do, even in times of mighty outpouring. Some of them may go to extremes, and some of them may be deceived in part. This can happen, and it must be guarded against. The problem is, the moment we see such error, we tend to throw the whole thing out, and this can be an error too. The fact that one Pentecostal leader falls does not make the whole Pentecostal movement bad. The fact that one Reformed teacher gets deceived about the end times does not mean that the whole Reformed movement is wrong. It's the same with revival. We should be careful and we should definitely not accept every new thing that comes down the pike. But we shouldn't toss it all out so quickly either!

> VIII. If some, who were thought to be wrought upon, fall away into gross errors, or scandalous practices, it is no argument that the work in general is not the work of the Spirit of God.

Remember Judas Iscariot? Does his fall from apostleship disprove the ministry of Jesus or throw into question the validity of the other 11 apostles? Or how about Church history? Does the Church's unspeakably bloody persecution of the Jewish people negate the truth of the gospel? It's the same with revival. If the overall fruit of a so-called revival is bad, then it was obviously not a true revival. But that there should be some bad fruit is to be expected, and that some good fruit should go bad is no surprise.

> IX. It is no argument that a work is not from the Spirit of God that it seems to be promoted by ministers insisting very much on the terrors of God's holy law, and that with a great deal of pathos and earnestness.

My, how things have changed! Today we need to argue that just because some revival preachers make almost no mention of God's law and His judgments, we cannot therefore reject the whole work. Maybe a first wave of refreshing is coming through sincere but superficial vessels, and the next wave will go deeper. Or maybe God responded to someone's desperate faith and deep spiritual hunger, raising them up to shake His Church, in spite of their doctrinal flaws. In Edwards' day, the concern was about too much hell-fire preaching; nowadays, the concern is about almost no hell-fire preaching. Still, God can send His Spirit in spite of an overemphasis on hell or an underemphasis on hell.

Of course, that doesn't mean that we sit back and let things get totally out of balance. A more biblical message will produce more biblical believers, and we should strive to preach "the whole counsel of God"—with great sensitivity of the "now" message of the Spirit. But doctrinal pickiness has no place in times of refreshing.

Getting back to Edwards, that is the list of distinguishing marks by which a so-called revival could not be immediately disqualified. What were the positive marks? Although the English of Edwards may not always be clear to a modern reader, the signs he gave are really simple and clear, especially when we remember that God's purpose for mankind is to get for Himself an obedient, holy people, recreated in the image of His Son. If the end result of a revival is a godly, devoted Bride, then the work was from heaven![4]

> I. When the operation is such as to raise their esteem of that Jesus who was born of the Virgin, and was crucified without the gates of Jerusalem; and seems more to confirm and establish their minds in the truth of what the gospel declares to us of his being the Son of God, and the Saviour of men; it is a sure sign that it is from the Spirit of God.

Has Jesus become more precious to His people? Has He become more highly exalted in their eyes? Do they believe in Him more fervently, love Him more deeply, and long to commune with Him more and more? Then the Spirit did the work!

> II. When the spirit that is at work operates against the interests of Satan's kingdom, which lies in encouraging and establishing sin, and cherishing men's worldly lusts; this is a sure sign that it is a true, and not a false spirit.

Is there genuine repentance? Are people casting off their sins and becoming pure in thought, word, and deed? Is there a lasting break with the lusts of the flesh and the world? That is a work of the Spirit! Satan will not work against himself.

> III. The spirit that operates in such a manner as to cause in men a greater regard to the Holy Scriptures, and establishes them more in their truth and divinity is certainly the Spirit of God.

False cults and counterfeit Christian religions never want you to really get into the Word. They want you to follow their unique interpretations and use their study guides and teaching tools alone. According to them, it's not the Word that will help you, it's their additional revelation that you need. That is heresy, plain and simple, but a true revival will ultimately exalt the Scriptures and increase confidence that the Bible truly is God's Word. And here is something to chew on: While many mainstream Christian denominations have become liberal and have rejected the absolute authority of the Scriptures, the Pentecostal-Charismatic movement has remained extremely conservative in its view of Scripture. Does this say something to critics who claim that tongues, prophecy, and words of knowledge take us away from faith in the Word of God?

IV. If by observing the manner of the operation of a spirit that is at work among a people, we see that it operates as a spirit of truth, leading persons to truth, convincing them of those things that are true, we may safely determine that it is a right and true spirit.

First John 4:6 makes this perfectly clear. There is a spirit of truth (the Holy Spirit) and a spirit of error (from the devil). We can tell the difference! If someone falls to the floor during a revival service, shrieks, shakes, lies motionless for six hours, then gets up, confesses to previously hidden transgressions, makes restitution for sins against his business clients, recognizes the error of his ways and turns around, becoming an honest, upright person, we can recognize the Spirit of truth at work. The devil doesn't do that to people!

V. If the spirit that is at work among a people operates as a spirit of love to God and man, it is a sure sign that it is the Spirit of God.

Maybe the meetings are different than what we were used to. Maybe the speaker seemed a little offensive. Maybe we didn't appreciate the music. But if the meetings resulted in genuine devotion to the Lord and compassion to man, if missionaries were birthed out of these services, if ministries of mercy rose up, if there was a decided increase in prayer meetings and outreaches, if the people of God walked in greater love towards one another, then it is obvious that the Spirit was powerfully at work, even if there were some human flaws.

Forget the issues of style or denominational affiliation; forget the question of which version of the Bible was used or whether or not there was a choir; forget about the specific outward manifestations. Is there lasting fruit? Have the saints become more like Jesus? Have sinners been genuinely converted? Do God's people take His Word more seriously?

Have they been revived, refreshed, and renewed? Then the work in general is of the Lord!

That doesn't mean that we can't bring correction to those the Spirit is using, and it doesn't mean that we have to accept everything that is happening. All the specifics may not be right, and there may be clear, carnal excesses. We always need to go back to the Word and seek the Lord for His wisdom and leading, looking also to learn from some of our own experiences as well. But a real move of God doesn't come every day, and it would be a pity to disqualify a true visitation just because the Spirit didn't do things our way!

The ministry of Charles Finney came under heavy criticism from the clergy, because of his doctrinal beliefs and because of his so-called "New Measures"—like publicly identifying those who were under conviction and having them sit in "anxious seats" towards the front. He also preached in a straightforward manner, arguing his case like a lawyer in court instead of using lofty rhetoric like most of the other ministers of his day. And he disliked wearing clerical knickers! Yes, he got some real opposition.[5]

But what were some of the results of his labors? This was what John S. Tompkins reported in an article entitled, "Our Kindest City," printed in the July 1994 issue of *Reader's Digest*. Tompkins wondered why it was that the city of Rochester, New York was rated the kindest, most altruistic city in the nation in two separate polls, one taken in 1940 and the other from 1990 to 1992. He discovered the surprising answer. In 1830,

> Finney spent six months in Rochester and converted hundreds of residents—lawyers, doctors, judges, tradesmen, bankers, boatmen, workers, master craftsmen—to born-again Christianity. He scorched their consciences and

urged them not to follow the selfish ways of the world. Finney angrily denounced the evils of selfishness and deliberately aimed his message at the wealthy and powerful....

Having converted the affluent, Finney's final step was to get them to direct their energy and wealth into beneficial philanthropies. He was amazingly successful. Rochester embarked on a church-building boom. Rochesterians went on to establish a university, organize charities and self-help agencies, build a public-school system, fight against slavery (the city was a station on the Underground Railroad, which smuggled slaves into Canada), form unions and reform prison system. Rochester became a city where love for one's fellow man was more than an empty phrase.[6]

That's what you call lasting fruit! One hundred sixty years have passed, and the effects of the revival are still being felt. How's that for proof?

I have known men out on the fields, others at their weaving looms, so overcome by this sense of God that they were found prostrate on the ground. Hear the words of one who felt the hand of God upon him: "The grass beneath my feet and the rocks around me seem to cry, 'flee to Christ for refuge.' " This supernatural illumination of the Holy Spirit led many in [the Hebrides] revival to a saving knowledge of the Lord Jesus Christ before they came near to any meeting connected with the movement. I have no hesitation in saying that this awareness of God is the crying need of the Church today. "The fear of the Lord is the beginning of wisdom"; but this cannot be worked up by any human effort, it must come down.

Duncan Campbell, *The Lewis Awakening*

Cold, formalistic preaching never raised the dead! Only a demonstration of divine power will do that, such as took place in the days of Whitefield when it was a common sight for sinners to "cry out, as in the agony of death." ... During the great Scottish Revival in 1850, when James Turner, the fiery Methodist preacher, went down to Pontrochie to preach, so great was the conviction of sin that many businesses had to close down in order that the people might get right with God! Large numbers of drunkards were changed by the Power of God. Meetings lasted from 14 to 18 hours. Sinners, hearing their lost condition, swooned away, but came round praising God for acceptance.

Owen Murphy, *"When God Stepped Down from Heaven"*

Chapter Seventeen

The Holy Presence
and the Word on Fire

What is revival? It is God "stepping down from heaven" and baring His holy arm. He comes and acts and speaks. There is a holy Presence and a word on fire. God is in the midst of His people. The Lord is shaking the world. That is revival! It is a time of visitation.

If it is confined to one church, it is not revival. If it is confined to the meetings themselves, it is not revival. If it can all be traced to the efforts of man, it is not revival. If it does not ultimately affect the society, it is not revival.

When Jesus was on the earth, He explained to His disciples that it was better for Him to go away so that the Holy Spirit could come. Jesus could only be in one place at one time, but the Holy Spirit could be everywhere. Jesus could directly touch only those who heard and saw Him, but the Holy Spirit could directly touch people anywhere at any time—even if they were resisting and running. He transcends all human agency!

In revival, the Holy Spirit moves deeply and widely, supernaturally and powerfully. He goes into the homes and schools, into the places of business and the places of sin, and He brings the sense of the reality of God. He brings conviction! It is impossible to flee from God during revival.

The words of the Lord in Jeremiah 23 and the words of the psalmist in Psalm 139 are always true, but their reality is fully sensed during times of revival:

> "Am I only a God nearby," declares the LORD, "and not a God far away? Can anyone hide in secret places so that I cannot see him?" declares the LORD. "Do not I fill heaven and earth?" declares the LORD. (Jer. 23:23-24)

> Where can I go from Your Spirit? Where can I flee from Your presence? If I go up to the heavens, You are there; if I make my bed in the depths, You are there. If I rise on the wings of the dawn, if I settle on the far side of the sea, even there Your hand will guide me, Your right hand will hold me fast. If I say, "Surely the darkness will hide me and the light become night around me," even the darkness will not be dark to You; the night will shine like the day, for darkness is as light to You. (Ps. 139:7-12)

During the Welsh Revival, it was commonly reported that men would go into the bars to drink, not wanting to go to their homes, because they knew their wives were praying and the Presence of God was there. But they couldn't escape Him in the bars! As they would take the drink in their hands, an unseen Hand would stop them, and they would run from that place to their homes and get saved.

As the Spirit converted many of the profane, ungodly coal miners, His Presence went with them to work, and they would start their days with prayer and worship. It was said that you could feel His Presence in the coal mines as much as you could in church!

Once, some visitors were asking for directions to the meetings in one part of Wales. They were told to take the train to such and such a place and get out there. "But how we will know when we are there?" they asked. "You'll feel it!" was the reply. And they did! After getting out from the train, they asked for further directions. They were told to walk to a certain place and turn there. Again they asked, "But how will we know where to turn?" "You'll feel it!" was the answer again. And they did!

That holy Presence is not geographically limited, as Arthur Wallis documented:

Ships as they drew near the American ports [in 1858] came within a definite zone of heavenly influence. Ship after ship arrived with the same tale of sudden conviction and conversion. In one ship a captain and the entire crew of thirty men found Christ out at sea and entered the harbour rejoicing. Revival broke out on the battleship "North Carolina" through four Christian men who had been meeting in the bowels of the ship for prayer. One evening they were filled with the Spirit and burst into song. Ungodly shipmates who came down to mock were gripped by the power of God, and the laugh of the scornful was soon changed into the cry of the penitent. Many were smitten down, and a gracious work broke out that continued night after night, till they had to send ashore for ministers to help, and the battleship became a Bethel.[1]

I heard a story about a man here in the States who had witnessed to his unsaved friend and prayed for him for years. One day, that friend came over to borrow a tool, but no one was home. So he went to the toolshed to find what he was looking for when, suddenly, the Presence of God overtook him. He was convicted of his sins and broke down, putting his faith in Jesus at that very moment.

When he told his Christian friend what had happened to him, he found out there was a simple explanation: That faithful believer had prayed with tears for his salvation for a period of years, making intercession for his soul in that very shed. The Holy Spirit was there!

Now, multiply that picture a thousand times over and spread it across cities, counties, states, and even nations, and you have a glorious picture of revival.

After the night of prayer in the Hebrides when the house literally shook with the Presence of the Lord, Duncan Campbell relates:

> The following day when we came to the church we found that the meeting house was already crowded out. A stream of buses had come from the four quarters of the island. Who had told them of the services? I have no way of knowing; God has His own manner of working when men are praying in faith. A butcher's van brought seven men from a distance of seventeen miles.
>
> We gathered in the church, and I spoke for about an hour. The Spirit of God was at work. All over the building men and women were crying for mercy. And on the road outside, I could hear the strong cries of weeping men. I saw both men and women swooning, some falling into trances. Many were crying, "Oh, God, is there mercy for me?"
>
> A young man beneath the pulpit prayed, "Oh, God, hell is too good for me."
>
> The seven men who came in the butcher's van were all gloriously converted that night.
>
> In the field of evangelism today, the desperate need is for conviction of sin—conviction that will bring men on their faces before God.[2]

When the service was about to end and the last people were leaving, the young man by the pulpit, himself a new convert, began to pray, and his prayer lasted for 45 minutes.

Somehow, word got out that the meetings were to be held all night! People began to return from all over, packing the church. The service lasted until 4:00 a.m.! But the story doesn't end there. At 4:00 a.m. Campbell received a message: "Mr. Campbell, people are gathered at the Police Station, from the other end of the parish. They are in great distress. Can anyone here come along and pray with them?"[3]

Who drew them there? Who convicted them? Many of these people had been strongly opposed to the gospel right up to that very day. What was happening? The Spirit was at work! This is a true picture of revival:

> We went to the Police Station and I shall never forget the scene that met our eyes. Under a starlit sky, with the moon gazing down upon us—and angels, too, I believe, looking over the battlements of glory—were scores of men and women under deep conviction of sin. On the road, by the cottage side, behind a peat stack, they were crying to God for mercy. Yes, the revival had come!

> For five weeks this went on. We preached in one church at seven o'clock [in the evening], in another at ten, in a third at twelve, back to the first church at three o'clock [in the morning], then home between five and six, tired, but glad to have found ourselves in the midst of this Heaven-sent movement of the Holy Spirit.[4]

Remarkably, in the first parish where revival hit, Campbell reports that 75 percent of the converts were born again *before* they arrived at the meeting place! There was also an amazing revival among the young people. In those days, not a single young person attended any public worship services in any of the churches, but the very first evening—without announcement or advertisement—the awareness of God in the dance hall at midnight became so great that the young people left there and crowded into the church! And so the revival continued, spreading in like manner to the neighboring counties.[5]

Why can't we believe God for similar outpourings in our day? Why cheapen revival by dragging it down to the feeble level of our unbelief-ridden, flesh-dependent expectations? Why not ask God for the real thing? And here's a good checkpoint for Pentecostals and Charismatics: With all our emphasis on the power of God and miracles, another sign of revival for us will be true, frequent New Testament healings in our midst. They will not be the exception to the rule, but they will be the norm. Such things cannot be fabricated! But as long as our healing ministers reach multiplied millions of sick people through TV, radio, book, tape, and magazine, yet continue to have relatively meager results, we have little to boast about. All the more should we cry out for a real visitation that will not disappoint!

In 1922, when Smith Wigglesworth was ministering in Wellington, New Zealand, he called for a special prayer meeting with a group of 11 leaders. After each of them had prayed, Wigglesworth rose to seek the Lord, and the Presence of God began to fill the room. Soon the glory of God became terrible. The light became too bright, the heat too intense. The other men couldn't take it any longer. Every one of them left the room! Only Wigglesworth could continue in the midst of the Shekinah.

Another minister heard what had happened and determined at the next gathering, no matter how strong the Presence of God became, he would stay until the end. Once again, the scene repeated itself: Wigglesworth began to pray, the holy Presence of God filled the room, and the glory became unbearable. Everyone left, except this one leader. He would not be overcome and driven out by the manifest Presence of the Lord. But it was too much; Wigglesworth was caught up in the Spirit, radiant with holy fire, and even the determined minister couldn't stand the intensity. Soon enough, he was gone too![6]

That is the Presence of God that comes with revival. It becomes unbearably intense. Its light breaks through the darkness. Its heat raises the temperature all around! It cannot be localized or confined. By its very nature, it must make an impact on its surroundings, otherwise it is not true revival. And while it will not completely change the world, it will make a radical impact. It will drive sin out!

With this in mind, we can speak quite clearly about revival in America today: As long as homosexuals march brazenly down our streets and serve in leading positions in our governments; as long as abortion clinics and pornography theaters thrive; as long as "Christian" young people watch MTV and "Christian" adults watch HBO; as long as the jails have too many prisoners and the mission fields have too few laborers; as long as greed and materialism rule most of the world and much of the church; as long as humanists, new agers, and atheists dominate our college faculties; as long as these things are at the forefront of our society, we are not experiencing revival! Sweeping revival in America would mean upheaval. The holy Presence would change the complexion of our nation dramatically.

And what if *all* of America does not experience revival? Then its powerful impact will be felt in select towns, cities, or states. And even with these limitations, the far-reaching effects of revival will be experienced well beyond local church walls. The divine invasion—actually, to most Americans, a return to New Testament reality would be as abrupt and shocking as an invasion—will cause a shakedown and a shakeup.

Of course, we praise God for the refreshing that He is now bringing to many of His people. We thank Him for the joy and encouragement. Yet we can roll on the floor and laugh every night until three in the morning, but if the world around us remains unchanged, that is not revival. If the way we live outside the building does not become characterized by holiness and sacrificial love for the Lord and the lost, that is not revival. And if everything that happens in our revival meetings comes through the hands of human vessels—without the supernatural visitations outside the Church, without the abiding Presence, without the clear evidence that God Himself has stepped down from heaven in power—that is not revival.

For many ministers, that's frustrating. We like to do it ourselves! If revival is truly a heavenly visitation, that means that we can't manufacture it or produce it. We are utterly dependent on God. But that's the best place to be! He wants to bring revival more than we want to see it. He wants to bless more than we want to be blessed. He has invested far more into this dying world than we have, and He has far more at stake. What better place to be than at the feet of the Lord in fervent prayer, crying out, "Revive Your people, O God!"

And when He comes in power, He will not only act. He will speak! Revival is characterized by the Word of God on fire. It is not simply a matter of making time in every service for teaching and preaching. It is not just giving the Word its proper place. We've had our fill of lifeless pulpits that "honor the Word," and many believers today are "taught to death." No, it is a matter of the Word on fire, a matter of holy unction, a matter of hearing the urgent message of the hour.

The effects of the Welsh Revival at the beginning of this century were far-reaching and worldwide. Clearly, these were days owned by the Lord. But the revival was not perfect, and many believe that it could have had an even greater and more lasting impact—especially in Wales itself—if there had been a deeper, more consistent ministry of the Word of God.

It's so easy to get caught up in the fervor of revival, in the excitement of the manifestations, that we forget about something critical: God wants the heart, and through the Word of God, He probes the heart and changes the heart. The excitement will pass, and the manifestations will wane. But if the trumpet has been sounded, if the awakening cry has been raised, if the burden of the Lord has been delivered, if the radical call to follow Jesus in a radical way has gone forth, that will determine just how deeply individuals will be changed. *The Word is the road map for the revival's future.*

Trivial, nonchallenging messages will not lead the way. Those who were nourished by lightweight meals will falter during the hard times. They will find themselves swerving and veering, lacking clear direction. Soon enough, they will rebuild the walls that revival tore down and revert to the habits from which revival delivered them. Within a few years, they will be living on memories and trying to perpetuate those memories through now-dead forms. If only there had been a prophetic, piercing, challenging, truthful proclamation of the Word! If only there had not been so much entertainment and frivolity!

Matthew records that "Jesus went throughout Galilee, teaching in their synagogues, preaching the good news of the kingdom, and healing every disease and sickness among the people" (Matt. 4:23).

Do we know better than Jesus? He gave Himself to teaching and preaching as well as healing, and He taught without compromise. (His words are so disturbing!) He taught with authority. What better time than during true revival to bring the uncompromising, prophetic call? What better time to preach the cross than during times of renewal when Jesus is seen in His glory?

Even in the intensity of the spiritual outpouring in the Book of Acts, the anointed Word was still central:

> Every Sabbath [Paul] reasoned in the synagogue, trying to persuade Jews and Greeks. When Silas and Timothy came from Macedonia, Paul devoted himself exclusively to preaching, testifying to the Jews that Jesus was the Christ. ... So Paul stayed for a year and a half, teaching them the word of God. (Acts 18:4-5,11)

Do we know better than Paul?

But someone will say: "Oh, in our current revival meetings, there is always time devoted to the Word of God"— especially before the offerings, I might add! But putting that aside, when the Word is preached, what is the substance? One prominent leader has asked some questions about the current preaching emphasis. Does it exalt Jesus? Does it produce a real burden for the lost? Does it present the wrath of God along with the love of God? Does it challenge and convict?

God used Charles Finney mightily in the first half of the nineteenth century, but his words still speak today. His sermons on revival preached in New York City in 1832 were subsequently published as *Lectures on the Revival of Religion*, and these messages have gone around the world in multiple languages. Through the anointed word, the revival lives on. At the turn of this century, Jonathan Goforth, the Canadian missionary to China and Manchuria, began to get reports about the Welsh Revival. At the same time, he began reading Finney's *Revival Lectures*, and he put into practice what he read. A move of God swept the cities where he ministered!

The Great Awakening and the Methodist Revival ended more than 200 years ago, but the messages of Edwards and Wesley still challenge us today. They being dead yet speak; their words still burn and set our hearts aflame.

Now look for a moment at the compromised worldly Church of America. We know almost nothing of the dedication, sacrifice, fervor, or faith lived out daily by our brothers and sisters around the world. We know almost nothing of the gospel of martyrdom. We have little understanding of the cross. What does the Spirit want to say to us? Do we need froth or fire? What is the divine prescription for the sick patient? Do we need surface manifestations or serious movings, frivolity or fervor, glitz or glory? Enough with all the fluff!

We must never forget: Revival is a supernatural work of the Holy Spirit (not the Happy Spirit—although He brings great joy; not the Hollow Spirit—in spite of the impression given by some of our empty meetings; and not the Hollywood Spirit—in spite of our superstar preachers; He is the Holy Spirit). I have heard Him described as "wild," "exciting," and "creative." But have we forgotten that He is holy? His manifest Presence is holy, and His work is to make us holy. Peter wrote that we "…have been chosen according to the foreknowledge of God the Father, *through the sanctifying work of the Spirit*, for obedience to Jesus Christ and sprinkling by His blood" (1 Pet. 1:2).

The Spirit is not a showman; He is a Sanctifier. He may cause us to weep or laugh or stagger or fall, but His goal is holiness. His goal is separation. His goal is to make us like the Son, shining in His glory and radiance.

What is holiness? According to Samuel Logan Brengle, "Holiness is pure love." Holiness is beautiful, not binding, and wonderful, not wearisome. Holiness is being like God— in character and inner nature, in heart and soul. What a blessed state! It is marked by Christlikeness instead of corruption, by divine attributes instead of devilish attitudes, by loyalty instead of lust, by generosity instead of greed, by devotion instead of drunkenness. Holiness is perfect goodness. Holiness is purity of life.

But holiness will not be attained by spiritual excitement alone. It is not an abstract, nebulous "something" existing "somewhere," no more than God Himself is just an abstract "something" existing "somewhere." Holiness does not float in and skip out. Holiness means definite, concrete, radical change. It means a whole new way of living. And it is grounded in the Word of God.

Without a clear call to holiness, revival will run amuck. If the standards of the Lord are not clearly lifted up, the people will soon fall down (and I don't mean in the Spirit). If their experience is not grounded in the Scriptures, they will have the long-term stability of a feather blowing in the wind. When the shouting dies down, disappointment will set in. Some will even turn against their initial, transforming experience. Why? It didn't last. It had no solid foundation!

Revivals have been famous for their revival preachers, and true revival preaching—not emotional ranting and raving or pseudo-spiritual rambling—must become central once again. Otherwise we will quickly lose our bearings. Otherwise we will drift!

There are at least six things the Holy Spirit will commonly do in times of revival: He will sanctify (Heb. 9:13-14); convict (John 16:8-11); glorify Jesus (John 16:14); deliver and heal (Acts 10:38); empower (Acts 1:8); and refresh (Acts 3:19). He can do all these things by means of His inner, secret work on our hearts, but just think of how much more effective the working would be if it was coupled with His voice!

The Holy Spirit was upon Jesus to preach the good news and to liberate the captives (Luke 4:16-18). In fact, it was through His anointed Word that the captives were set free. The Spirit does not contradict the Word, compete with the Word, or confine the Word; He *confirms* the Word (Heb. 2:1-4).

Seven times in Revelation 2 and 3 Jesus addressed His Church. Seven times John recorded the Lord's exact words, and all seven times He ended by saying, "He who has an ear, let him hear what *the Spirit says* to the churches" (Rev. 2:7, etc.).

Jesus speaks to His people by His Spirit! Are we hearing His voice today? The Spirit speaks His words. During revival, those words thunder forth. The message has not changed; we have changed. We need to get back to the Word! (Of course, most of our churches boast about their faithfulness to the Word, and some are even called "Word" churches, yet there's a lot more to the Word than what you may hear in some of these places.) We need truly anointed, holy pulpits and truly anointed, holy preachers. This generation is crying for a fresh word from above. As Leonard Ravenhill expressed,

> Evangelistic preaching is often a heart massage. Revival preaching is heart surgery. We have had varieties of evangelistic preaching—million dollar gospel crusades, charismatic healing evangelism. It is now time for confrontational preaching of holiness unto the Lord. Evangelism touches the emotions. Revival preaching touches the conscience.[7]

Although the Welsh Revival did not have an emphasis on public preaching or teaching, it began with a message of immediate repentance and instant obedience. That remained as the foundation of the Spirit's work. The Azusa Street outpouring was known far and wide for its Pentecostal manifestations, and some of its leaders strayed into strange doctrines like British Israelitism. But if you look at the doctrinal statement they drew up, you will see something very clearly. It put repentance first, second, third, fourth, and fifth—leading to a holy, Spirit-baptized life.[8]

Has that become passé? Is such a message no longer needed in this hour? Have we advanced beyond repentance and holiness? Has the Lord finally decided to look the other way? Is He choosing to ignore the fact that most of the American "Spirit-filled" (or, as I have said many times before, "Spirit-frilled") Church is hardly distinguishable from the world?

I think back to the fire-baptized preachers of past generations—to the Whitefields and Tennents, to the Savonarolas and Foxes, to the Finneys and Campbells—and I long to see a new breed of no-compromise leaders arise in our day. I think back to their heartrending messages, their challenging calls to get right with God, their tearful offers of the mercy of the Lord, their fearless proclamation of the cross, their devastating descriptions of the state of the lost, and their wonderful promises of the glory to come, and I can only shudder when I compare this to most of our contemporary North American "revival" preaching.

Do the people of God today need a master surgeon or a circus master? Do we need to be provoked or primped? Do we need our leaders to tell us the truth or to tell us a joke?

The world is self-destructing without God. The harvest is more ripe than it has ever been. The need for holy laborers is absolutely pressing. The time to go for it without reserve is *now*. What are we waiting for?

Implore the Lord of the harvest to raise up spokesmen who will bring His prophetic message. Ask Him to bring to the fore those who will "cry out and spare not" (Is. 58). Beseech Him to speak clearly and directly to His people. We cannot afford a shallow revival. We cannot afford a spurious work.

Pray for the Word on fire that will set us on fire so we can go and set the world on fire—for the glory of God. The time is short. The potential is breathtaking. Let's not miss the opportunity of a lifetime. Now—not never.

Revival is often a preparation for suffering that will follow, and the suffering itself becomes a test of the quality and reality of the revival.... Within ten years [of the 1904-05 Welsh Revival], thousands of young men who had been converted in the revivals were fighting and dying in the choking mud of the Great War [World War I] battlefields. How many of these were men who, but for the revival, would have had no hope of eternal life, only eternity will tell. Revival came to East Africa in the 1930s and prepared the church for the eight years of terror under Iddi Ammin in the 1970s when more than half a million were brutally killed. It also prepared Kenya for the Mau Mau atrocities in the 1950s and the terrible inter-tribal wars in Rwanda and Burundi. Revival came to the Congo in 1953, preparing the church for the cruel Simba rebellion ten years later when many leaders, members and missionaries were massacred.

Brian Edwards, *Revival: A People Saturated With God*

For I will pour water on the thirsty land, and streams on the dry ground; I will pour out My Spirit on your offspring, and My blessing on your descendants. They will spring up like grass in a meadow, like poplar trees by flowing streams.

Is. 44:3-4

Come, let us return to the LORD. He has torn us to pieces but He will heal us; He has injured us but He will bind up our wounds. After two days He will revive us; on the third day He will restore us, that we may live in His presence. Let us acknowledge the LORD; let us press on to acknowledge Him. As surely as the sun rises, He will appear; He will come to us like the winter rains, like the spring rains that water the earth.

Hos. 6:1-3

Ask the LORD for rain in the springtime; it is the LORD who makes the storm clouds. He gives showers of rain to men, and plants of the field to everyone.

Zech. 10:1

Chapter Eighteen

A Warning and a Promise

In the year 642, Manasseh, king of Judah, died. He had reigned for 55 years, and according to the testimony of the Word, Manasseh "…shed so much innocent blood that he filled Jerusalem from end to end—besides the sin [of idolatry] that he had caused Judah to commit, so that they did evil in the eyes of the LORD." (2 Kings 21:16). Although he repented and brought reformation at the end of his life (see 2 Chron. 33:11-19), his sins and the sins of the people had been so great that heavy judgment had to fall on Judah and Jerusalem. There was no choice!

Manasseh's 22-year-old son Amon succeeded him, continuing in Manasseh's evil ways. After two years, he was assassinated, and Amon's young son Josiah, just eight years old, became king in his place.

He did what was right in the eyes of the LORD and walked in the ways of his father David, not turning aside to the right or to the left. In the eighth year of his reign, while he was still young, he began to seek the God of his father David. In his twelfth year he began to purge Judah and Jerusalem of high places, Asherah poles, carved idols and cast images. Under his direction the altars of the Baals were torn down; he cut to pieces the incense altars that were above them, and smashed the Asherah poles, the idols and the images. These he broke to

pieces and scattered over the graves of those who had sacrificed to them. He burned the bones of the priests on their altars, and so he purged Judah and Jerusalem. (2 Chron. 34:2-5)

Under this godly young king, Judah experienced a national
revival. Idols were smashed; the Word of God was brought
back from oblivion. Pure worship was restored. The holy
days were observed again. Things changed dramatically.

But one thing couldn't change: Judgment still had to
come! The blood of the slain was still crying out for justice.
The Lord still had to fulfill His Word. Divine retribution
could only be postponed; it could not be annulled. And so, as
soon as Josiah was removed from the scene—cut down by
enemy archers in the midst of a foolish military venture—the
judgments began to fall. Within one generation, the Temple
was demolished, there was no Davidic king and no Davidic
throne, and multitudes of Jews were carried into exile in
Babylon.

> The LORD sent Babylonian, Aramean, Moabite and Ammonite
> raiders against [Jehoiakim, the son of Josiah]. He sent them to
> destroy Judah, in accordance with the word of the LORD pro-
> claimed by His servants the prophets. Surely these things hap-
> pened to Judah according to the LORD's command, in order to
> remove them from His presence because of the sins of
> Manasseh and all he had done, including the shedding of inno-
> cent blood. For he had filled Jerusalem with innocent blood,
> and the LORD was not willing to forgive. (2 Kings 24:2-4)

Revival had purchased a respite. It had given the nation
one last opportunity to get right with God before calamity
came. It had given fresh strength to the righteous, and it demonstrated the justice and mercy of God. He gave them another chance, but no sooner was Josiah dead than the people
went back to their own ways.

Church of America, listen well! There is a message for us here. There is a lesson for us to learn. Why does God want to send revival to our land? Certainly, it is because He loves us and wants to bless us. Certainly, He is responding to the prayers and petitions of His people. Certainly, He is jealous for His reputation and the honor of His Son. Certainly, He wants to equip us and thrust us out to reap the vast harvest. But there is something more. Could it be that He is preparing us for the hard times? Could it be that He is sending a glorious renewal to enable us to endure the coming calamities?

A veteran missionary of the Zaire Evangelistic Mission, Harold Womersley, said, "The blow that fell in 1960 was the greatest since the inception of the Mission in 1915. A threatened annihilation of the Church. Pastors, elders, missionaries were senselessly slaughtered, churches burned down, whole congregations hacked to pieces while worshipping, blood running like water. It looked as though the church was finished." But the gates of hell could not prevail against a church that was built upon the Rock. Through revival the Great Unseen Head of the Church had been preparing His people for their fiery trial.[1]

Of course, if the Church gets on fire and confronts the world, many will get saved, and many others will not. Some will become holy, others will become hostile—and I mean *hostile*. The world will finally have a good reason to persecute the people of God, and red-hot believers will stir up a hornet's nest of attack. As Vance Havner said, "A real fire brand is distressing to the devil and when a wide-awake believer comes along, taking the Gospel seriously, we can expect sinister maneuvering for his downfall."[2]

Revival will make us ready! The lasting joy and victory will help us to persevere and not back down or shut down, back up or shut up. The flames will keep burning in our hearts even where darkness reigns. We will rejoice in the midst of persecution. We will overcome!

But it's not just the devil that we'll be dealing with. Our very nation will be shaken by God! The closing chapters of the closing book of the Bible give a stunning picture of the wrath of God—His wrath against the world, not the Church. Vials and vials of wrath will be poured out! The Book of Revelation speaks of "the cup" of God's wrath, "the great winepress" of His wrath, "seven golden bowls" filled with His wrath, and "the wine of the fury of His wrath." Of Jesus it says:

> Out of His mouth comes a sharp sword with which to strike down the nations. "He will rule them with an iron scepter." He treads the winepress of the fury of the wrath of God Almighty. (Rev. 19:15)

We must grasp the devastating fact that overwhelming judgment will come to America. God is still the Judge, not the Joker.

Forget about date-setting prophecy books and Second Coming speculation. Forget about trying to figure out exactly where we stand on the end-time eschatological calendar (or else make sure that you write in pencil!). Forget about even wondering whether these verses in Revelation have anything to do with the United States specifically. It is enough to understand these three things: 1) The closer we get to the end of the age (and we know we are getting closer), the more staggering the manifestation of God's wrath will become. It will not just be merry mercy and giddy grace. 2) The testimony of the whole Bible makes it clear that the Lord is righteous and just, that He will not leave the guilty unpunished, and that He will execute vengeance in this world here on earth. There is judgment in the hereafter, and there is judgment in the here and now. America will be judged. 3) Judgment begins with the house of God (1 Pet. 4:17). The Church is exempt from God's wrath (1 Thess. 5:9), but not His purifying judgment. He examines the righteous before He destroys the wicked (Ps. 11:4-6).

Now consider this absolutely terrifying thought. What if God sent waves of refreshing and revival to His people in America today and we spurned His grace and took for granted His visitation? What if we continued to live as we live and thumbed our nose at a totally amazing display of mercy and kindness? What would happen to our land? The words of Jesus come jumping off the page:

> As He approached Jerusalem and saw the city, He wept over it and said, "If you, even you, had only known on this day what would bring you peace—but now it is hidden from your eyes. The days will come upon you when your enemies will build an embankment against you and encircle you and hem you in on every side. They will dash you to the ground, you and the children within your walls. They will not leave one stone on another, because you did not recognize the time of God's coming to you." (Luke 19:41-44)

I am deeply and passionately jealous for the pure, powerful move of God to come to its full potential here. I can't imagine us missing the Lord's visitation in our day. I tremble at the thought. May it not be!

But there's something else that is sobering too. Even if we receive everything God has for us, even if we see true revival sweep our land from coast to coast, even if we have a radical awakening, America's past guilt won't just go away. Our past crimes won't simply be overlooked, and the consequences of our massive national transgression won't simply disappear. If people knew that revival would eliminate judgment, then they could just sin to the max and repent at the last moment. And if God answered with revival, then they would have gotten away with their sins. It would be so easy! But it's not.

Think of a murderer who kills a young mother and then runs from the law. As a fugitive, he hears the gospel and gets saved. His sins are forgiven, and He is wonderfully transformed. He grieves over his past and finds mercy from heaven, but justice still demands that he turn himself in and serve time in jail (or even suffer the death penalty). The stain of his sin is washed away, but there is still a consequence to his actions. And there is still a husband without his wife and children without a mother because of this man's violent crime. What does this tell us about America's future?

Sometimes revival comes because the mercy of the Lord is so great that He extends yet another opportunity to sinners and rebels to turn back before it's too late. His justice would have long since wiped them out, but His long-suffering and compassion moved Him to make one last public display of grace. But after that comes the judgment!

Is it just a coincidence that less than ten years after a powerful revival swept this country in 1857 through 1858, the Civil War claimed hundreds of thousands of young American lives? Mercy and unmerited favor were poured out in abundance before the consequences of the horrid sin of slavery were meted out in our nation. And even during the Civil War, revivals continued. In fact, there are stirring accounts of visitation and outpouring among both the Confederate and Union troops.[3] God was still displaying His mercy!

There is a biblical principle that applies directly here: To whom much is given, much is required (Luke 12:48). Once the Church is revived and the world has gotten a real taste of the true gospel, once the alarms have been sounded and the warnings proclaimed, there is nothing left to hold back retribution. What will "pay day" look like for America?

Of course, neither you nor I know exactly what the future holds. We can't make absolute predictions about every detail of what is coming, when it's coming, and how it will come. But this much is sure: The Lord is *not* sending us revival so we can get fatter and more complacent. We are not being renewed in order to enter a time of even greater peace and prosperity. That's what killed us in the first place! The pleasures and lusts of this world, the idols of materialism and entertainment, the deception of luxury and wealth have been our undoing. We don't need a "prosperity" revival. We don't need a "success in life" renewal. We need reality!

Let the truth be told. This generation of American believers is more accustomed to Christian cruises than to the cross of Christ and more familiar with the programs in the *TV Guide* than with the preaching of the terrors of God. Persecution for the faith seems old-fashioned, while suffering hardship for the Lord is deemed negative. And any talk of God's wrath on the disobedient is considered totally out of place. Judgment on America? Perish the thought! We want another spiritual high.

The message of repentance and the promise of revival is anything but trite. And the consequences of rejecting a genuine move of God's Spirit are terrible. Yet with so much talk of revival and visitation, who is warning America and the nations? With all the anointing, where are the watchmen? Where are the prophetic voices (not just the dreamers and the customized "personal prophets," but the voices)? How many are pleading with men and women to repent before it's too late? How many ministries emphasize this? Not only are we not sober, we're not sobering up our nation![4]

Listen to the warning of Jesus: "Be careful, or your hearts will be weighed down with dissipation, drunkenness and the anxieties of life, and that day will close on you unexpectedly like a trap" (Luke 21:34).

This is not party time for the Church. This is the time for holy watchfulness. This is the hour to be alert. While the world gets caught up with the lusts of the flesh and deceptions of the devil, dazed by drugs, bound by immorality, enslaved by greed, hypnotized by entertainment, stupefied by alcohol, paralyzed by fear, we who drink the Spirit's new wine will be sober. We will not be deceived. As for those who only prophesy peace and prosperity—beware!

> While people are saying, "Peace and safety," destruction will come on them suddenly, as labor pains on a pregnant woman, and they will not escape. But you, brothers, are not in darkness so that this day should surprise you like a thief. You are all sons of the light and sons of the day. We do not belong to the night or to the darkness. So then, let us not be like others, who are asleep, but let us be alert and self-controlled. For those who sleep, sleep at night, and those who get drunk, get drunk at night. But since we belong to the day, let us be self-controlled, putting on faith and love as a breastplate, and the hope of salvation as a helmet. For God did not appoint us to suffer wrath but to receive salvation through our Lord Jesus Christ. (1 Thess. 5:3-9)

Listen again to the words of Jesus. There are prophetic principles here, truths that apply to all generations, regardless of specific dates, times, and seasons, regardless of exactly when the Lord returns. The warnings still apply:

> Just as it was in the days of Noah, so also will it be in the days of the Son of Man. People were eating, drinking, marrying and being given in marriage up to the day Noah entered the ark. Then the flood came and destroyed them all. (Luke 17:26-27)

Do you understand what the Lord is saying? He is not describing here the sinful behavior of that generation. He is describing how life went on as it always had, right up to the moment of destruction: "People were eating, drinking, marrying and being given in marriage up to the day Noah entered the ark." Everything was normal, and then the flood of judgment came. People of God, it's wake-up time!

We have had more warnings than the people of Noah's day had—even to the point of calamities coming to our nation by flood and fire in different locations on the very same day. This has happened more than once! There was even a river of fire that swept through the prosperous city of Houston in the Fall of 1994. Less than a year before that, the front cover of *USA Today* featured a full-color picture of a blazing inferno of fire raging behind a large development of beautiful homes in southern California. The caption read, "Nothing to stop that fire!" Are these signs of things to come?

Why should America today be any different than Judah in the days after Josiah? Judah was a special covenant nation spoken of thousands of times in the Bible; America is not directly mentioned in the Word even once. God Himself said that He would be a wall of fire around Jerusalem, and whoever touched Jerusalem was touching the apple of His eye (Zech. 2:5,8); He made no such promises to Washington, DC! Yet He brought down Jerusalem and Judah, even though it meant that His name would be blasphemed among the nations. His holiness and justice demanded it. Where does that leave us?

What if refreshing comes to us, only to prepare a people who will be ready for the fire? What if God says, "I must have real, dedicated people to endure the real, disastrous times that are coming!"? Do we understand the hour in which we live? This is not a Nintendo game we're talking about. This is not an HBO movie. This is reality! It's going to get wild down here. Are you ready for the shaking? Only a revived people will endure in victory.

> LORD, who may dwell in Your sanctuary? Who may live on Your holy hill? He whose walk is blameless and who does what is righteous, who speaks the truth from his heart and has no slander on his tongue, who does his neighbor no wrong and casts no slur on his fellowman, who despises a vile man but honors those who fear the LORD, who keeps his oath even when it hurts, who lends his money without usury and does not accept a bribe against the innocent. *He who does these things will never be shaken.* (Ps. 15)

> I have set the LORD always before me. Because He is at my right hand, *I will not be shaken.* (Ps. 16:8)

> My soul finds rest in God alone; my salvation comes from Him. He alone is my rock and my salvation; He is my fortress, *I will never be shaken.* (Ps. 62:1-2)

When God comes in revival might, He shakes all things that can be shaken—from dead traditions to habitual sins; from man-made kingdoms to human wisdom—so that only eternal, God-ordained things may remain (see Heb. 12:25-29). He shakes His people free, so that we can be secure in Him, immovable, confident, and unshakable. Our trust is no longer in what we can see. We have been revived!

Like Moses, we endure by seeing Him who is invisible (Heb. 11:27). Like Paul, we count all things loss because we know the Lord, because Jesus has become our all in all (Phil. 3:7-8). Like Daniel, we do not fear the edict of the king, because our God is able to deliver us (Dan. 6). We are alive and sold out to Him. Revival is totally practical!

I hope and pray that judgment will be delayed as long as the Lord is willing to delay it. And I want to see the works of the evil one muzzled as much as is spiritually possible. We don't gloat over death and destruction. We don't sit back glibly and watch a nation fall. But we had better not fool ourselves. Things will be getting intense!

It could well be that God will send refreshing to His people to serve as the anesthesia before the surgery. It could well be that a renewing stream had to come first because the Church was so sickly and sluggish, so compromised and carnal, so battered and bruised, so distant and downtrodden, and then *after* this the Lord will really get down to business. What if intense conviction comes then? What if wailing and mourning follow joy and laughter? What if the purging judgments then sweep through the Body, followed by an even greater release of victory and joy?

It is not that God is trying to confuse us. He is certainly not sitting back and mocking His Church. No, He is doing what He is doing for our good and for His glory, but He's doing things His way. And He will get His results!

Brian Edwards reminds us again that:

There is no revival without deep, uncomfortable and humbling conviction of sin. It is this terrible conviction of sin that led the Congolese Christians, during the revival in 1953, to sing a chorus of their own making:

Receive salvation today,
This is the hour of judgment.

The missionaries wanted to change the words to "This is the hour of mercy," but were pointed to Malachi 3:2-3: God had come as "a refiner's fire."[5]

Revival brings God near—in His mercy and His majesty, in His joy and His judgment, in His power and His purity. Are you ready for the Lord?

Early in his ministry, D.L. Moody began to feel the need for a greater, deeper anointing from heaven. He realized the necessity of a real baptism in the Spirit, and he cried out earnestly to the Lord, diligently seeking His face. When the definite answer came, it was so overwhelming that Moody finally begged the Lord to stay His hand. It was more than he could take! And think of how mightily Moody was used. The baptism of power had its effect!

Friends, there is no limit in God. There is no shortage in heaven's supply. The ocean of the Spirit will never run dry. Let's cry out for visitation until it's too much. Let's intercede for the showers to fall until there is a river that no one can cross—deep enough to swim in (Ezek. 47).

Jesus rebuked the hypocrites because they cleaned the outside of the cup, but inside they were full of self-indulgence and greed (Matt. 23:25-26). Many of us have cleaned the inside of the cup and now our hearts are pure, but our cups are empty! Others have gone one step further. We have not only cleaned the inside of our cups, but we have become filled. That's wonderful, yet there's something more. God wants our cups to overflow!

Is there anything too hard for Him? He sends the overflowing supply. He pours forth His overabundance—in us, on us, around us, and through us. Are you a candidate for the deluge? Do you qualify for the inundation?

Right now, make a break with known sin. Right now, weed out the compromise in your heart. Right now, put away all questionable behavior. Right now, renew your hunger for the Lord. Tell Him you want Him more than anything in this world, more than life itself. Tell Him that you can't live without a radical visitation—the likes of which you've heard about but never experienced. Tell Him that if His Word is true, you absolutely must see the Book of Acts—and more!—lived out in your day, in your land, in your life. And tell Him you'll obey!

"Speak Lord, Your servants are listening! Move Lord, Your children are waiting! Act Lord, Your honor is at stake!"

Don't settle for anything less than everything the Spirit has. Don't stop until Jesus is truly glorified as the head of the Church. Don't give up until the world is shaken. Now is the time for revival!

We don't need a squirt or a pinch. We must have a mighty outpouring! This is not the day for "a little dab 'ill do ya." We must be drenched! The devil is on the rampage. Broken homes have become so common that the cities of America have become the great garbage dump of the family. What is God's answer to the flood of filth and the volcano of violence? What is God's antidote to the horrors of homosexuality and the abomination of abortion? Revival is His answer! Revival is His antidote! Revival will do the work.

In the midst of calamity, the Lord will build His Church. In the midst of perversion, the Lord will strengthen His people. In temptation we will triumph; out of fears our faith will rise! The promise to Jerusalem speaks also to us:

Arise, shine, for your light has come, and the glory of the Lord rises upon you. See, darkness covers the earth and thick darkness is over the peoples, but the LORD rises upon you and His glory appears over you. (Is. 60:1-2)

Will America fall and then recover? Will this land become great once again? Do we have five years or 50 years to go? Only the Lord knows in full. The secret things belong to Him. But this much we do know: He wants to move and bless and revive. He wants to glorify His Son and purify the Bride. He wants to make His name known among the nations.

He wants to reap the harvest of human souls. He wants to redeem His creation. He wants to bring revival! Is there anything that still hinders or holds back?

Some teachers have cautioned us: "Be careful not to exaggerate earlier revivals. Don't fall into the error of overglorifying the past. Every visitation has had its problems. No move of God has been anything near perfect. Be realistic, not nostalgic." Yes, I agree, without a doubt. But by all means—and I say this with a pleading heart—don't make excuses for the pitiful state of much of the modern Church in our land. Don't say, "Well, things weren't perfect then, and they're not perfect now." No!

In this day, we need to remember what Watchman Nee said: "By the time the average Christian gets his temperature up to normal, everybody thinks he's got a fever."[6] Or, in the words of Leonard Ravenhill: "The church has been subnormal for so long that when it finally becomes normal, everybody thinks it's abnormal."[7]

Now is the time to get hotter—until others think we're burning with fever. Now is the time to become "normal," like Elijah and Paul, Moses and Stephen, Jeremiah and Peter; normal according to the example of Jesus and the promise of the Spirit.

Have you ever been trapped behind a big, slow truck meandering its way down a two-lane, no-passing highway? Have you ever driven by that scene from the opposite direction and seen the long row of cars trailing that truck? I don't want to lead like that! I don't want to set that kind of example. I don't want my life and attitude to hinder, frustrate, discourage, and slow down others. It's time to move, not meander; to attack, not atrophy; to plunge in, not putter around. It's time to set others ablaze, not put their fires out. It's time to really believe!

Don't negate the testimony of the Gospels and Acts. The things recorded there really happened. They can happen again through us! Don't make the ministry of Jesus and the apostles look like a modern healing meeting on TV. There *was* more and there *is* more. Keep on dreaming your dreams!

There *was* something different about Charles Finney and Evan Roberts. God *did* use George Whitefield and Duncan Campbell in extraordinary ways. Whole cities *were* shaken. Multitudes of lives *were* radically transformed. Revivals changed the course of history.

May God send true revival in this day! Are you ready? Are you willing? Are you desperate?

Once, while preaching near Buffalo, I visited Niagara Falls together with Jennifer, our older daughter. As we walked along the bank towards the Falls, there was a clear, strong tide pulling the waters along. The thought struck me: *That is the state of a growing Church. It is progressing and moving forward. But that is not revival.*

Then we got nearer to the Falls. The flowing stream had turned into raging rapids! The water was capped with white waves, and the tide was almost violent in its pull. Again the thought came to mind: *That it what most of us today call revival. It's a great increase over the normal state of things, much more is happening, and it looks really exciting. But it's still not revival!*

Then we came to the Falls. They were absolutely awesome! I had seen them as a little boy, but the reality was so much more powerful than the memory. They were not just grand and impressive. They were staggering!

But I wasn't content just to see the Falls. I wanted to experience them. So Jennifer and I joined a group of other interested tourists, rented out some big, yellow raincoats, left our shoes in a locker, and went down to the rocks at the base of the Falls. The closer we got, the more overwhelming it became.

Torrents of water—so much water!—crashed like thunder. In a moment we were soaked. The wind—where did it all come from?—blew so hard it actually took our breath away. We were no longer spectators; we were participants, caught up in the pounding, swirling, churning, flooding display of natural glory. There, in a face-to-face encounter with the raw power of God, with the majesty of the Creator exploding all around me, I could only raise my hands and praise Him who lives for ever and ever. I was swallowed up in the Falls.

That is a picture of revival. Are you ready?

Endnotes

Chapter Two

1. Günter Krallman, ed., *Deeper Life in Christ: Guidelines towards Christlikeness and Power for Service, Selected and Edited from Writings of Andrew Murray* (Hong Kong: Jensco, 1995), 30.

Chapter Three

1. Charles Finney, *Reflections on Revival* (Minneapolis: Bethany, 1979), 94.

2. See Duncan Campbell, *The Lewis Awakening: 1949-1953* (Edinburgh, Scotland: The Faith Mission, n.d.), 30.

3. Ibid.

4. For summaries of some of these revivals, see Colin C. Whitaker, *Great Revivals* (Springfield, MO: Gospel Publishing House, 1984), 105-88.

5. Charles Finney, *Reflections on Revival* (Minneapolis: Bethany, 1979), 93.

6. Smith Wigglesworth, *Ever Increasing Faith* (rev. ed., Springfield, MO: Gospel Publishing House, 1971), 118.

Chapter Four

1. I.V. Neprash, "The Spirituality of the Welsh Revival," in Richard Owen Roberts, ed., *Glory Filled the Land: A Trilogy*

on the Welsh Revival of 1904-1905 (Wheaton: International Awakening Press, 1989), 193-94.

Chapter Five

1. John G. Lake, *Adventures in God* (Tulsa: Harrison House, n.d), 53-54.

2. For an honest assessment of the contemporary Pentecostal-Charismatic movement by an insider, see the present author's *Whatever Happened to the Power of God: Is the Charismatic Church Slain in the Spirit or Down for the Count?* (Shippensburg, PA: Destiny Image, 1991).

3. See Albert M. Wells, Jr., *Inspiring Quotations: Contemporary and Classical* (Nashville: Thomas Nelson, 1988), 13, no. 124.

4. See James A. Stewart, *Invasion of Wales by the Spirit through Evan Roberts* (Asheville, NC: Revival Literature, n.d.), 56.

Chapter Six

1. Arthur Wallis, *In the Day of Thy Power*, (Fort Washington, PA: Christian Literature Crusader, 1988), 26.

2. Brian Edwards, *Revival: A People Saturated With God* (Durham, England: Evangelical Press, 1990), 218.

Chapter Seven

1. Duncan Campbell, *The Price and Power of Revival: Lessons from the Hebrides Awakening* (Dixon, MO: Rare Christian Books, n.d.), 23.

2. "The Watchword," no. 48, 1.

3. Günter Krallman, ed., *Deeper Life in Christ: Guidelines towards Christlikeness and Power for Service, Selected and Edited from Writings of Andrew Murray* (Hong Kong: Jensco, 1995), 17.

Chapter Eight

1. For the entire account, with detailed background notes, see Garth M. Rosell and Richard A.G. Dupuis, eds., *The Memoirs of Charles G. Finney* (Grand Rapids: Zondervan, 1989), 271-72.

2. Arthur Wallis, *In the Day of Thy Power* (Fort Washington, PA: Christian Literature Crusade, 1988), 68.

3. Duncan Campbell, *The Lewis Awakening: 1949-1953* (Edinburgh, Scotland: The Faith Mission, n.d.), 29, 27-28.

4. See William Reid, ed., *Authentic Records of Revivals* (Wheaton: International Awakening Press, 1980), 119-120.

5. Elfion Evans, *The Welsh Revival of 1904* (Wales: Evangelical Press of Wales, 1969), 68.

6. See conveniently, William T. Summers, comp. *The Quotable Matthew Henry* (Old Tappan, NJ: Fleming Revell, n.d.), 221.

7. "George Whitefield," *Christian History*, no. 38, 22.

8. Ibid., 23.

9. See conveniently, Harry Verploegh, comp., *Oswald Chambers: The Best from All His Books*, vol. 1 (Nashville: Oliver Nelson, 1987), 263.

10. See Summers, *The Quotable Matthew Henry*, 129.

11. From the hymn "Arise My Soul, Arise."

12. Reid, *Authentic Records*, 121.

13. Ibid., 123-24.

14. Ibid., 122-23.

15. Colin C. Whitaker, *Great Revivals* (Springfield, MO: Gospel Publishing House, 1984), 158.

16. Arnold Dallimore, *Spurgeon: A New Biography* (Carlisle, PA: Banner of Truth, 1988), 17.

17. Ibid., 15.

18. Ibid., 20.

19. Ibid., 14.

20. James A. Stewart, *William Chalmers Burns and Robert Murray M'Cheyne* (N.p.: n.p., n.d.), 77, available now through Revival Literature, Asheville, NC.

Chapter Nine

1. James Edwin Orr, *Campus Aflame*, ed. Richard Owen Roberts (Wheaton: International Awakening Press, 1994), 220-21.

2. Ibid., 221.

3. For more on the prophetic significance of Israel's calendar, see the present author's *Our Hands Are Stained With Blood: The Tragic Story of the "Church" and the Jewish People* (Shippensburg, PA: Destiny Image, 1992), 35-41.

4. See Albert M. Wells, Jr., *Inspiring Quotations: Contemporary and Classical* (Nashville: Thomas Nelson, 1988), 103, no. 1347.

5. See conveniently I.D.E. Thomas, ed., *The Golden Treasury of Puritan Quotations* (Carlisle, PA: Banner of Truth, 1989), 159.

6. A.W. Tozer, *When He is Come* (Harrisburg, PA: Christian Publications, 1968), 15.

7. See Thomas, *Golden Treasury*, 159.

8. Ibid., 158.

Chapter Ten

1. Emyr Roberts and R. Geraint Gruffyd, *Revival and Its Fruit* (Wales: Evangelical Library of Wales, 1981), 35.

2. Leonard Ravenhill, *Why Revival Tarries* (Minneapolis: Bethany, 1962), 83.

3. See *The Works of John Wesley* (Grand Rapids: Baker, 1986), 1:210 (this is the journal entry from 7 July 1739).

4. Arthur Wallis, *In the Day of Thy Power* (Fort Washington, PA: Christian Literature Crusade, 1988), 75.

5. See Duncan Campbell, *Revival in the Hebrides* (Springfield, MO: Gospel Publishing House, n.d., Tract No. 4673), 6.

6. Brian Edwards, *Revival: A People Saturated With God* (Durham, England: Evangelical Press, 1990), back cover.

7. Ibid.; Campbell, *Revival in the Hebrides*, 6-8.

8. Wallis, *In the Day of Thy Power*, 78.

9. Michael L. Brown, *The End of the American Gospel Enterprise* (Shippensburg, PA: Destiny Image, 1989), 63-69.

10. This is the famous account of Peter Cartwright; see Bill Britton, *Quotes from the Past...*(taken from *History of Tennessee,* Springfield, MO: Goodspeed Publishing Co., n.d., 645-65), 5; for a brief summary of some of the Cane Ridge manifestations, see Mark A. Noll, *A History of Christianity in the United States and Canada* (Grand Rapids: Eerdmans, 1992), 167.

11. Roberts, *Revival and Its Fruit*, 7.

12. Ibid., 21-22.

13. Ibid., 9.

14. The article was entitled, "Holy Kickers Baptized 138. Remarkable Scenes at Terminal Yesterday."

15. Roberts, *Revival and Its Fruit*, 8.

16. Ibid., 20-21.

17. Reported in the *Los Angeles Times*, 6 September 1906, fully illustrated under the caption, "Hand-Made Chicken Tracks on Paper," and with an alleged translation as well. The linguist cited in the article was "the profound Oriental scholar" Baba Bharati.

18. From a secular newspaper article entitled, "Rolling on Floor in Smale's Church," exact date and source unavailable to me.

19. Oswald Chambers, *My Utmost for His Highest* (reprinted in many editions and by various publishers), August 1.

20. Gordon Lindsay, ed., *Spiritual Hunger and Other Sermons* (Dallas: Christ for the Nations, 1987), 80.

Chapter Eleven
1. For the life of Judson, see Courtney A. Anderson, *To the Golden Shore: The Life of Adoniram Judson* (Valley Forge: Judson Press, 1987).

2. See John Holt Rice and Benjamin Holt Rice, *Memoir of James Brainerd Taylor* (London: Frederick Westley and A.H. Davis, 1834), 207.

3. Jonathan Edwards, *Jonathan Edwards on Revival* (Carlisle, PA: Banner of Truth, 1987), 12-13.

4. Arthur Wallis, *In the Day of Thy Power* (Fort Washington, PA: Christian Literature Crusade, 1988), 63.

5. H.A. Baker, *Visions Beyond the Veil* (Springdale, PA: Whitaker, 1979), 88-89.

6. James A. Stewart, *I Must Tell* (N.p.: n.p., n.d.), 34, available now through Revival Literature, Asheville, NC.

7. Ibid., 85.

8. Ibid., 85-86.

9. See K.P. Yohannan, *Living in the Light of Eternity* (Longwood, FL: Longwood Communications, 1993), 99-102.

Chapter Twelve

1. For discussion of the Hebrew expression used here (*pî shenayim*), see T.R. Hobbs, *2 Kings,* Word Biblical Commentary (Waco, TX: Word, 1985), 21: "The phrase indicates twice as much as any other heir, not double the amount Elijah had."

2. John Gillies, *Historical Collections of Accounts of Revivals* (Carlisle, PA: Banner of Truth, 1981), vi.

3. Ibid., ix-x.

4. James A. Stewart, *William Chalmers Burns and Robert Murray M'Cheyne* (N.p.: n.p., n.d.), 22.

5. Gillies, *Historical Collections*, 351.

6. See Albert M. Wells, Jr., *Inspiring Quotations: Contemporary and Classical* (Nashville: Thomas Nelson, 1988), 63-64, no. 788.

Chapter Thirteen

1. Arthur Wallis, *In the Day of Thy Power* (Fort Washington, PA: Christian Literature Crusade, 1988), 81.

2. James A. Stewart, *Evangelism* (4th ed.; Asheville, NC: Revival Literature, n.d.; this edition was first published in 1955), 11-12.

3. Lyle W. Dorsett, *Billy Sunday and the Redemption of Urban America* (Grand Rapids: Eerdmans, 1991), 88.

4. See James A. Stewart, *I Must Tell*, (N.p.: n.p., n.d.), 68-69.

5. James A. Stewart, *Evangelism*, 15-16.

6. Ibid.

7. Samuel Chadwick, *The Way to Pentecost* (Fort Washington, PA: Christian Literature Crusade, 1976), 13.

8. James A. Stewart, *Evangelism*, 12.

9. Ibid., 14.

10. See "George Whitefield," *Christian History*, no. 38, 22.

11. Duncan Campbell, *Revival in The Hebrides* (Springfield, MO: Gospel Publishing House, n.d., Tract No. 4673), 15, "arranged from an address given by Duncan Campbell as Keswick Convention in 1952."

12. James A. Stewart, *Evangelism*, 13.

13. Basil Miller, *Praying Hyde* (Grand Rapids: Zondervan, 1943), 44.

14. Edward and Lillian Harvey, *Missionaries and Revival*, vol. 3 of *How They Prayed* (Hampton, TN: Harvey & Tait, 1987), back cover.

15. Samuel Chadwick, *The Way to Pentecost* (Fort Washington, PA: Christian Literature Crusade, 1976), 12-13.

16. David Hogan, founder and president of Freedom Ministries, working specially among the impoverished native Indians of Mexico and Central and South Americas.

17. Richard Owen Roberts, ed., *Glory Filled the Land: A Trilogy on the Welsh Revival of 1904-1905* (Wheaton: International Awakening Press, 1989), 174.

18. See Albert Wells, Jr., *Inspiring Quotations: Contemporary and Classical* (Nashville: Thomas Nelson, 1988), 177-78, no. 2340.

19. James A. Stewart, *Evangelism*, 18; for the final line, see Wells, *Inspiring Quotations*, 178, no. 2350.

20. See Wells, Ibid., *Inspiring Quotations*, 178, no. 2347.

21. Campbell, *Revival in the Hebrides*, 3-4.

22. Smith Wigglesworth, *Ever Increasing Faith*, rev. ed. (Springfield, MO: Gospel Publishing House, 1971), 100.

23. See James A. Stewart, *William Chalmers Burns and Robert Murray M'Cheyne* (N.p.: n.p., n.d.), 7.

24. Leonard Ravenhill, *Why Revival Tarries* (Minneapolis: Bethany, 1962), 112.

25. Ibid., 113.

26. Jack Hywel-Davies, *The Life of Smith Wigglesworth* (Ann Arbor: Vine Publications, 1988), 161-62.

Chapter Fourteen
1. The missionary was David Hogan (see endnote 16 in chapter 13).

2. Andrew Bonar, ed., *The Memoirs and Remains of R.M. M'Cheyne* (Carlisle, PA: Banner of Truth, 1987), 23.

3. Taken from Andrew Bonar, ed., *The Letters of Samuel Rutherford* (Carlisle, PA: Banner of Truth, 1984), page number not cited.

4. From his newsletter, "The Voice of the Martyrs."

5. See Richard Wurmbrand, *The Overcomers* (Tunbridge Wells: Monarch, 1993), 97. The Romanian pastor was Bishop Vladimir Ghica.

6. Ibid., 18-19.

7. See Cyril J. Davey *Sadhu Sundar Singh* (Waynesboro, GA: STL Books, 1980), 101-02.

8. See "William Carey," *Christian History*, no. 36, 34.

9. See James A. Stewart, *Evangelism* 4th ed. (Asheville, NC: Revival Literature, n.d.; This edition was first published in 1955), 14-15.

Chapter Fifteen

1. All these examples were taken from Vinson Synan, *The Holiness Pentecostal Movement in the United States* (repr., Grand Rapids: Eerdmans, 1983).

2. Clarence Larkin, *Dispensational Truth* (Philadelphia: Larkin, 1920), 102.

3. R. M'Cheyne Patterson, in Captain E.G. Carré, ed., *Praying Hyde* (S. Plainfield, NJ: Bridge Publishing, 1982), 136-37.

4. Ibid., 70.

5. See Harry Verploegh, comp., *Oswald Chambers: The Best from All His Books*, vol. 1 (Nashville: Oliver Nelson, 1987), 191.

Chapter Sixteen

1. Robert Glen Gromacki, *The Modern Tongues Movement*, 2nd ed. (Nutley, NJ: Presbyterian and Reformed, 1972), 151.

2. Donald C. Palmer, *Explosion of People Evangelism: An Analysis of Pentecostal Church Growth in Colombia* (Chicago: Moody, 1974), 123.

3. For the following points, see Jonathan Edwards, *Jonathan Edwards on Revival* (Carlisle, PA: Banner of Truth, 1987), 89-108.

4. For the following points, see ibid., 109-20.

5. For an overall discussion, see Keith J. Hardman, *Charles G. Finney, Revivalist and Reformer* (Syracuse: Syracuse University Press, 1987).

6. John S. Tompkins, "Our Kindest City," *Readers Digest*, July 1994): 55.

Chapter Seventeen

1. Arthur Wallis, *In the Day of Thy Power* (Fort Washington, PA: Christian Literature Crusade, 1988), 68.

2. Duncan Campbell, *Revival in the Hebrides* (Springfield, MO: Gospel Publishing House, n.d.), 7-8.

3. Ibid., 8.

4. Ibid., 8-9.

5. I have these facts from a cassette tape message recorded by Campbell (original date and source unknown).

6. See George Stormont, *Smith Wigglesworth: A Man Who Walked with God* (Tulsa: Harrison House, 1989), 69-70.

7. From a private letter written to me (received 2 August 1994) in response to chapter eight of this book ("Conviction!"), used with permission. These could well be Ravenhill's last words in print.

8. See the doctrinal statement printed in W.J. Hollenweger, *The Pentecostals*, trans. R.A. Wilson (Peabody, MA: Hendrickson, 1988), 513.

Chapter Eighteen

1. Colin C. Whitaker, *Great Revivals* (Springfield, MO: Gospel Publishing House, 1984), 135.

2. See Albert M. Wells, Jr., *Inspiring Quotations: Contemporary and Classical* (Nashville: Thomas Nelson, 1988), 56, no. 686.

3. For an account of awakenings among the Confederate troops, see W.W. Bennett, *A Narrative of the Great Revival which Prevailed in the Southern Armies* (Harrisonburg, VA: Sprinkle Publications, 1989).

4. For more in-depth treatment of these themes, see the present author's books *How Saved Are We?* (Shippensburg, PA: Destiny Image, 1990); *Whatever Happened to the Power of God: Is the Charismatic Church Slain in the Spirit or Down for the Count?* (Shippensburg, PA: Destiny Image, 1991); *It's Time to Rock the Boat: A Call to God's People to Rise Up and Preach a Confrontational Gospel* (Shippensburg, PA: Destiny Image, 1993).

5. Brian Edwards, *Revival: A People Saturated With God* (Durham, England: Evangelical Press, 1990), 116.

6. See Wells, *Inspiring Quotations*, 27, no. 298.

7. I heard this orally, but it has frequently been expressed by Ravenhill in speech and writing.

ICN Ministries has prepared a complete resource catalog of materials by Dr. Michael L. Brown. Included in this catalog are books, audiotapes, videotapes, and self-study courses dealing with:

- Repentance and Revival
- Spiritual Life
- Prayer and Intercession
- Holiness
- Prophetic Ministry
- Divine Healing
- The Church and the Jewish People
- Answering Jewish Objections to Jesus
- Debate and Dialog with Rabbis and Anti-Missionaries

To request our resource catalog, write, call, or fax to:

ICN Ministries
P.O. Box 7355
Gaithersburg, MD 20898-7355
Phone: 301-990-4303
FAX: 301-990-4306

Other
Destiny Image titles
you will enjoy reading